Pious Postmortems

Pious Postmortems

ANATOMY, SANCTITY, AND THE
CATHOLIC CHURCH IN EARLY
MODERN EUROPE

Bradford A. Bouley

PENN

UNIVERSITY OF PENNSYLVANIA PRESS *Philadelphia*

THIS BOOK IS MADE POSSIBLE BY A COLLABORATIVE GRANT
FROM THE ANDREW W. MELLON FOUNDATION.

Published by
University of Pennsylvania Press
Philadelphia, Pennsylvania 19104-4112
www.upenn.edu/pennpress

Printed in the United States of America
on acid-free paper

10 9 8 7 6 5 4 3 2 1

Library of Congress Cataloging-in-Publication Data

Names: Bouley, Bradford A., author.
Title: Pious postmortems : anatomy, sanctity, and the Catholic Church
    in early modern Europe / Bradford A. Bouley.
Description: 1st edition. | Philadelphia : University of Pennsylvania
    Press, [2017] | Includes bibliographical references and index.
Identifiers: LCCN 2017012494 | ISBN 9780812249576 (hardcover :
    alk. paper)
Subjects: LCSH: Canonization—History—16th century. |
    Canonization—History—17th century. | Autopsy—Europe—
    History—16th century. | Autopsy—Europe—History—17th
    century. | Human body—Religious aspects—Catholic Church. |
    Religion and science—Europe—History—16th century. | Religion
    and science—Europe—History—17th century. | Catholic Church—
    Europe—History—16th century. | Catholic Church—Europe—
    History—17th century.
Classification: LCC BX2330 .B68 2017 | DDC 235/.24094—dc23
LC record available at https://lccn.loc.gov/2017012494

CONTENTS

Pious Postmortems

On March 26, 1612, the Bishop of Coimbra exhumed the body of Queen Isabel of Portugal (1271–1336), which had been buried for 275 years. Isabel's body, according to witnesses, exuded a sweet odor and appeared not to have rotted despite almost three centuries in the ground.[1] These phenomena, which seem unusual to the modern reader, were standard elements of sanctity that dated back to medieval traditions.[2] But how could one tell if a body's sweet smell and failure to rot were signs of a miracle and not just unusual, but natural phenomena?

For the Counter-Reformation Church, which was seeking to reassert both its identity and the validity of the cult of the saints, traditional signs of holiness had to be rigorously validated and defensible both to the faithful layman and to canonization officials.[3] It was for this reason that the letters opening Isabel's canonization process deputed two physicians and one surgeon to examine her body.[4] In their thorough investigation of the corpse, these experts found that Isabel's face was still "covered by white flesh," her head was "full of hair," which seemed as if it had been "just washed," her "eye sockets, ears, and nose were whole," and her breasts were "similarly totally white and dry" and, upon probing, "remained solid and firm."[5] Judging what they found against their experience with other bodies, the medical men ruled that what had occurred to Isabel's corpse was "beyond nature."[6] In the lexicon of early modern natural philosophy, "beyond nature" was not a vague term at all; rather, it delimited a specific realm of phenomena created by God.[7] These medical professionals were saying that, in their medical opinion, a miracle had occurred in the body of Queen Isabel.

Isabel's case was not unusual, however, and, in fact, Catholic officials ordered the posthumous examination of nearly every prospective
saint in the first hundred years after the Council of Trent (1545–1563).
During these examinations, medical professionals found a variety of
abnormalities in saintly cadavers including miraculous incorruption,
evidence of extreme asceticism, and wondrously unusual anatomy. In
many of these cases, the evidence of the body, interpreted by medical
experts, became part of the demonstration of the individual's sanctity. In a period of crisis, the Church looked to experts on the natural
world—medical practitioners—to help them demonstrate the existence of supernatural realities such as miracles and saints.[8]

This book provides a comprehensive study of the role played by
anatomical evidence in the creation of saints. Although several studies have explored the ecclesiastical interest in medicine by examining
the role of medical professionals in canonization proceedings, few
have discussed the numerous postmortems performed on prospective
holy men and women.[9] The studies that have looked at postmortem
examination, which include works by Katharine Park, Nancy Siraisi,
Gianna Pomata, and Elisa Andretta, have focused either on an earlier period or on only a select few of the most famous cases.[10] Archi-
val evidence demonstrates, however, that such examinations became
especially widespread in the late sixteenth and seventeenth centuries.
From 1550 until about 1700, corpses of nearly every pope, prospective saint, and many other esteemed individuals underwent postmortem examinations, sometimes including a full autopsy, as part of the
search for the holy.[11] Indeed, at least one prospective saint, Isidore the
Laborer, was exhumed after 500 years so that medical practitioners
could assess his body against the new standards of sanctity.[12] Francis
Xavier's corpse was examined in faraway Goa and then reevaluated
in Rome by other, better known and more prestigious medical practitioners.[13] The Catholic Church, it would seem, cared deeply about
the anatomy of prospective holy men and women and went to great
lengths to ensure that medical criteria were used in evaluating the
unusual qualities of saintly cadavers.

The Church's alliance with anatomical studies invites a reassessment of the relationship between Catholicism and medicine in the
early modern period. Certainly, the narratives that once cast the
Church, and religion more generally, as the enemy of science have
given way to more complex theses.[14] Various trends have been identified by modern scholars that demonstrate the ways in which religious

authorities alternately collaborated with philosophers in studying the natural world, viewed natural philosophy as a separate sphere of knowledge, or, indeed, even opposed certain investigations into nature.[15] The collaboration thesis has been subject to a great deal of scholarship in recent years as studies by John Heilbron, Sachiko Kusukawa, Marcus Hellyer, Rivka Feldhay, and others have provided convincing evidence that religion and natural philosophy frequently cooperated across a range of fields that were occupied with understanding nature.[16] In medicine in particular, Maria Pia Donato describes the relationship between religion and medicine as involving a complex set of interactions characterized by "collaboration, competition, and conflict."[17] In short, knowledge of the natural world frequently consisted of a negotiation between various ways of understanding the interactions between man, nature, and the divine. In this respect, the attempt to locate the holy in human cadavers conforms to what is currently accepted about science and religion in the early modern period: medical professionals, theologians, and canon lawyers frequently worked together, and occasionally at odds, in defining what could be considered the miraculous in the human body.

Nevertheless, the Catholic Church's extensive use of anatomy to verify the bodies of prospective saints also provides a distinctly new perspective on the interaction between the Church and medicine in the early modern period. On the one hand, such extensive use of medical expertise should alter how scholars understand the reassertion of Catholic identity after the Reformation. Medicine and anatomy acted as a buttress to Catholic claims about the saints. Indeed, the examination of the bodies of a wide variety of holy people—ranging from popes down to local mystics (some of whom were denounced as heretics)—became fundamental for the definition of Catholic identity in the early modern world.[18] Through their corpses these individuals could offer confirmation of their connection with the divine or, conversely, reveal themselves as traitors to the faith. Anatomy, interpreted by skilled medical practitioners, was the key to knowing the true nature of an individual, physically and spiritually.[19] Anatomy defended Catholicism. Indeed, the importance of anatomy to Catholic identity suggests that rather than the body becoming desacralized—as one recent scholar has argued—through the early modern expansion of anatomical studies, the opposite seems to have occurred.[20] Anatomical understanding harnessed to a Counter-Reformation agenda could invest the body with greater religious significance.

On the other hand, the extensive involvement of medical professionals in canonization proceedings in the late sixteenth and seventeenth centuries should also alter how we understand the ways in which the medical profession came to be defined. Church patronage of anatomical study helped sanction ongoing trends in the medical field related to who was allowed to make knowledge about the natural world and how that knowledge was made. The Church, for example, appears to have endorsed the position that university-trained physicians sought to claim for themselves: placing them at the top of the evolving medical pyramid. As many scholars have noted and various chapters of this book explore, the healing professions in early modern Europe encompassed a broad range of practitioners that included household healers, apothecaries, midwives, noblewomen, empirics, barber-surgeons, and physicians, to name only a few of the vast array of healers in this period.[21] Physicians, who were defined by their university training, sought at various points to assert their preeminent role at the top of this hierarchy.[22] Such preeminence, however, was not always necessarily apparent to patients who might seek the expertise of a variety of practitioners or, indeed, even have preferred other types of healers to physicians.[23] Yet canonization officials were clear in their preference for physicians in verifying bodily miracles. The evidence about Francis Xavier's incorrupt corpse, for example, which was initially established by a *medicus* in a colonial outpost, required reinterpretation by an eminent Roman physician, Angelo Vittori, before it could be considered for his canonization.[24] Teresa of Avila's holy body was examined three times, but only the last examination—undertaken by a university professor—seems to have counted in her final canonization process.[25] During the canonization of Giacoma della Marca, a physician's testimony was used to invalidate a surgeon's testimony.[26] Numerous other examples attest to this preference for university training in the Church's expert witnesses. The reason for this predilection is clear: such education distinguished the physician as more able to discuss philosophical and theological issues related to a miracle.[27] The Church's marked preference for physicians in this way gave religious sanction to a professional divide, which further enhanced a distinction that was already becoming more pronounced at this moment in history.

Church-organized anatomical investigation of prospective saints also helped promote and endorse a new way in which medical professionals produced knowledge in the early modern period: through empirical evidence. Firsthand experience, which had largely been considered at best a low form of knowledge or at worst not knowledge at all, began to be deployed with greater frequency in this period. Recent scholarship has shown that in the fifteenth and sixteenth centuries individuals in a number of fields, including astronomy, alchemy, metallurgy, geography, and law, began to rely on experience as a guide to knowledge making.[28] However, medicine—considered both an art and a science—clearly and early on began to deploy new empirical evidence as both useful and problematic for the articulation of its discipline. Chiara Crisciani, Katharine Park, and Michael McVaugh have shown that as early as the fourteenth century, some elite medical practitioners had begun already to draw new conclusions based on their own clinical experience.[29] By the sixteenth century, Gianna Pomata has recently argued, clinical observation had become important enough for medicine that a new style of writing arose to meet this need. Medical practitioners created a new genre, loosely inspired by Hippocrates, to respond to a new way of making knowledge—through individual experience. This new style, generally denoted with a publication including the title of *Observationes*, constituted, according to Pomata, an "epistemic genre." The *Observationes* format allowed medical practitioners to circulate knowledge among themselves that they deemed useful but was outside the accepted epistemologies of medical faculties.[30] Thus, by the sixteenth century many different ways of making knowledge from experience—"diverse, overlapping 'empiricisms,'" in Alisha Rankin's phrase—were emerging on the stage of European learning even before Francis Bacon articulated an accompanying epistemological program.[31]

Catholic officials lent their authority to these new empiricisms in medicine. In their attempt to demonstrate that a singular event—a miracle—had occurred in a human body, canonization officials relied on a number of techniques of making knowledge, including various empirical methods. A variety of medical practitioners, for example, examined Teresa of Avila's corpse on multiple occasions and in various weather conditions. Their goal in these repeated examinations was to test the corpse for incorruption.[32] The bodies of Isabel of Portugal, Francis Xavier, Giacomo della Marca, Luis Bertran, and numerous others were manipulated, prodded, and tested in various ways to demonstrate their holy nature.[33] The demonstration of Andrea Corsini's incorruption by a Florentine physician was notarized and then signed by seventeen witnesses.[34] When the cadaver of Thomas of

Villanova in 1611 (can. 1658) was unearthed, notaries recorded in thorough, firsthand detail their exact experience at the tomb and during the medical examination, a literary attempt to make the visit as real as possible.[35] All these techniques—repetition, testing, multiple witnessing, new narrative styles—have been seen as characteristic of the empirical programs of the later seventeenth-century experimental societies.[36] Although Catholic investigation of holy corpses was still a long way from systematic Baconian experimentalism, this was a moment in which religious authority sanctioned new ways of making knowledge about the natural world. Although there is no conclusive evidence, it is tempting to speculate that this support from such a powerful authority as the Catholic Church might have been partly why empiricism became a recognized way to make knowledge during the seventeenth century.

Through its collaboration with medicine, then, the Catholic Church should be seen as a major contributor in early modern attempts to understand the natural world. Church officials helped articulate who should investigate nature, what sort of evidence should be used in this investigation, and even to some extent what potential subjects of study were, since they funded numerous investigations into the boundaries of the human and the divine in the bodies of prospective saints. That is, rather than being a tale of science versus religion, the narrative that arises through posthumous examination of saintly bodies is one in which emerging scientific practice was supported and defined by religion.

This book explores these posthumous examinations of saintly cadavers across five chapters. As the central issue behind these medical examinations was the Church's concern over its ability to correctly judge saintliness, Chapter 1 begins by discussing broadly the changes to canonization in the period after the Council of Trent (1545–1563). Saints have been a focus of a great deal of scholarship in recent years, and extensive studies by André Vauchez, Michael Goodich, Donald Weinstein, and Rudolph Bell, among others, have analyzed saints statistically in an attempt to gain a general overview of the qualities that defined holiness.[37] However, such monographs tend to either focus on the Middle Ages or downplay the differences between the early modern and medieval periods. This is problematic, because the medical examination of saints' bodies was only one of several major changes affecting the making of saints in the early modern period. Chapter 1, therefore, looks at a number of specific cases to examine what had changed in the practice of canonization.

Chapter 2 then looks specifically at the advent of anatomical expertise as a means to discern sanctity. It follows the growing trend whereby holy bodies became no longer matters decided by popular acclaim, but medical subjects understood by experts. The impetus to create a medical context for the holy came, however, not from the Church authorities, but from the medical practitioners, who had become interested in unusual case studies. That is, reports on unusual anatomies of holy individuals began to appear in the epistemic genre of *observationes*, discussed by Pomata.[38] Shortly after medical practitioners began writing about unusual saintly anatomy, promoters of various prospective saints' canonization attempted to use these medical case studies to defend claims of bodily sanctity. Such interest in anatomy by ecclesiastical officials grew out of existing practices of autopsy both within medical and in religious settings. Officials in Rome first ignored these attempts by local officials. However, by the early seventeenth century such case studies began to feature prominently in canonization proceedings. This chapter charts the eventual acceptance of new types of medical evidence by canonization officials.

Chapter 3 looks at one specific type of bodily wondrousness: miraculous incorruption after death. Incorruption was the most common sign of holiness, and medical professionals examined nearly every saint canonized during this period to confirm his or her failure to rot. Decomposition, however, was still a relative, subjectively viewed quality. Understanding whether a body was incorrupt relied on a number of ambiguous medical and theological signs.[39] Therefore, when medical practitioners testified about the bodies of incorrupt saints, they were also engaging in a negotiation between members of their community, their profession, and the Church hierarchy over the meaning of the corpse in question. Holiness, like other knowledge created in early modern Europe, was a profoundly local and contextual phenomenon.[40]

The fourth chapter explores the role of asceticism as evidence of saintliness. Like incorruption, the perception of bodily asceticism was influenced by a number of cultural factors, including, in particular, social rank and gender. Medical professionals opened the bodies of far more men than women to confirm wondrous feats of asceticism during life. In this way, medicine and anatomy bolstered preexisting notions of sanctity, which connected asceticism to male ecclesiastical authority. Medical evaluation of women, on the other hand, tended to provide an outlet for preexisting skepticism over female sanctity.

The final chapter turns to a more thorough analysis of the ways that gender was fundamental, both to early modern categories of sainthood and the establishment of medical expertise. Despite the rise to prominence of several early modern female saints—such as Teresa of Avila, Rose of Lima, and Maria Maddalena de' Pazzi—early modern sanctity based itself on the rearticulation of clear gender hierarchies. Ecclesiastical authority defined and articulated itself after the Reformation as being in opposition to feminine weakness.[41] Holy women who had a public role, therefore, had to act masculinely in life to the point of even becoming physiologically like men. Such a stance was in itself threatening to hierarchies, and so after death the posthumous medical examination reasserted the feminine and sexual nature of women's bodies, thereby subordinating them to ecclesiastical authority. Male bodies, in contrast, were completely stripped of their sexuality and made both asexual and hypermasculine after death. In assigning gender in this way, though, the medical practitioners involved in these cases also strongly reasserted their own masculinity. Indeed, this chapter argues that the act of performing a postmortem, especially an autopsy, on a prospective saint of either sex established gender roles for all involved—physicians, surgeons, bishops, and the bodies under the knife—and therefore reinforced the correct ordering of Catholic society. The practice of autopsy was a gendered and gendering activity.

In sum, the fact that canonization officials ordered medical examinations of almost every canonized saint and many more holy people who did not achieve canonization deeply affects how we understand a number of issues related to religion and medicine in the early modern period. It should encourage further reevaluation of the Church's interaction with science, its reaction to the Protestant Reformation, the development of the early modern medical profession, and the interrelated way in which gender, sanctity, and nature were understood.

SOURCES AND METHODS

The overwhelming majority of the sources used for this book come from the processes of canonization conducted by the Congregation of Rites and housed in the Vatican Secret Archives. These are the official records of the canonization trials that were used by the Rota Tribunal, the Congregation of Rites, and the pope in deciding whether to confer sainthood. They are, therefore, ideal pieces of evidence for understanding what qualities the Church sought among those whom it canonized. In the course of this research, I examined records for all the saints canonized from 1588 until 1700, with the expectation that these successful cases would most clearly indicate what was required for canonization. In addition to successful cases, I also reviewed a number of failed canonization attempts, which fizzled either before any rank was achieved or after the blessed status was conferred. In choosing which, among many, failed cases to review, I based my decision on whether bodily holiness formed part of the saint's cult. To supplement the rites processes, I have also examimed printed hagiography (*vitae*), letters, pamphlets, papal bulls, and inquisition trial dossiers. The Inquisition trial dossiers on which I focused were the cases of false or affected sanctity in the archives of the Roman Inquisition, which are now housed in the Archivio della Congregazione per la Dottrina della Fede. As only a few volumes, representing several dozen cases, survive, I examined all the records from the seventeenth century that exist in this archive.

These sorts of documents have many virtues but are not without pitfalls. As Dyan Elliott has observed, a canonization process is a trial that unfolds very much the same way a case before the Inquisition would.[42] Canonization officials, usually including a notary and several religious authorities such as a bishop and a few members of his entourage, interviewed witnesses at a central location. The notary would record the questions asked in Latin, but the witnesses' words were supposed to be recorded verbatim in the vernacular. Thus, as in the case of Inquisition trials, canonization proceedings might seem to allow a rare opportunity to hear a range of ordinary, "non-elite" people speak in their own voices.[43]

In contrast to this view, several scholars have argued that such sources should be seen as at best a mix of official and local voices composed through multiple authorship, rather than an unmediated report of what a witness thought. Carlo Ginzburg has suggested that the distance between an educated churchman's view of a supernatural phenomenon and that of an uneducated peasant was so great that in recording the latter's words, the former almost certainly distorted somewhat his intended testimony.[44] Similarly, in both Inquisition and canonization proceedings, the interviewers at times asked leading questions. Indeed, for all early modern canonizations the interviewers had a list of questions that were asked.[45] In answering them, witnesses unwittingly followed the questioner's logic, rather than speaking according to his or her own ideas about the individual in question. The intimidating nature of the setting—normally in a church before prelates who were generally of much higher rank than the witness—might also predispose the witness to follow the questioner's logic. Thus, an argument could be made that a canonization process only narrowly tells us about what the judges understood holiness to be and not about what the believers or even medical professionals more broadly thought about the saint or the saint's body.

Still, pieces of evidence point to the fact that testators frequently saw a canonization process as an opportunity to voice their opinion about the holiness—or lack thereof—of someone from their community. For example, in giving evidence for the canonization of their sister Caterina Ricci, two nuns dictated statements that lasted for more than twenty manuscript pages.[46] When Andrea Castaldi testified for the founder of his order, Gaetano dei Conti di Tiene, his testimony took up thirty-six pages.[47] Testifying for a saint was a rare opportunity to talk to the elite, and many seized upon it.[48] The length of their testimony implies that much of their personal opinion about the person in question, and therefore the definition of holiness in general, entered into the deposition. It also would seem to imply that many of these witnesses saw the testimony before these elite churchmen as something of a performance, which they may have rehearsed multiple times before telling it to the notary. In this way, then, such testimony might tell us more about what people in a given area thought sainthood should be rather than about the deeds of the individual in question.

On a similar note, witnesses occasionally expressed hostility toward canonization judges and testified in a way that was clearly against the intention of the question. When asked about the miracles carried out by Fra Felice of Cantalice—a Capuchin put forward for canonization in the sixteenth century, but only elevated to the rank of saint in 1712—his fellow Capuchin, Fra Giovanni da Bergamo, stated in what were less than glowing terms that "this was a great miracle from the life of Fra Felice. He studied in these three things, that is: the disregard of himself, obedience, and prayer."[49] A knowledgeable listener would have recognized da Bergamo's explicit denial that Felice had carried out any miraculous works. In a similar vein, medical witnesses did not invariably tell the canonization judges exactly what was expected.

What can be concluded is that the record of a canonization trial was a negotiated piece of evidence in which the voices of the believers blended with those of the ecclesiastical authorities who were attempting to turn local holiness into universal Catholic sainthood. It is those negotiations, especially as they pertain to the body of the saint, that this book examines. From a thorough review of extant sources, it emerges that the meaning of the saintly body, whether interpreted by laymen, medical practitioners, or theologians, itself had no single, fixed, or absolute meaning. Rather, the holy body was defined by local context and circumstances. This study documents the Church's attempt to make local belief and local knowledge into universal Catholic truth.

CHAPTER I

Expertise and Early Modern Sanctity

On November 25, 1602, Pope Clement VIII (r. 1592–1605) convened a group of eminent cardinals, jurists, and theologians to discuss what he saw as a central problem facing the Catholic Church: the veneration of saints.[1] Although Clement supported the cult of the saints, he told the assembly that he was deeply concerned about a number of dubious practices that had become commonplace. His list of more than twenty items included the printing of vitae, the selling of images, and the distribution of relics from those who had not yet been recognized as saints.[2] In short, Clement was worried that enthusiasts were pushing forward individuals as saints who in reality had no right to be recognized as holy.

Clement's concerns encapsulate the issues surrounding saints following the Reformation. Saints were one of the most popular aspects of Catholicism and one of the most effective ways to evangelize the masses.[3] The Church needed saints. The enthusiasm that saints inspired, however, could lead believers into error and had put the Church under attack. Believers might, for example, venerate individuals who were not truly holy or even those who had been condemned by the Church. Veneration of Girolamo Savonarola, the condemned heretical Dominican, for example, flourished in the sixteenth and seventeenth centuries, while in the medieval period many venerated as a saint a greyhound who had saved an infant boy.[4] Such practices went decidedly against the reform aims of the Catholic Church following the Reformation.

Along with such veneration of unworthy or unapproved individuals, other believers might popularize miracles that had little evidence to support them and that seemed little related to the faith. Such dubious miracles provided easy fodder for Protestant reformers, who saw in the cult of the saints an emblem of everything that was wrong with Catholicism.[5] Veneration of the saints could thus act as both powerful propaganda in favor of Catholicism as well as damning criticism against it. In reaction, the Catholic Church halted official canonization for much of the sixteenth century. After this long hiatus, when papal canonization resumed in 1588, according to Peter Burke, "the distinction between sacred and profane was made sharper than it had been, while recruitment procedures for the saints were made uniform and formal."[6]

The ways in which this new rigor was applied in practice and how it differed from earlier procedure for medieval saint-making has, in some ways, been difficult to define. In theory, medieval canonizations already were subjected to a degree of central control and involved a number of legal devices designed to separate the holy from the mundane.[7] Recent scholars have attempted to identify the changes to canonization in the sixteenth century by focusing either on the numerous institutional changes to the Church in the early modern period or by looking at specific case studies.[8] The present chapter differs from and yet draws on these previous strands of scholarship: the goal here is to examine the practical methods whereby canonization officials verified the miracles and the lives of the saints. The papacy in the late sixteenth and early seventeenth centuries drew on medieval precedent, but also created new legalistic and bureaucratic devices to evaluate the holiness of those proclaimed saints including, in particular, an increased role for various outside experts and new methods of assessing evidence. In looking at these new procedures, this chapter provides a broader background for the specific innovation, medical verification of bodily sanctity, which is detailed in later chapters.

Despite the fact that the authorities in Rome introduced more and increasingly lengthy procedures to the canonization process, it never became simply a matter of central authority dictating how veneration should be practiced. Rather, the veneration of a holy individual began with a groundswell of popular support in his or her local community. This popular belief in a person's sanctity turned into canonization through the actions of a number of patrons, who can be considered negotiators or lobbyists between the Curia and the localities. In fact, even the numerous techniques of verification used by the Holy See were, in many ways, part of that negotiation which turned local ideas about holiness into ones accepted by Rome and therefore suitable for veneration by the universal Church.[9]

In explaining how early modern negotiations of sanctity unfolded, two central themes need to be examined. First, as even the definition of what it meant to be a saint has changed across the long history of the Catholic Church, this chapter begins with the evolving classification of saints in the Church leading up to the period after the Reformation. The focus then turns to the actual process of canonization, from the importance of establishing sanctity at a local level to the role of patronage, and finally, the application of a variety of methods to verify both the holiness of the individual's life and the truth behind his or her miracles. This last section ends with a survey of the increased role of a variety of experts, including legal professionals, artisans in a range of specialties, and medical professionals, in demonstrating a prospective saint's miracles. These experts used techniques based on practices in their own fields, drawing on a number of different empirical practices when it came to vetting the potentially holy.

THE EVOLVING MEANING OF SAINTHOOD

The history of saints in the Tridentine period can be characterized as a struggle between established local belief practices and the attempt on the part of the papacy to exercise greater control over saint-making. This was not always the case. In the early Church, until the twelfth and thirteenth centuries, the papacy played almost no role in defining sainthood.[10] The first real efforts to make canonization a papal prerogative came in the thirteenth century, when a series of legally trained popes, including Innocent III (1198–1216) and Gregory IX (1227–1241), formalized procedure and increasingly made it necessary and desirable to seek papal approval for the veneration of a saint. This was not just a top-down phenomenon, though, since during this period of heightened papal power, local believers frequently sought papal recognition of a saint cult because such affirmation enhanced the stature and credibility of the cult. The Fourth Lateran Council (1215), convened by Innocent III, made such approval not just desirable but necessary, as it forbade the veneration of relics that had not been approved by the papacy.[11]

Nevertheless, the picture should not be overdrawn. As Aviad Kleinberg has observed, many scholars have overestimated the role that the papacy had in canonization at this point.[12] Local veneration without papal approval still continued unabated. Furthermore, any progress made toward centralization was soon lost when the papacy's prestige and power sank to a nadir during, first, the Avignon Papacy and, later, the Great Schism (1378–1417).[13] André Vauchez points to the fifteenth century and the papacy's return to Rome as the moment when a more central authority emerged.[14] But even at this juncture, local veneration of noncanonized saints continued. Thus, despite the fact that the papacy became more cautious about whom it canonized, its return to Rome had little effect on local veneration.[15]

Similarly, the Reformation has been debated as a turning point in the history of saints. The Protestant attack on the cult of the saints is well known.[16] It was demonstrated most violently in acts of iconoclasm including, in particular, the attack on Saint Benno of Saxony. Canonized in 1523, Saint Benno was shortly thereafter denounced by Martin Luther as an example of Catholic superstition and priestly fraud. In the following year, a mob in Saxony paraded horse bones, claiming that they were relics equally valid as those of the deceased Benno.[17] In 1539, as the Reformation spread to new areas, Benno's shrine and the site of his burial in Meissen were desecrated.[18] Following Benno's canonization, no new saints were proclaimed by the papacy for sixty-five years, the longest break since the practice began in the Middle Ages. Peter Burke has seen in this halt a "failure of nerve" on the part of the papacy in the face of Protestant attack.[19] Other scholars, among them Miguel Gotor and Ronald Finucane, claim that the pause was characteristic of a papacy that already was slowing canonization frequency as it sought to rearticulate the methods whereby saints were verified.[20] Likely both views are correct and the halt is symptomatic both of internal divisions caused by Protestant attack and long-standing papal desire to increase the centralization and rigor of canonization.

This mid-sixteenth century halt in canonization brought in its wake significant changes to both how saints were venerated and how they were made. The foundation of the Roman Inquisition in 1542 was the first innovation that altered local practices of veneration. In addition to extirpating heresy, the tribunal of the Inquisition was also tasked with rooting out forms of worship that could damage the Church. Hence, the Inquisition began in the 1560s to systematically suppress the veneration of holy individuals that had not received papal approval.[21] This was despite the fact that the Council of Trent (1545–1563) had decreed that bishops could still approve the veneration of local holy people.[22] In using the Inquisition in this way, the papacy exerted control over canonization, overruling the authority of local bishops. That this was a statement of papal power is especially clear since, as several scholars have recently demonstrated, the tribunal itself functioned to a great extent as an instrument of the papacy.[23] Thus, despite what the Decrees of Trent stipulated, the Inquisition, and by extension the papacy, began for the first time to regulate local patterns of veneration.

Nevertheless, the Inquisition's activities might have been more significant for what they symbolized than what was actually achieved. The Inquisition lacked the ability, especially in its early years, to penetrate into many of the communities that it officially oversaw. An example of its lack of authority is the saint cult for Gaetano da Thiene (d. 1547), which sprang up in Naples in the years following his death. This cult continued into the seventeenth century without any official approval until da Thiene's beatification eighty-two years later, in 1629.[24] The files of the Roman Inquisition contain numerous cases that stretch well into the eighteenth century, in which unapproved veneration had proceeded unchecked—sometimes for decades. Each of these cases came to the attention of the Inquisition only when someone denounced the local cult.[25]

Nevertheless, by the 1560s the papacy had taken a significant and symbolic step in centralizing saint-making through its creation of this permanent congregation—the Inquisition—that was loyal to the pope and that was officially tasked with halting unapproved veneration.

The second part of the rearticulation and centralization of canonization was the foundation of a congregation that oversaw the approval and proclamation of saints. This came in 1588 when Pope Sixtus V (1585–1590) promulgated the Bull, *Immensa aeterni Dei*, establishing fifteen congregations to oversee the life of the Church and the Papal States, including the new Congregation of Rites. This Congregation was in charge of two central areas of Church life: (1) the rites, liturgy, and ceremonies of the Church, and (2) the canonization of saints. From 1588 onward, the Congregation of Rites was the main body in the Church charged with vetting the applications of saints and presenting results to the pope.[26] Five cardinals made up the membership in this Congregation and they reported directly to the supreme pontiff.[27] In theory, the founding of the Congregation of Rites should therefore have marked the transition of canonization into an entirely papal prerogative.

Again, however, the situation was in practice more complicated than this ideal. In reality, the Congregation of Rites relied heavily on local enthusiasm and belief for processes of canonization to begin and move forward. Furthermore, especially in the early years after the founding of the Congregation of Rites, its activities were frequently aided if not shared by the Tribunal of the Rota. This Tribunal dated to the fourteenth century and was the highest court of appeal in the Church. Prior to the foundation of the Congregation of Rites, and even for decades later, the Rota judged the quality of the evidence in processes of canonization and ensured that certain standards were met.[28] Thus, even as the Congregation of Rites marked an institutional change in how saints were made, in reality the importance of both local veneration and old institutions involved with verifying sanctity persisted.

The institutional changes to the Church in the sixteenth century, then, are only part of the story. In addition to the continuing role of local veneration, strong patronage was important, and the new methods of verification greatly influenced who was chosen to be put forward as a saint and whether or not such promotion was ultimately successful.

HOW TO BECOME A SAINT

The early modern process of canonization involved a series of investigations carried out at a local level, followed by multiple reexaminations of the evidence in Rome. Much of this process had been in place by the late Middle Ages.[29] Yet as the papacy worked to centralize canonization procedures, it also enacted a variety of new regulations designed to verify, before the Church canonized an individual, that he or she was indeed a saint. These included new phases in the process of canonization, more careful evaluation of evidence, and greater oversight by officials in Rome.

During the sixteenth and seventeenth centuries, canonizations still normally began at a local level with the first—or ordinary—process opened by a bishop. In most cases, the bishop was responding to a swell of popular support. After interviews of an initial set of witnesses had established the prospective saint's holy life and miracles, the bishop then sent the dossier of testimony and other evidence for canonization to Rome. There, the Tribunal of the Rota and then the Congregation of Rites decided whether there was sufficient evidence to continue with a canonization. If these authorities approved, they sent their recommendation to the pope, who gave the command to issue remissorial letters deputing officials to carry out the second, or apostolic, phase. The Rota Tribunal usually drew up these letters.[30]

Although frequently many of the same testators from the ordinary process would be called during the apostolic, during this period the apostolic phase was made completely distinct from the ordinary. That is, whereas in the past the same documents and testimonies might simply be reused as evidence during this new phase, after Trent the entire process was carried out again. By redoing all the interviews and other evidence collection, the papacy clearly distinguished papal from local authority when it came to canonization. The apostolic phase proceeded with questions drawn up in Rome, with judges selected by the papacy, and across any number of locations where the prospective saint lived for an extended period of time.[31] Furthermore, the apostolic process frequently was split itself into two phases during this period: *in genere*, which sought to demonstrate an individual's saintly reputation, and *in specie*, which examined specific virtues and miracles attributed to the holy person.[32] During the *in specie* phase of the apostolic process, a number of new methods of verification, including medical examination of the corpse, were required as early as the turn of the seventeenth century.

At the completion of the apostolic phase, the dossier of testimony was sent back to the Tribunal of the Rota in Rome for additional consideration. If the Rota was convinced that the prospective saint possessed both the requisite pious life and evidence of miracles, its members approved the canonization process. The Rota then created a summarized compendium on the deceased that they forwarded to the pope and the Congregation of Rites.[33] The cardinals in the Congregation of Rites reviewed this summary. They then pronounced on whether or not they deemed the individual fit for beatification and sent their recommendation to the pope. After receiving initial approval from the Rites and Rota, the pope could beatify an individual without further consultation.[34] Beatification, or becoming "blessed," was a term without clear meaning until the seventeenth century.[35] Over the course of the early seventeenth century, though, it came to designate an individual who had received preliminary approval from the Church and therefore could be venerated by local believers or within a certain religious community, such as a religious order.[36]

To proceed from beatification to canonization required an addendum to the apostolic phase to verify any new miracles that might have occurred in the intervening years, since frequently at least a decade passed between beatification and canonization.[37] The Congregation of Rites reassessed both these new miracles and the saints' previous virtues and miracles. If the saint's qualities were deemed sufficient, the pope convened a series of three consistories to discuss the prospective saint's merits. Eminent cardinals and prelates of the Holy See attended these consistories in which speakers, generally consistorial lawyers, prepared orations on the virtues and miracles of the candidate in question. At the last consistory, the assemblage voted on whether or not the individual should be canonized. If the vote was positive, the pope set a day to proclaim the canonization in a ceremony at Saint Peter's.[38] Such canonizations resulted in huge festivities, both inside and outside Rome. The promoters of the individual's sanctity printed vitae of the saint, and a variety of imagery circulated that proclaimed the sanctity of the individual.[39] Thus, a large propaganda effort that attempted to spread veneration of the saint across the Catholic world followed canonization. In this way, local belief was integrated, made official, and turned into universal veneration.

In general, the process of canonization constituted an extremely complicated bureaucratic and legalistic procedure. But underpinning the various iterations of the canonization process there were a few, central elements that unified every successful canonization: the enthusiasm of believers, the continued support of a patron, and the successful navigating of the various legal criteria for sainthood.

MANAGING THE ENTHUSIASM OF BELIEVERS

Despite the modifications to canonization in the early modern period, one important aspect of sanctity remained unchanged: for a canonization proceeding to begin, the basic requirement was people who believed in the holiness of the deceased individual. Yet local enthusiasm for a holy individual was not a simple matter. Even when it already existed at a person's death, those who favored canonization sought to manipulate, stoke, and channel it in ways that could be productive for canonization efforts. When such fame and enthusiasm were not manifest, promoters of a saint went to great lengths to generate it. Others also attempted to capitalize on the fame of a saint in order to play on local divisions or for goals other than canonization.

Thus, the first stage in canonization—the belief that an individual was holy—represented a moment in which the raw power of faith could be harnessed to agendas that might either be beneficial or detrimental to Church unity. It was exactly this power of faith that concerned Clement VIII in 1602, when he convened the meeting with which this chapter began.

A number of late sixteenth-century cases demonstrate how the fame of a holy individual could create intense emotion and devotion, which could be difficult for the papacy to control. When Filippo Neri died in 1595, for example, contemporary *avvisi*, or newsletters, from Rome reported that a "huge concourse of people" formed along the processional route that Neri's body traversed in Rome. Everyone, it seemed, wanted to touch the body.[40] His fellow Oratorians displayed his cadaver for a full day after his death, during which time a great throng of Romans came to see the deceased. Giacomo Bacci, one of Neri's first hagiographers, describes the crowd's frenzy: "Some cut off pieces of his [Neri's] vestments, though the fathers [members of Neri's Order, the Oratorians] did all they could to hinder it; others cut off some of his hair, or of his beard, and even portions of his finger-nails, which they kept by them as relics. Among the crowd were many ladies who out of devotion drew the rings from their fingers and put them on the fingers of the Saint, and then replaced them on their own."[41] Clearly, Romans viewed Neri as an especially holy person. Neri's supporters encouraged such displays of emotion by creating situations in which veneration could flourish. His well-staged autopsy that night, which is explored in the next chapter, further stoked the flames of devotion to the deceased Oratorian.[42] It was due to such clear enthusiasm for Neri that Clement VIII specifically listed his cult as one that concerned him in 1602.[43]

In another case, after Felice of Cantalice died in Rome in 1587, his fellow Capuchins encouraged the massive enthusiasm for the saint by managing access to his body. Initially, the Capuchins laid out the corpse in their Church of San Bonaventura and invited the populace in, allowing them to interact with the body. An enormous crowd responded, excited to be able to touch the deceased friar. Some mourners kissed the hands, feet, and face of Felice while others, who may have been more concerned with relics, tore off pieces of his clothes, tufts of his beard, two of his teeth, and some flesh from his head. Those who were not able to get close enough to physically touch the friar used canes or other implements to reach over the crowd and poke the cadaver.[44] In the midst of such enthusiasm, the father general of the Capuchins suddenly expelled the crowd and closed the church, citing the danger that such a large crowd could cause on such a hot day.[45]

Although he may have been genuinely concerned about the welfare of the believers, the father general's decision to prevent access to Felice's body also further stoked the crowd's enthusiasm. The assembled believers now surrounded the building and began to demand access to the corpse. In the midst of this spectacle, Cardinal Anton Maria Salviati elbowed his way into the church and advised the Capuchin leaders to either send for the Swiss Guards or immediately bury the body so as to remove the object of the crowd's devotion and thereby calm it.[46]

Salviati's involvement was likely a purposeful intervention by the papacy in a scene it had deemed excessive. After all, Salviati was a high-ranking cardinal who was a member of the apostolic chamber, had served the Curia on a number of dangerous diplomatic missions, and had worked to extend papal power and Catholic interests against Protestant ones.[47] Given his diplomatic background and elite status, he was the perfect agent of papal authority to defuse this tense situation. Immediately after Salviati's intervention, Fra Felice was placed in a wooden coffin and laid in the Capuchin cemetery attached to San Bonaventura. That the Capuchins had not done this earlier suggests that they were deploying Felice's holy cadaver to incite the passions of believers in Rome.

Cantalice's case was not unique. Promoters of sanctity regularly managed access to and staged interactions with a prospective saint's body in an attempt to build enthusiasm and establish a cult. In the small town of Rossano in Calabria, for example, local Capuchins attempted to put forward one of their brothers as a saint. They therefore staged viewings of his body, which was said to miraculously resist rot. His corpse was moved from a group tomb to the sanctuary of the church. His brothers then allowed small groups of local parishioners, and especially local women, to enter the sanctuary to see and venerate the body. As lay believers, in particular women, normally would not have had access to this section of the church, the experience was designed to inspire wonder and awe. In fact, these activities soon generated a strong local following, despite the fact that the exact identity of the deceased brother was unknown.[48]

In addition to managing access to the body of a prospective saint, supporters could engage almost in a sort of multimedia campaign to encourage belief in an individual's holiness.[49] Those who sought to forward the cult of Girolamo Mani in Verona in the 1650s, for example, began to print and distribute vitae depicting the prospective saint with holy rays of light coming from his head, implying that he already was a saint. This use of the printing press soon helped to create a sizeable local following for Mani.[50] In 1632 in Benevento, in Campania, the local Jesuits unearthed and displayed the body of Caterina Margiacca, whom they believed to be holy.[51] They then distributed her bones as relics and printed portraits of her holding a halo-like crown.[52] In this case, the circulation of both relics and imagery helped spread and enlarge her cult. Portrait statuary was also made of prospective saints and displayed publicly to stir devotion. Such was the case for one prospective saint who had the name "venerable" placed underneath a statue carved in his likeness, which was then strategically located above the central altar in his parish church.[53] In each of these examples, the promoters of sanctity clearly sought to encourage and focus the veneration of deceased individuals whom they deemed holy. A variety of media was thus employed to convey the message. These cases, which are among a few dozen that appear in the archives of the Roman Inquisition, are likely just the tip of the iceberg and represent generally how saints were promoted.[54]

The effort expended to canonize Ignatius of Loyola (d. 1556) probably represents the most elaborate attempt to promote a saint's cult in this period. After Pope Clement VIII denied Loyola's canonization process in 1599 on the grounds that too few miracles had been attributed to the Jesuit founder, several supporters undertook a campaign to generate belief in Loyola's saintliness. They sought to fashion a reputation for him as a miracle worker. Cardinal Cesare Baronio (1538–1607), author of the famous *Ecclesiastical Annals*, along with the first Jesuit cardinal, Francisco Toledo, conducted displays of devotion at Loyola's tomb. These displays focused on the healing powers of the holy man's relics.[55] The campaign extended into other media as well, with the cardinals and the Jesuits commissioning new vitae and even portraits by Peter Paul Rubens that cast Ignatius as a miracle worker. These actions were successful and the promoters of Loyola's sanctity persuaded Pope Paul V to open the process of canonization just a few years later, in 1605. Loyola was canonized in 1622.[56]

Although Loyola's case was successful, this crowd-fueled promotion of sanctity became suspect in the sixteenth and seventeenth centuries, and most cases discussed here come from Inquisition trials. Such concern was not without basis: the promotion of an individual's sanctity by inflaming the masses did not necessarily dovetail with official, papal views on how the faith should be promulgated and could be counterproductive, leading to resistance to central authority. In 1655, for example, a woman named Francesca da Montimaggiore from the diocese of Fano, part of the Papal States on the Eastern coast of Italy, claimed to have enjoyed a vision in which the locally venerated saint Oliver (d. ca. 1050) revealed to her that he was buried under a large stone in a nearby parish church.[57] He had been there for some time, but now "no longer wanted to be buried."[58] News spread within the local community, and based on the strength of Francesca's vision, a large group of believers began to worship at the rock in the small church. The bishop, concerned about this growing cult, ordered that the rock be removed so that "the truth could be made clear."[59] Once the bishop's agents moved the stone, the gathered faithful found no body. The cavity that the rock covered was left open for several hours, permitting the worshipers to use the evidence of their own eyes to recognize that Francesca's vision was false.

The cult of "Saint" Oliver became a rallying point for local believers against the Church hierarchy. Undeterred by the lack of a body, the faithful came up with two theories: either the body had been moved secretly by the bishop at night or, given the lack of veneration shown to him by the religious authorities, Saint Oliver chose to hide his remains when the stone was moved.[60] In short, when the bishop did not support their faith in Saint Oliver, the local parishioners became convinced that he was either attempting to deceive them or was perhaps not a very faithful Catholic. Lacking the corporeal remains of the saint, believers took pieces of the rock as "relics."[61]

Oliver's absent remains catalyzed old divisions in the community and accentuated a preexisting divide between the bishop and his parishioners. Indeed, the cult acted to support Francesca's claims to sanctity through her ability to prophesy—an ability viewed with skepticism by local ecclesiastical leaders. The inquisitor, who had now been deputed to deal with this case, quickly brought the matter to a close by sealing the doors of the church and preventing access to the stone.[62] There is no coda explaining what the parishioners of that church did when it was sealed, but it is likely that they either ceased going to services or dispersed to other nearby churches. In either event, the suppression of this burgeoning cult disrupted local patterns of worship and quelled growing religious enthusiasm.

Much of the initial phase of canonization, therefore, entailed encouraging and then managing the cult of a saint. The Curia, however, viewed such activities with increasing concern. The Roman Inquisition was already tasked with suppressing any such unapproved veneration. These efforts, which were somewhat ineffective, were aided in the 1620s, when Pope Urban VIII promulgated a series of decrees designed to deal with the problem of unapproved veneration. In particular, in 1628 he forbade the canonization of any holy person until fifty years had elapsed since his or her death.[63] Thereafter, the opening move in any canonization proceeding was to establish that no cult had existed sooner than fifty years after the saint's death.[64] This served a double purpose: such a time lag was assumed to lead to a more careful consideration of the saint's merits, as enthusiasm waned, and by forcing the promoters of sanctity to ensure that no public cult had formed prior to canonization, authorities thereby ensured that no unapproved veneration counted for official canonization.

Given these changes and innovations, why was Loyola's case, which clearly represented unapproved veneration, allowed to go forward whereas so many others were not? The answer lies in patronage. Political and economic support determined to a great extent how nearly any aspect of a canonization unfolded. In Loyola's case, there were two eminent cardinals and the entire Jesuit order that pressed forward approval for his canonization. The next section examines how such patronage worked in a number of other cases.

THE IMPORTANCE OF PATRONS

As we have seen, "unapproved veneration" first won a degree of approval when a local authority—usually the bishop—opened the ordinary phase of the process of canonization. The success of this preliminary evaluation depended heavily on the strength of the patron in the local community. If the bishop was absent or disliked, old religious or political divisions were often reignited. For instance, in 1612 a metropolitan canon opened the canonization of Francisco Girolamo Simon in Valencia because the episcopal seat was temporarily vacant and thereby sparked riots in the city.[65] Shortly after the opening of the ordinary process, conflicts between Dominicans and

Franciscans in the city exploded, with the former decrying the veneration of Simon as excessive and unjustified. In response, some of Simon's supporters—inspired by Franciscan preaching—marched to the Dominican convent and demonstrated—even firing arquebuses at the building in protest.[66]

Even when there was not a great deal of acrimony in the opening of a process, the bishop or other official still needed a fair amount of locally accepted support to begin this extended undertaking. Canonizations began with a sermon in which the bishop or one of his agents announced that he would collect testimony about the holy life and miracles of the prospective saint. A location—usually a local church—and a time were then set for testimony to be taken. The bishop and a notary carefully recorded the testimonies. This process could be lengthy, as hundreds of witnesses might come forward for an especially popular saint: 139 testators appeared for Felice of Cantalice in 1587 alone, while Filippo Neri had 351 people testify for him between the opening of his ordinary process in 1595 and the beginning of the apostolic process in 1610.[67]

The resources that were required—both financially and organizationally—to maintain a notary to record hundreds of witness testimonies over months, if not years, were large. Therefore, even initially, a patron was required who was willing to devote resources and who had the authority to cajole or inspire local believers to come forward. And a single denunciation, even at this stage, could open an entire negative Inquisition proceeding, which would derail the process.[68]

Once the bishop or other official sent the ordinary process to Rome for review, another sort of patron was required: one who could grease the slow-moving wheels of the papal curia and hold the audience of successive popes. For most successful canonizations, support from a patron was made explicit from the moment the dossier arrived in Rome. For example, lay and clerical ambassadors from the city of Milan, who had been given a special commission not only by the city but also from the king of Spain, brought Carlo Borromeo's process to Rome in 1604.[69] Similarly, letters from the leaders of the Jesuit order and John IV of Portugal accompanied Francis Xavier's ordinary process.[70] Teresa of Avila's ordinary process was approved and her apostolic opened only after the king of Spain, Philip III, and his wife specifically wrote to the papacy to express their devotion to the prospective saint.[71] The petitions for the opening of Francisco de Borja's official canonization process included letters from many eminent people throughout the Iberian Peninsula, including the Spanish monarchs, the Duke of Lerma, and high-ranking members of the Jesuit order.[72] Thus, demonstrations of support from the elite ranks of society were important even during this early phase of the canonization process. Promoters had to illustrate that their prospective saint enjoyed the support of powerful patrons within the Roman Church for the bid to even be considered.

After the process began to move along the track to approval and was under review by first the Rota and then the Congregation of Rites, it could stall if there was not sufficient pressure placed on these bodies to move the canonization along at a steady rate. Each institution had more than just one canonization to consider and ruled upon a variety of other matters that had nothing to do with saints.[73] Furthermore, when a pope died, his successor often had different interests and so might direct efforts away from the canonization of a given holy person favored by the previous pope. A powerful patron was thus needed to drive a saint's cause if it was to remain a priority long enough for the bid to succeed.

Even Carlo Borromeo's process of canonization, which was the most rapidly carried out in this period, stalled in 1605 as it shifted from the ordinary to the apostolic process.[74] As the process dragged on for two years without much advancement, crowned heads throughout Europe began to flood the Curia with letters urging the completion of Borromeo's canonization. Philip III of Spain wrote the pope about his desire to see Borromeo canonized, as did Sigismund III, the king of Poland. The Dukes of Savoy, Parma, and Mantua, as well as several Swiss Catholic communities, expressed their support for Borromeo's canonization bid.[75] The process picked up speed and the Church canonized Borromeo in 1610. Indeed, the pressure exerted by these powers on the papacy may explain why Borromeo avoided the intermediary phase of beatification—the last saint to do so.[76]

The necessity of patronage is further revealed by the failed canonization attempt of Pope Gregory X (1271–1276). Pietro Maria Campi (1569–1649)—the main supporter of the cause—worked tirelessly for years in the early seventeenth century to gain official acceptance for Gregory's sanctity. While Campi did manage to win some support for Gregory through the powerful Farnese family, it was never enough to overcome the evidentiary issues that hindered the process. The Farnese family was just one Roman family, not a crowned head of state, and not even entirely unwavering in its support of Gregory.[77]

Even at a late stage in the canonization of Saint Hyacinth, the king of Poland, Sigismumd III (1587–1632), was careful to maintain explicit support. Prior to the final presentation of evidence on behalf of this prospective saint, the king sent an official to hold a gathering—reminiscent in many ways of a political rally—at a palace near Campo de' Fiori. Then, when he presented the evidence, this official marched to the Vatican with an amazing show of support, accompanied by "many curial officials, noble men, Roman barons, and other prelates."[78] Given the size of this rally and its route through major thoroughfares, much of the city's population was aware of it. It can be no surprise, then, that Hyacinth's canonization was approved shortly thereafter.

Although patronage sped the bureaucratic process of canonization, it also was required to pay for the increasingly expensive costs of canonization. The supporters of a saint cult paid for every phase in a canonization process from the diocesan inquiry up to the ceremony in which the pope proclaimed the newly minted saint to the world. Until the last phases of the canonization, these payments were made without any assurance that it would actually lead to the desired outcome. Given the enormous expense—both in time and in money—of canonization and the insecurity of the investment, putting one's money into a prospective saint was in itself a great act of faith. It was also an act that required a patron with access to extensive economic resources.

Lists of expenses do not normally appear in canonization *processi* and so it is only occasionally that we get a glimpse of how extraordinarily expensive canonization could be. The cost for Carlo Borromeo's canonization, records show, amounted to the staggering sum of about 30,000 ducats.[79] This was nearly the same amount it cost Venice to keep its largest warship in action for an entire year, including pay for all the men on board and for the equipment.[80] The cost comparison demonstrates how very important Borromeo's canonization was to Milan. The city and episcopacy of Milan, which footed the bill for this canonization, spent amounts on Borromeo's canonization that easily could have paid for the extension of city walls, numerous troops, or other important defensive measures during a period of regular warfare. That it chose instead to support a canonization bid confirms that saints were considered an essential good for the community in which they were venerated on par with, if not more important than, physical defense of the city.

Although it is not clear how all the money in Borromeo's cause was spent, the well-documented expenses for Francesca Romana's canonization (1608) give a great deal of information about the individual costs of saint-making in the early modern period. The price tag for her canonization, which seems to have represented only expenses from the apostolic phase of her process from 1604 to 1608, came to 19,000 scudi.[81] In addition to this general expense, various gifts, gratuities, and bribes had to be given to those involved at the moment of canonization. As a gratuity for the canonization, the promoters paid 500 scudi to the pope and 200 scudi to Franciso Peña for his role as deacon of the Rota; each of the other two Rota judges involved received 100 scudi, and Cardinal Pinello, the head of the Congregation of Rites, was awarded 200 scudi.[82] The list contains quite a few other people who were paid lesser sums: Giambattista Spada, the fiscal lawyer for the canonization, received twenty-five scudi, an unnamed papal physician received twelve, and even the Swiss Guards who attended the pope received four scudi each.[83] For comparison, artisans in the city of Rome made about three scudi a month, while police officers made four.[84] Thus, these "tips" were rather large financial awards with even the least payment equivalent to a whole month's salary for many Romans.

In addition to monetary remuneration, many also received costly garments and accessories in thanks for their efforts on the canonization. The pope was given a stole for processions, as well as a silk cord to cinch it, another stole for saying masses, a taffeta shirt, sandals and socks, an apron, a bag, and a mat with which he could cover his desk.[85] Others received silk garments, with a variety of embellishments depending on rank and status. The famous jurist Prospero Farinacci received a gown made of blue silk with a hood "like the consistorial lawyers wear."[86] The papal doctor was given a red garment with a hood.[87] Thus, canonization required a wide array of goods and monies that only truly eminent and wealthy patrons could be expected to furnish.

Perhaps due to such additional costs that could spiral out of control, Pope Benedict XIV (1740–1758), more than a hundred years later, sought to fix prices for canonization.[88] Benedict forbade the giving of gifts, even if they were only edible items, to those involved with canonization, and set the amount that could be given as a gratuity at a fairly low value.[89] Furthermore, he specified how much individual pieces of the canonization ceremony should cost. The prices were still surprisingly high: the Bull and Decree of canonization cost a total of 1650 scudi—just for the document.[90] Expenses for the festival to be held in Saint Peter's to celebrate a saint's election amounted to 20,400 scudi.[91] Given these efforts at setting prices, which we might imagine could be circumvented when one wanted to press for a canonization, saint-making continued to be an enormously expensive endeavor well into the eighteenth century. These high prices and expensive bribes, furthermore, were a burden that continued to be shouldered by the promoters of the saint's cause.

Patrons therefore acted as brokers for a saint's cult in a number of ways. First, they translated the veneration that was occurring locally into a dossier, vouched for by their good name, that might be acceptable to Rome. Then, throughout the process the patron kept the canonization moving forward through a combination of financial incentives and political displays. In many ways, the patron helped, in the words of Simon Ditchfield, to "universalize the particular."[92] That is, the patron tried to ensure that local patterns of belief became part of the overall tapestry of Catholic faith. Canonization officials in Rome, though, had their own apparatus whereby they evaluated evidence that came from the parishes and sought to determine whether or not it was in accordance with the belief system of the universal Church.

VERIFYING SANCTITY

The Church's increasingly rigorous attempt to demonstrate beyond all doubt that an individual should be recognized as a saint really began with the opening of the apostolic process of canonization.[93] Although certainly the ordinary phase of the process sought to establish that a person lived a holy life and worked miracles, especially in the seventeenth century, the apostolic phase represented a much more rigorous and centrally directed procedure. The pope opened the apostolic phase by issuing remissorial and compulsorial letters, which designated three local officials to oversee the canonization process in each locale and that specified which questions should be asked.[94] The letters required that a notary be present for all testimony to provide the stamp of law to the proceedings.[95]

The questions asked during the apostolic phase were carefully designed to establish whether certain criteria for holiness were met as well as to evaluate witness probity. The questions asked in the 1650 apostolic process in Valencia for Francisco de Borja are typical.[96] At the outset, witnesses for Borgia were first warned that it is a grave sin to commit perjury.[97] Following this initial admonition, the first round of questions sought to affirm the identity of the witness. Investigators asked witnesses for their first and last name, who their parents were, where they were from, how wealthy they were, and how they made their money.[98] Next the officials sought to assess the witness's probity: each was asked about his or her spiritual state, when and where they last confessed, if they received communion, and if they had ever been excommunicated. They also asked witnesses whether they had ever been convicted of a crime.[99] Finally, the judges asked if the witness's testimony had been coached in any way.[100]

Following the inquiry into the character of the witness, the judges then turned to questions about the saint. Frequently, these questions were open-ended. In the case of Borja, the judges asked a series of questions about his life that might lead to a range of answers, including whether the witness knew if Borja had a reputation for being a saint, what miracles he might have worked, and how the witness knew that what had occurred was actually a miracle.[101] Again, this set of questions appears to have been standard and was routinely asked in apostolic phases of canonization.[102] The motives behind such questioning were threefold: to ascertain whether the witness in fact knew the prospective saint, judged him to be holy, and understood what criteria were required to establish that an individual was a saint. Such distinctions were crucial since a witness's reliability was predicated on his ability to effectively understand what was happening when a miracle occurred.[103]

Following these initial questions, the Rota judges then sought specific details about the saint. The letters regularly supplied lists of miracles and virtues that witnesses could potentially confirm. Rota judges drew this list from testimony given in the ordinary process or the *in genere* phase of the apostolic process. Officials did not require witnesses to speak about each point on a list, but to select the items which they knew something about. In the case of Maria Magdalene de' Pazzi, this list for the Florentine phase of her apostolic process consisted of twenty items. The first group posited some basic facts about de' Pazzi—for example, that she was born legitimately, the identity of her parents, the date of her baptism, and how she was educated.[104] The next sections consisted of statements about her virtues. Testators were asked to affirm, for example, that "she had the greatest charity for her neighbor[s], longing for their salvation, and she cared for weak nuns, both looking after some novices, and instructing other nuns."[105]

Finally, the investigators turned to miracles, including specific ones to be certified. For de' Pazzi, they asked, for example, if "a fluid, similar to oil, emanated from her corpse and if a sweet odor came forth from her tomb."[106] Other topics, such as whether the deponent had witnessed many people attending the tomb of de' Pazzi, also appeared in the list.[107]

The questions and then the list of virtues and miracles were part of the apparatus whereby canonization officials attempted to demonstrate that the prospective saint merited canonization. The idea here is that proof is cumulative in nature and that the weight of many reliable witnesses to an event provided the most effective demonstration of its reality.[108] Thus, when the Rota compiled the apostolic process, for each miracle to be considered, a short summary would be created where each witness's account of what happened is produced in extract form.[109] The weight of the testimony for each miracle was thereby clearly laid out for readers to see.

In addition to soliciting testimony from witnesses who knew about the miracles of the prospective saint, the judges in an apostolic process sought testimony from experts in a wide variety of disciplines. In one case, an inquisitor who was investigating the veracity of a saint's relics called upon a woodworker as an expert. He asked the woodworker to use his knowledge to determine how much of the original relics survived in a wooden casing for a long dead saint. The inquisitor was prepared to quash the veneration if there was not enough of the saint left for devotion still to be shown toward the reliquary.[110] In another case, when the survival of a woman through a difficult childbirth was declared a miracle, midwives from the city of Rome were asked to evaluate whether it did in fact exceed the realm of the natural.[111]

In judging these cases, both the woodworker and the midwives relied on their own experience and on specific observations to respond to the canonization judges' questions. That is, the Church employed artisanal experts using empirical techniques to create knowledge about the holy in the sixteenth and seventeenth centuries. This matches what Pamela Long and Pamela Smith, among others, have uncovered, namely, that artisanal techniques of hands-on manipulation and direct observation began to enjoy status as viable methods of making knowledge during this period.[112]

In addition to using artisans as expert witnesses, Church officials employed techniques characteristic of various trades, those accustomed to using experience as a guide to practice, when it came to assessing the holy body. When canonization judges and medical professionals unearthed the body of Thomas of Villanova in 1611 (can. 1658), they recorded in thorough, firsthand detail their experience at the tomb. They visited his sepulcher on October 13 at the third hour of night.[113] The notary recounted in minute detail the appearance of the church and of Thomas's tomb, noting the exact dimensions of the room in which it sat as well as the number of votive tablets, candles, and other instruments of worship that believers had placed on the sepulcher.[114] When it came time to reveal Thomas's corpse, the notary stated that his actual tomb was "four and a half palms in length, two in width, and another two in depth covered in a purple veil propped up by gold pedestals and studded with gilded bolts [but] not properly closed or locked." He further gave the name of the woodworker, Simon, who opened the coffin.[115] Upon opening, the notary recorded what the medical team said and wrote down every bone that they found.[116] This level of detail appears to have been normal in canonization proceedings and also occurs, for example, in the visitation of Lorenzo Giustiniani's tomb in Venice.[117]

This extensive recounting of details in examining saintly bodies along with an emphasis on direct observation was a narrative technique characteristic of contemporary travel writing, legal studies, medicine, and, later, early experimental societies in order to make eyewitness testimony into a historical reality.[118] Spanish pilots sailing to the New World, for example, were asked by Spanish cartographers to record extensive descriptions of what they saw so that the cartographers could be sure of its accuracy.[119] Detail implied authenticity. Later in the seventeenth century, experimentalists with the Royal Society would use such elaborate detail to demonstrate that a real historical event or experiment actually had happened. Robert Boyle, for example, would engage in long descriptions of minutiae prior to and during an experiment. These details would demonstrate that no part of what had occurred was omitted and therefore the unusual event had occurred as described.[120] Canonization officials thus engaged in a culture of observational empiricism so as to demonstrate the reality of miracles as they occurred in the bodies of saints.

Perhaps the clearest combination of empiricism and expertise in canonization proceedings came during the physician-led examinations of saintly bodies, which is the focus of the remainder of the book. The evaluation of Andrea Corsini's body will serve as a preliminary example, though, which well illustrates the Church's embrace of such techniques. In 1606 local canonization judges in Florence asked the physician, Angelo Bonello, to evaluate the state of Corsini's corpse. Upon examining the body, Bonello "wondered at and admired the body's preservation [which was] beyond the bounds of nature."[121] That is, Bonello considered the preservation of the body to be miraculous.[122]

To bolster his testimony and conclusions about the body, though, Bonello enumerated a number of features that led him to his conclusion, including the cadaver's skin color, flexibility, and the contents of the abdomen, which he opened during his investigation.[123] In Bonello's own words: "Therefore I, Angelo Bonello, Florentine, extensively saw, touched, and smelled Corsini's body."[124] That is, he made an empirical survey of this corpse in which he observed and tested the corpse against his theoretical and practical knowledge of human cadavers and decay. Furthermore, he demonstrated what he found in a semi-public autopsy in which seventeen other witnesses were present. These witnesses added their names to Bonello's notarized description of the event. The signatories were men of standing, consisting of some of the most eminent contemporary Florentine citizens: a senator, a member of the Guiccardini family, the Florentine inquisitor general, a local surgeon, and many other illustrious prelates.[125] The document for Corsini's wondrous corpse thus represented a rich tapestry of evidentiary devices including empirical demonstrations, common assent, and philosophical discussion of the boundaries of nature. As this example illustrates, canonization officials relied on a number of techniques at this moment, including various forms of empirical knowledge making, to help make a miracle appear not just believable but a verifiable reality.

Physicians, therefore, represented ideal expert witnesses for the Church because they could deploy so many evidentiary devices in their testimonies about miracles. It was for this reason that canonization officials frequently asked physicians to reinterpret miracles that might have evidentiary issues. During the canonization process of Lorenzo Giustiniani, for example, Domenico Maffeo testified to Giustiniani's miraculous healing of his son, also named Lorenzo, who was suffering from epilepsy. Maffeo was a less than optimal witness, however, having previously been accused of killing a person; in addition, his son, a few years after the miraculous cure, died.[126] Thus, both the testator and the subject of the cure were not considered reliable. In evaluating this evidence, the Tribunal of the Rota turned to Paolo Zacchia, a famous Roman physician and author of a treatise entitled *Medical-Legal Questions*, a foundational work of forensic medicine.[127] That the Rota asked Zacchia, rather than consult with one of the local surgeons who resided near Maffeo, suggests the Church's preference for prestige and a physician rather than direct observation of an event. Zacchia was asked to reevaluate this supposed miracle and see if it could be made to meet Rome's evidentiary standards.[128] Zacchia diagnosed the boy's illness as a specific disease, came up with a prognosis, and concluded that there was no natural way that the body could have been healed.[129] Through a mix of theoretical training and experience, Zacchia was able to conclude that the boy's healing was miraculous. Thus, Zacchia thereby turned questionable testimony produced outside Rome into evidence acceptable to the Roman Curia. Expert witnesses, and especially physicians, functioned in a role somewhere between agents of papal authority and negotiators between local and official sanctity.

As these examples show, canonization processes introduced a number of techniques whereby evidence produced at a local level in the parishes was reinterpreted and reevaluated through agents of the Roman Curia. These techniques married both the empirical methods characteristic of artisanal practitioners with the natural philosophic modes of interpretation available to physicians and theologians. In this way, ideas about sanctity generated locally were integrated into and made acceptable for the universal Church. Canonization after Trent was both an imposition of central authority and an act of negotiation between the center of the Catholic world and its peripheries.

The final act in the reform and introduction of more rigor into canonization after the Reformation was the creation of the office of *promotor fidei* by Pope Urban VIII in 1631. The individual holding this office was deputed to sit with the Congregation of Rites when they vetted the apostolic process. However, his job was an unusual one: his goal was to find errors with the process and potential reasons why a candidate should not be canonized, thus earning the unofficial nickname of the "Devil's Advocate."[130] In practice, this meant that after the testimony for the miracles and the virtues of a prospective saint were summarized, the promotor fidei would attack individual elements of the argument for canonization. He might impugn the reliability of witnesses, argue that a miracle may have been invented or exaggerated, or question whether testimony about miracles stemmed more from a misunderstanding about how nature worked rather than an actual appearance of a miracle.

The evaluation of the promotor fidei carried out during the apostolic phase of the canonization of Alfonso Toribio in 1675 (can. 1712) represents nicely the way in which these agents vetted canonization processes. The promotor in this case was Prospero Bottini (1621–1712), the Archbishop of Myra. He evaluated the evidence for a number of miracles that Toribio supposedly had carried out both in life and after his death. The information produced during his evaluation was printed in a type of document called a *Positio super dubio*. Such works were published to demonstrate the extreme care and caution that the Church took when evaluating the lives and miracles of the saints. The *Positio* for Toribio contains an initial summary of the evidence for each miracle, then Bottini's objections to it, followed by rebuttals to Bottini's arguments either by a consistorial lawyer, Federico Caccia, or the eminent physician Paolo Manfredi. The choice of Manfredi as expert medical witness was not casual: he was at the forefront of medicine in the seventeenth century. In the years immediately prior to giving testimony in this case, he had carried out some of the earliest experiments on blood transfusion and undertaken careful anatomical research into the structure of the eye and the ear.[131] He responded to Boccini's objections in many of the medical cases, while in several cases both Caccia and Manfredi offered rebuttals.[132] Thus, any miracle accepted for Toribio's canonization had been considered by multiple experts before it was actually deemed verified.

This debate between the promotor fidei, medical practitioners, and lawyers over the miracles for Toribio demonstrates the ways in which the negotiation for sanctity had evolved in the seventeenth century. First, each of the expert witnesses involved in this case was selected by the Roman Curia and resided in Rome. In addition, their arguments focused on specific and expert pieces of knowledge that were beyond the ability of most parishioners to evaluate.[133] Thus, sanctity was a matter removed from its original, locally constructed beginnings. In some sense, the introduction of the promotor fidei could be seen as the final act of centralization of canonization under the papacy.

Yet even in this case, the importance of local belief and the role of patrons is evident. All the testimony came from Lima, Peru, where Toribio had died, and the experts in Rome took it at face value—that is, they evaluated and accepted Toribio's holiness according to the testimony of those residing in the New World. Furthermore, patronage is everywhere evident. Not only had all this testimony been sent from Peru to Italy, but it had also been translated into Latin and circulated in print form. All this would have cost time and money. Finally, the current Archbishop of Lima was present for some of the miracles that had occurred, implying some sort of involvement by this local patron who was perhaps looking for miracles enacted by the prospective saint.[134] He was acting, as Baronio had for Loyola, as a promoter who sought to encourage veneration for his deceased predecessor.

CONCLUSION

The long history of saints in the Catholic Church might appear to be a struggle between central authority and local belief. Yet in many ways, this is more appearance than reality. Prior to the sixteenth century, attempts to regulate local veneration were either non-existent or only very unevenly applied. Then, even after a number of institutional changes altered significantly the bodies associated with saint-making in the sixteenth century, local veneration continued along older models.

The real changes came in the early seventeenth century, when repression of local cults was unified with increasing standardization of the techniques whereby parochial veneration turned into universal canonization. Such an act of canonization required enthusiastic support both at home and in the form of eminent patrons. These patrons translated the local enthusiasm into a dossier of evidence that brought the saint's case to Rome, where a process of negotiation began. This meant the potential holy individual was subject to an increasingly rigorous evaluation. The Church employed a variety of methods to ascertain the truth of an individual's sanctity, including verification of witness probity, the use of multiple witnesses for an event, and the deployment of new narrative techniques designed to validate miracles. Many of these techniques mirrored the empirical methods employed by artisanal practitioners in a number of fields. The Church's use of such techniques very likely contributed to the legitimation and eventual appropriation of such empirical methods by those who studied the natural world.[135]

In addition to these techniques, the Church also came to rely heavily on experts in their attempt to demonstrate the reality of miracles. Lawyers, craftsmen, and a variety of medical practitioners began to make regular appearances at the meetings of the Tribunal of the Rota and the Congregation of Rites. Although medieval churchmen had used experts during canonization, the early modern Church relied extensively on expert testimony to help it verify the most important miracles. Through reliance on such testimony, canonization became less a matter of popular acclaim and more an exercise in expertise.

The remaining chapters of this book focus on one set of experts—medical professionals—and their attempts to turn popular ideas about bodily signs of holiness into evidence that demonstrated the reality of a saint's miracles. The next chapter charts the rise to prominence of the expert medical witness and the increasingly important role anatomy played in this evolution.

CHAPTER 2

A New Criterion for Sanctity

On March 12, 1622, Pope Gregory XV (1621–1623) forcefully reasserted the validity of the cult of the saints when he simultaneously canonized five individuals: Isidore the Laborer (d. 1130), Francis Xavier (d. 1552), Ignatius Loyola (d. 1556), Teresa of Avila (d. 1582), and Filippo Neri (d. 1595). With the exception of Isidore, each of these saints lived after the Reformation and had been active in encouraging new piety and devotion to the Church. Although several canonizations had taken place following the long break after the Reformation, such a large "group canonization" of early modern saints clearly proclaimed the renewed strength of the faith and the confidence of Church leaders in their ability to discern saints.[1]

In addition to reasserting the validity of the cult of the saints, this group canonization also introduced a new standard that would henceforth be used in vetting the potentially holy: the corpses of prospective saints would undergo medical examination. Each of the saints canonized in 1622 and most of those considered for canonization during the remainder of the seventeenth century were subjected to posthumous medical evaluations, frequently including full autopsies.[2] This new standard formed part of the process of centralizing canonization, which was described in the last chapter. The medical expert became an agent of papal authority who turned local, particular ideas about holiness into universal, Catholic ones.

Nevertheless, the advent of the medical witness as the verifier of bodily sanctity was not simply a top-down imposition from Rome; rather, it represented the eventual adoption by canonization officials of new ways of making knowledge about the natural world. As this chapter argues, the initial push to introduce medical postmortems into canonization proceedings came from the promoters of a saint's cult. The body and the remains of the saint were central to the elaboration of his or her cult locally.[3] In the wake of the Reformation, however, undue veneration of noncanonized individuals could be considered suspect.[4] In an effort to justify such enthusiasm for the remains of local holy people, promoters of sanctity turned to the burgeoning field of anatomy.

The study of anatomy itself was undergoing profound changes during this period. In particular, the number of printed anatomical case studies exploded in the sixteenth and seventeenth centuries and represented part of a transition in the methods that were acceptable for making knowledge about the natural world.[5] Indeed, Gianna Pomata has argued that a new epistemic genre, the *Observationes*, arose in medicine at this point as a means to present firsthand observations as a guide for practice in order to gain knowledge about the body. This emphasis on experience and practical training, in turn, contributed to the rising prestige of anatomy.[6] By the end of this period, many believed physician-anatomists were uniquely able to read recondite signs found in the human cadaver and thereby say something about the deceased's life and death and possibly his or her interaction with the divine.[7] The postmortem investigation could provide a window into an individual's most private moments and therefore was of great use to canonization officials who wanted to know as much as they could about a prospective saint.

Canonization officials were, however, slow to recognize the utility of anatomical studies for verifying sanctity. The first saint canonized after Trent, Diego of Alcalá, was widely reported to have a miraculously incorrupt corpse, yet medical testimony never confirmed it. When promoters of the canonizations of Carlo Borromeo and Ignatius Loyola attempted to use anatomical details as part of the demonstration of these candidates' holiness, Roman authorities failed to recognize the validity of the evidence submitted. Yet over the course of succeeding decades, Roman officials—especially under the guidance of the important deacon of the Rota, Francisco Peña (1540–1612)—began to recognize and then require postmortem examination of prospective saints. Through its eventual adoption of the empirical methods that had been deployed to make knowledge in the field of anatomy, the Church began to change how it made saints. The medical practitioner transformed wondrous signs found in the human body into a miracle for the whole faith. By cooperating in this way, medical and religious understanding of the body were removed from their local context and made into universal knowledge. From tentative beginnings, anatomy became a recognized mode of demonstrating extraordinary human holiness that was central to the Church's reestablishment of canonization after the Reformation.

SAINT DIEGO'S WONDER-WORKING CORPSE

In 1588 Pope Sixtus V proclaimed Diego of Alcalá a saint, making him the first person canonized in sixty-five years. Diego had, in fact, long been considered a holy man by his local community, and following his death in 1463 a number of miracles were attributed to him. However, in the wake of the Reformation, many of his wondrous acts were contested.[8] In the subsequent debate, an unusually large number of physicians testified either for or against Diego. The prominence of medicine in this first canonization after Trent set the stage for the increased use of experts in canonization and what can be thought of as the "medicalization" of the holy body.

One of the most important and contested miracles counting for Diego's canonization was his postmortem healing in 1562 of Don Carlos, the seventeen-year-old son of King Philip II of Spain. Given the prominence of Don Carlos's family, this healing miracle gained for Diego almost overnight broad support for his canonization and an enthusiastic patron in the person of Philip himself. The tale of the miracle begins with Don Carlos stumbling down several stairs while chasing a "comely wench." He then smashed his head against the closed door at the bottom of the staircase with enough force to open a large gash. Although not initially considered life threatening, the wound became badly infected. At the prompting of King Philip II, a team of ten of the most eminent medical practitioners in all of Europe—including Andreas Vesalius—was called upon to attend the prince. Despite their efforts, these medical practitioners feared their young patient would not survive.[9]

That Don Carlos's wound did heal was attributed to Diego's intercession. The holy man's long-dead body was exhumed and brought to the ailing prince's bedside. According to numerous witnesses, the prince recovered only after his body made contact with Diego's corpse. Witnesses also noted that the corpse was strangely sweet-smelling and lifelike, despite having spent nearly one hundred years in the ground.[10] On the strength of this miracle and the wave of support that it engendered, Diego was canonized. This act was at least as much a political as a religious move. Pope Sixtus V used this canonization both to reward King Philip for his efforts in defending Catholicism and to encourage him in his planned invasion of England, which took place later that same year.[11] Thus, the papacy and the king of Spain desired this canonization.

Even with papal and royal support for Diego, medical opinion surrounding this healing of Don Carlos had been far from unanimous. Don Carlos's personal physician, Diego Olivares, declared that he did not believe the healing to be unusual in any way: "In my opinion it [the healing] was not [miraculous] because the prince was cured with natural and ordinary remedies, with which one usually cures others with the same injury or worse."[12] Olivares conceded that Don Carlos had likely been helped by God or his servants, but he cautioned that a miraculous healing must "exceed all natural forces" and this one had not done that.[13]

Another physician, Christobal de Vega, contradicted Olivares and specifically attributed Don Carlos's healing to the intercession of Diego's miraculous body. Indeed, de Vega argued that those medical practitioners who did not agree with this account of the cure were acting out of pride and they dissimulated in order to give the impression that the healing was caused "more by their own efforts than by the miracle."[14] De Vega's opinion carried the day, presumably because his discrediting of the other medical practitioners was entirely plausible—these men undoubtedly wanted to salvage their prestigious careers after Don Carlos's near death at their hands.

Almost completely unmentioned in these medical narratives was the miraculous instrument of the cure: the body of San Diego.[15] However, according to several nonmedical witnesses, Diego's century-old corpse had rotted so little that it appeared to be almost alive. As one witness noted with obvious astonishment, the corpse still "had its entire nose," which was normally one of the first parts of a body to decay.[16]

Despite the failure of the medical team to describe Diego's corpse, his hagiographers eagerly recounted its degree of preservation. Pietro Galesini, for example, who produced an official vita for the saint during his canonization, stressed the miraculous state of Diego's corpse during Don Carlos's healing.[17] Similarly, another biographer,

Francesco Bracciolini, recounted in detail the wondrous preservation of Diego's body upon exhumation.[18]

The prominence of Diego's incorrupt corpse in hagiography but its absence from the medical accounts suggests that postmortem analysis of holy bodies was not yet valued as part of canonization proceedings. Despite this medical disinterest, lay believers eagerly sought signs of the holy in the cadavers of the deceased and publicized their own interpretations of what they found. For them, Diego's incorrupt body was an obvious demonstration of his sanctity.[19] In the context of the Counter-Reformation, such enthusiasm was both useful and problematic: the Church wanted passionate believers, but sought to avoid accusations that miracles were merely the inventions of overly enthusiastic disciples. How, then, were Church reformers to make such classical signs of holiness rigorous and also controllable?

At this juncture, the eminent Spanish canon lawyer Francisco Peña, spurred by the canonization of San Diego, in which he took part, realized the usefulness of medicine in both justifying and controlling the interpretation of bodily evidence of the holy. In his role as a member of the Tribunal of the Rota, the highest ecclesiastical court, which judged evidence in canonization proceedings, Peña helped make the medically verified holy body a key miracle for any potential saint.[20] In so doing, Peña removed a key aspect of local piety from the bishops' authority and thereby contributed to the overall strength of the papacy in the early modern period.[21]

Francisco Peña was well suited and ideologically motivated to make a significant change to the understanding of sanctity in the early modern Catholic world. Born in Villaroya de los Pinares, near Saragossa, Spain, he was a highly learned individual, holding doctorates in Roman and canonical law as well as in theology from the University of Valencia. King Philip II of Spain introduced Peña to the papal court during the reign of Pope Pius IV (1566–1572). Despite this introduction, which might have prompted feelings of loyalty to the Spanish monarch, Peña immediately embarked on a number of projects that served to expand papal power and jurisdiction. These ventures included the censoring of works that criticized papal power, a revision of the standard manual on inquisition procedure, and the publishing of a number of hagiographies.[22] Although these tasks might seem disparate, the proclamation of saints and the actions of the Roman Inquisition both increasingly came under papal purview and eventually were considered expressions of papal authority during the late sixteenth and early seventeenth centuries.[23]

According to Peña's personal testimony, the task to which he most seriously applied himself was the canonization of the saints. As he asserted in his vita of Carlo Borromeo (canonized 1610), canonization was the "most important and most arduous thing that the Holy See controls."[24] In stating this, as first auditor and then deacon of the Tribunal of the Rota from 1588 until his death in 1612, Peña perhaps indulged in slight self-aggrandizement; this assignment of preeminence made him a central figure in the Curia since the Rota was the highest court in the Church and was charged with weighing the evidence in canonization trials to ensure that it was sufficient and sufficiently accurate before a process went forward. Peña thus had a major role in determining who was a saint during the very years in which sainthood was first being articulated after the long hiatus of the sixteenth century. In particular, Peña was deeply involved in the canonization proceedings of Hyancinth of Poland, Raymond of Penafort, Francesca Romana, Carlo Borromeo, Filippo Neri, Teresa of Avila, Elizabeth of Portugal, and Andrea Corsini.[25] Additionally, as he oversaw the Rota during the early proceedings for Isidore the Laborer, Francis Xavier, and Ignatius of Loyola, Peña likely exercised a strong influence over these canonizations. During these proceedings, which stretched over thirty-five years, from 1594 (Hyancinth) to 1629 (Andrea Corsini), the medical examination of the corpses of prospective saints became regular. Peña was, at least in part, responsible for this new emphasis on the body as is documented in many of his writings.

Revealingly, an early sign of the importance that Peña attached to the holy body emerges from the vita he wrote for Diego of Alcalá. Like other hagiographers, Peña commented on the failure of Diego's cadaver to rot and on its sweet smell despite having spent nearly a century in the ground. However, unlike hagiographers before him, Peña used a full eight pages to provide details about the corpse and its appearance.[26] In this section of this vita, he suggested various methods to establish an incorrupt corpse, including a detailed description of its level of preservation, the evaluation of firsthand witness reports, and the listing of similar, medieval cases in which this miracle was approved.[27] In short, Peña deployed a mix of empirical evidence and historical precedent to document how Diego's body had miraculously resisted rot. Clearly, Peña was preoccupied with the ways in which the miracle of an incorrupt body, in particular, could be established.

Peña's emphasis on the importance of the incorrupt body as a sign of sanctity is a repeated theme in his printed works. In his vita of Saint Raymond Penafort, for example, Peña argues that "the sweet odors that issue from the tombs of the dead are miraculous" and furthermore are "the sign that within them resides the Author of life [God]."[28] In his vita for Francesca Romana, Peña states that there is only space to discuss her most important miracles, "among which was the sweet odor that issued from her body, with which Divine Mercy well demonstrates the holiness of his servant."[29] Additionally, he concludes, "it was a wondrous thing that her body had not spoiled or rotted, but remained soft, flexible, and tractable, as if it were alive."[30] Although the incorrupt body was clearly an important miracle for Peña, in none of his printed saintly vita does he explicitly state that expert witnesses—e.g., physicians—should be used to confirm such miraculous phenomena. Only in an inquisition manual did Peña advise judges to use experts from other fields, including medical practitioners, to help in vetting the potentially holy.[31] Nevertheless, in his official and private canonization documents, Peña routinely began to call upon medical professionals to confirm the miraculous incorruption of saints' bodies.

As deacon of the Rota, Peña oversaw the composition of the letters that opened the apostolic phase of a canonization.[32] These letters specified how the proceedings should be conducted, including what sort of questions should be asked and which miracles and virtues were to be verified. Beginning early in the seventeenth century, in several cases directed by Francisco Peña, these letters included a clause ordering that the tomb of the purportedly holy individual be surveyed and the body unearthed. This clause apparently meant that medical professionals should conduct a postmortem survey of the corpse, since in these cases a medical investigation immediately followed the visitation of the body.[33] Later letters explicitly required medical intervention. Those opening the apostolic phase of canonization for Peter Alcantara in 1618, for example, specified that his body must be examined by "one or two physicians and one surgeon or other experts with the skills for inspecting the body, the bones, and remains of the servant of God, Peter of Alcantara."[34] In this way, by the early seventeenth century, postmortem examination of a holy body became part of the Rome-directed apostolic process of canonization. This new reliance on expertise represented an extension of centralized papal authority into local communities and a new requirement for canonization.

Peña, who already addressed the problem of demonstrating the incorruption of a corpse, was a major figure behind the creation of the new standard. With this innovation, however, he both exploited an old alliance between medicine and religion and benefitted from the newly recognized power of anatomy to make sense of the human body.

THE CHURCH AND MEDICINE

The Church's alliance with medicine was long standing, and as early as the thirteenth century medical professionals testified to healing miracles in canonization proceedings.[35] Medical professionals were asked to take part in these proceedings because they could authenticate the testimonies of "simple people" that might have otherwise been dubious. Local physicians in particular were important as they could rule out possible natural explanations for a healing.[36] Joseph Ziegler, however, has observed that such testimony was not a requirement in canonization proceedings and was based on local availability of medical practitioners.[37] Medical testimony about healing miracles in late medieval canonization proceedings was therefore ad hoc and represented a nice addition to other witness testimony rather than a replacement of it.

Historians of early modern Europe, including Fernando Vidal and David Gentilcore, note that after the Council of Trent (1545–1563) verification of healing miracles in canonization proceedings changed in two significant ways. First, testimonies became more technical, with medical witnesses relying both on experience and philosophical training to rule out natural explanations for a miraculous cure. Second, medical verification of a healing miracle became regular in this period and, eventually, a specific requirement.[38]

Despite this recent detailed research on the role of medical professionals in confirming healing miracles, little has been written about their role in the posthumous examination of the corpses of deceased holy men and women. Although Katharine Park has studied examinations of holy bodies in the medieval period, those works that have touched on the early modern period tend to focus on the most famous, printed cases of autopsies, such as those of Filippo Neri, Carlo Borromeo, and Ignatius Loyola.[39] The postmortems on prospective saints, however, form an important part of the interaction between Catholicism and medicine in the early modern period both because they were so widespread—nearly every canonized saint and many other holy individuals were subjected to a posthumous examination—and because they demonstrate that the Church valued new medical practices and ways of making knowledge.

Confirming a healing miracle as opposed to judging a body to be miraculously irregular required a different set of skills and implied a different relationship between medicine and religion. In order to confirm a healing miracle, a medical professional was forced to admit that he was unable to explain how the healing occurred and that, to his knowledge, the recovery that had happened was impossible. The success of healing miracles requires the failure of medicine. In contrast, to judge a body holy a physician employed experience, knowledge of modern and classic medical writers and philosophers, and surgical skill to isolate and explain unusual anatomical features.[40] Therefore, the postmortems on saints were a judgment by the Church of the positive contribution that medical professionals could make in defining the boundaries of the natural rather than, in the case of healing miracles, forcing such practitioners to admit the inadequacy of their skills.

The Church had good reason to view the medical profession, and especially anatomy, positively in the sixteenth and seventeenth centuries. The practice of opening human bodies was of long standing by the sixteenth century and had begun in the late medieval period for a number of reasons: (1) to embalm the elite for as part of burial practices, (2) to determine the cause of death, (3) to investigate murders, and (4) to check physical signs of a saint's holiness.[41] From at least the twelfth century, an additional reason why medical practitioners engaged in anatomical investigations was to support the knowledge they gleaned from classical sources. The medical school in Salerno carried out animal dissection even at this early date. The first recorded use of a dissection to explain conclusions in a medical treatise appeared in a work by Mondino dei Liuzzi in 1316. Nevertheless, these dissections were to serve a didactic function, not an exploratory purpose.[42] That is, they were meant to illustrate the principles observed in the canonical treatises of Galen, Aristotle, and Hippocrates, not challenge them. It was for this purpose that the Universities of Bologna and Padua established yearly, public anatomical dissections. The practice of public dissection was commonplace by the time they appear in the 1405 university statutes of Bologna and in the 1465 statutes of Padua.[43]

Therefore, when canonization officials turned to anatomy to help establish bodily miracles, they drew on a number of long-standing autopsy practices in Europe. The initial and ostensible reason that many saintly bodies were opened was to embalm the corpse for display. However, forensic motivations also inspired the dissectors, who sought anatomical explanation of either unusual ailments or behavior in prospective saints. Finally, since these medical men were testifying in a legal context, the established practice of using medical professionals as expert witnesses in criminal proceedings likely also inspired canonization officials. In short, that Peña and other canonization officials turned to anatomy to help demonstrate sanctity was in some ways a logical step, since the opening of human bodies had been commonplace in a number of related legal, funerary, and medical contexts. Indeed, Katharine Park has argued that it was a similar mix of motivations that led to the opening of female saintly bodies in the fourteenth century.[44]

Yet there were also new practices in medicine and anatomy that altered both who was involved with the postmortems on prospective saints and how the evidence found in the body was interpreted. In the medieval examinations of holy women, a physician generally was not present when the body was opened, whereas in the sixteenth and seventeenth centuries the Church required specifically that physicians undertake the examination.[45] This represents not just a change in personnel but also in what a physician's duties and knowledge areas were supposed to be. The physicians were expected both to find unusual details in the human body and interpret them in part of an overall discussion of what could be natural for this specific body. That is, canonization officials expected physicians to draw on both empirical and theoretical medical knowledge to speak both about human bodies in general and a specific corpse in particular.

The reason for the Church's new expectations for their physician-testators was based on ongoing changes in how knowledge was made in medicine in the early modern period. Although still rooted in classical medical authorities such as Galen and Hippocrates, medicine by the early sixteenth century was undergoing what has been termed a "Renaissance" in its understanding of the human body.[46] This was fueled by the increasing availability of old texts and a circulation of some newly discovered texts from the ancient world.[47]

During the sixteenth century, medicine increasingly emphasized firsthand experience of anatomy as a guide to understanding the human body. Traditionally considered a low form of knowledge making, one typically relegated to nonphysician practitioners, direct observation as a guide to practice was beginning to be recognized as more important for the medical profession. New works in fact circulated that sought to share such information widely—a clear indication of its value for the profession.[48] By the early sixteenth century, then, a few physicians, including Alessandro Benedetti, Jacopo Berengario da Carpi, and Niccolò Massa, had conducted autopsies with their own hands as a way of uncovering new knowledge about the workings of human anatomy.[49]

Real change in attitudes toward dissection is evident in the 1543 publication of Andreas Vesalius's *On the Fabric of the Human Body*. Despite his reliance on Galen in some respects, Vesalius also argued forcefully for the utility of firsthand knowledge of dissection.[50] Indeed, Vesalius represented a fusion of knowledge-making techniques, since he employed the empirical methods characteristic of surgeons and apothecaries as well as using classical texts as sources with which to make knowledge about the human body.[51] A number of anatomists, including Realdo Colombo and Charles Estienne, also engaged in this synthesis of empirical and learned practices and added their own arguments about the structure of the human body based on these methods.[52] By the seventeenth century, Vesalian methods of dissection, according to historian Roy Porter, "had become the golden method for anatomical investigation."[53] This perhaps overstates the case, however, as students at even the best medical schools still might have had irregular access to actual dissections and many practitioners remained unconvinced by the new methods.[54]

Nevertheless, the power of Vesalian techniques is amply demonstrated by the number of landmark anatomical studies that were produced around the year 1600. Such publications documented for the first time the valves in human veins, the mechanisms of digestion, the structure of female reproductive anatomy, and, finally, the circulation of blood.[55] Many physicians had now embraced an epistemology that fused empirical investigation with textual evidence as a way to understand the human body.

In sum, when the Church turned to physicians to conduct postmortems on holy individuals, it both drew on existing legal, funerary, and medical precedents relating to autopsies and embraced new trends about how medical professionals made knowledge about the human body. The following sections detail how this collaboration between medicine and religion developed over the course of the late sixteenth and early seventeenth centuries.

THE FIRST ATTEMPTS: IGNATIUS OF LOYOLA
AND CARLO BORROMEO

The postmortems performed on Ignatius of Loyola (d. 1556) and Carlo Borromeo (d. 1584) represent the first documented post-Reformation attempts to use anatomy to establish sanctity.[56] In each case, the examination occurred shortly after the holy man's death, and embalming was the initial reason for opening the corpse.[57] The embalming of elites had been routine since the late Middle Ages and was not unusual in these cases.[58] However, upon opening each corpse, the medical practitioners and other spectators involved discovered unusual anatomy. This anatomy then became the focal point of the postmortem. But the significance attached to the anatomy was not fixed: physicians, eager to promote their careers, saw in the bodies of saints the possibility of extending and illustrating their range of medical knowledge. In contrast, hagiographers who wrote about these postmortems sought to use anatomy as evidence of the divine. Each group engaged in the emerging genre of using direct observation to make knowledge so as to further a specific aim.[59] But the fact that the same anatomical details could be interpreted very differently demonstrates that the meaning of bodily evidence was unstable and subjective. This instability meant that the negotiations about the significance of specific anatomical irregularities led to the exclusion of this evidence from the list of miracles for each of these two saints.

The autopsy of Ignatius of Loyola, occurring shortly after his death in 1556, demonstrates clearly the different meanings and uses of holy anatomy in the mid-sixteenth century. Owing to his prominence as the founder of the Jesuit order, Loyola was opened by the most eminent physician currently residing in Rome, Realdo Colombo (1515–1559), the professor of anatomy at the University of Rome La Sapienza.[60] The declared reason for opening Loyola's body was an embalming effort requested by the Jesuits.[61] There may also have been forensic motivation, as Loyola's final ailment had not been considered life-threatening by his physicians.[62] Still, the autopsy was not initially expected to confirm any signs of sanctity. It was only because Colombo found such unusual anatomy inside the deceased Jesuit that he thought it worthy of documentation.

Colombo recounted the details of Loyola's postmortem in his anatomical manual *De re anatomica*, published in 1559 as part of a narrative that emphasized his own expertise. In fact, the entire text of

Colombo's *De re anatomica* was intended to promote its author's reputation and, to some extent, attack Vesalius, whom Colombo viewed as a rival.[63] Throughout the text, Colombo based his authority in part on the immense experience that he had with dissection and autopsy.[64] The section in which Loyola's autopsy appears, in particular, seems to have been designed to demonstrate Colombo's superior skill and knowledge as an anatomist. This section purports to treat "those things which are rarely found in anatomy."[65] Colombo emphasizes, though, that such rarities were in some ways not new to him: "I, however, from the beginning of my career have dissected innumerous bodies, and in the last fifteen years I have dissected an even greater number in the center of the well-attended academies of Pavia, Pisa, and Rome."[66] In addition, Colombo notes that he sometimes "dissected fourteen bodies in a year" and that "no type of body has been denied to me for dissection, except for a man who was mute from birth."[67] Thus, this section served to underline Colombo's skill and demonstrate that he had more knowledge of human anatomy than his contemporaries or than even the classical authorities on anatomy.

Colombo suggests in this section that he undertook a great many private autopsies, which added to his knowledge of human anatomy. As two editors of his work note, it would be difficult for a modern pathologist who performed hundreds of autopsies a year to see all the abnormalities that Colombo had observed, let alone a sixteenth-century practitioner who should have at most been opening a few dozen.[68] Cynthia Klestinec has argued that private, explorative autopsies were much more common and were considered surer ways of gaining knowledge of the human body than had previously been thought for early modern Europe.[69] By highlighting the extreme diversity that he had seen in human bodies, Colombo was suggesting to knowledgeable readers that he had opened far more bodies than would have been officially allowed. This would, in turn, imply that he had greater knowledge of the human body and accuracy in describing it than his competitors who did not go to such lengths. The postmortem on Loyola, which appeared in this section, was therefore part of a statement about Colombo's extensive knowledge acquired through firsthand investigation.

Colombo's narrative of Loyola's postmortem clearly emphasized his personal experience with anatomy and his extensive knowledge of the human body. He made it clear that he, rather than a surgeon or barber, opened the body and handled Loyola's entrails, stating that he "extracted with these hands innumerable stones from his penis and found stones of various colors in his lungs, liver, and in the vena porta. . . . I saw moreover pebbles in the urinary duct in the bladder, in the colon, in the hemorrhoidal vein and in his navel area."[70] Although these were unusual details, Colombo stated he had seen other bodies with similar problems.[71] The narrative, then, advertised Colombo's expertise: he had been invited to open the eminent leader of the Jesuit order, had performed the autopsy with his own hands, and found details that might be unusual to other anatomists, but which were familiar to him. The saint's anatomy was important not because of any miracle—in fact, Colombo explicitly states that Loyola's unusual anatomy is within the realm of the natural—but because it demonstrated Colombo's skill and the ability of the new anatomists to understand variation within the human body.

In contrast, Loyola's fellow Jesuit and attendant during his final illness, Giovanni Polanco, immediately interpreted the anatomical details in a religious light. His narrative of the postmortem appeared in a letter Polanco initially sent to the superiors of the Jesuit order. Shortly thereafter, this letter circulated in anonymous copies. That it was widely distributed can be surmised from the fact that copies survive in Latin, Spanish, and Italian versions.[72] The Jesuits' attempt to disseminate the knowledge of Loyola's anatomy suggests that even at this early stage, anatomy could demonstrate his sanctity. Furthermore, circulating Polanco's observations in a letter full of firsthand experience suggests that these Jesuits actively engaged in the epistemic genre of *Observationes* in an attempt to make knowledge about the holy.

According to Polanco, the autopsy provided evidence that Loyola had lived a remarkably ascetic life. Polanco's letter states that, upon opening Loyola's body, the physicians "discovered that his stomach and intestines were quite small and without anything inside them." The physicians then declared that they understood these irregularities to be a sign of the great feats of self-denial that Loyola had undertaken.[73] The numerous stones found in Colombo's body were reinterpreted as part of this narrative: Loyola's extreme asceticism had made his liver harden and produce stones.[74] These stones would, in turn, have been painful to bear. Thus, Loyola's anatomy demonstrated that he had lived a life of extreme ascetic rigor that caused a great deal of unseen hardship for the holy man.

This anatomical demonstration of Loyola's asceticism may have been especially necessary, since other accounts did not cast Loyola as bearing his final illness with the heroic patience of a saint. His friend Pedro Ribadeneira, who wrote the first posthumous biography of the saint, depicted Loyola as so "surrounded and oppressed by infirmities" that he wanted to "see himself with Christ," that is, die.[75] This yearning for death because of his pain was in contrast to the advice Loyola himself had given a friend just two years earlier. Loyola told his friend that an illness was "an occasion for merit and the exercise of virtue" in patient forbearance.[76] That Loyola was in so much pain that he wished for death implied that he was not, in fact, bearing his pain with virtuous patience. Furthermore, as Ribadeneira noted, "the doctors [medici] did not make much of Ignatius's illness, as it seemed to them to be his ordinary sickness."[77] That medical practitioners ignored the call of the famous leader of the Jesuits when he was ill, claiming that it was just his "ordinary sickness," indicates that Loyola regularly called doctors unnecessarily. In this depiction by his friend and well-disposed biographer, the holy man appears more sensitive to his personal discomfort than a true ascetic should have been. Colombo's autopsy, as reported by Polanco, vindicated Loyola as someone who bore with extreme patience his bodily infirmities.

Importantly for Loyola's saintly reputation, the autopsy also uncovered Loyola's first postmortem miracle. Polanco reported that, given his anatomy, Loyola only "lived due to a miracle for a great deal of time, since with a liver such as that, it would not be possible to live unless our Lord God, in providing for the necessities of the Company [of Jesus], made up for the weakness of his bodily organs and maintained him in life."[78] That is, Loyola's stones should have killed him long before; therefore God must have, through divine intervention, performed a continuous miracle through Loyola's body to keep him alive. Autopsy had uncovered new and hidden miracles.

Although drawing on similar anatomical evidence, Polanco's letter clearly attributed very different meaning to the evidence from that offered in Colombo's treatise. Polanco's letter, in addition, represents the emergence of a new genre, in which the anatomical case study was married to a work of hagiography. Anatomical details in it provided empirical evidence of the miracles and virtue of the saint. That contemporaries thought such a new type of narrative was both informative and important is demonstrated by the fact that Polanco's work circulated widely and that a contemporary Jesuit disseminated a separate treatise which repeated almost exactly the details that Polanco had written.[79]

Despite all this recording of physical evidence of holiness, canonization officials paid little attention to either Polanco or Colombo's accounts of Loyola's autopsy. Surviving documents for his canonization do not mention Loyola's unusual anatomy, and the official vitae for the saint do not discuss his holy body.[80] One reason this information failed to count for canonization might be that Polanco and Colombo did not agree on the meaning of Loyola's anatomy. Colombo cast it as within the realm of natural variation within the human body, whereas Polanco explicitly stated that Loyola's anatomy was miraculous.

That the lack of uniform interpretation was the reason for excluding Loyola's wondrous anatomy from his canonization is supported by the next case, in which the polyvalent meaning of Carlo Borromeo's anatomy also seems to have led to its exclusion from consideration for sainthood. Two separate accounts of Borromeo's autopsy circulated in sixteenth-century Europe, one medical and one hagiographical. Upon his death in 1584, Carlo Borromeo had long been the archbishop of Milan and was one of the leaders of the efforts to reform the Catholic Church.[81] Hence, as was usual for elite prelates, Borromeo's cadaver was opened shortly after his death for embalming.[82] Given Borromeo's fame, Giovanni Carcano Leone, the chair of anatomy at the University of Pavia, was tasked with the embalming effort. However, upon opening the corpse, Leone discovered that Borromeo had a most unusual anatomy. The details of this anatomy soon appeared in treatises designed to spread the fame of the deceased prelate.[83]

Despite his being the dissecting surgeon, Leone was not the first to write about Borromeo's anatomical irregularities. Rather, Borromeo's friend, the priest and diplomat Giovanni Botero, penned a letter almost immediately after Borromeo's death in which he touted the cardinal's anatomy as a clear sign of his sanctity.[84] In particular, he stated that Borromeo's liver and kidneys were found to be "destroyed and decaying," his heart and lungs were "overly large," and his body contained "not a trace of fat." Furthermore, he claimed, "nor was anything seen to exist for the penis, other than for some bony structure and rough skin [in that area]."[85]

These details emphasized Borromeo's connection with the divine. His ruined liver and spleen must have been acutely painful, yet Borromeo bore it patiently—signs of his devotion to asceticism. Similarly, the absence of fat in his body demonstrated that his fasting had been profound. Botero's description of Borromeo's large heart and lungs suggest that the man was full of love, as the heart was rich with such symbolism in the early modern era.[86] Finally, the lack of a penis implies that Borromeo had died a virgin and that his sexual organ had withered away from disuse, divine proof of his abstinent life. In short, his body provided clear testimony that Borromeo was an ascetic who fasted and remained celibate, while at the same time holding great love for his flock.

Botero's treatise was immediately popular. In six weeks it went through thirteen editions and was quickly translated from the Latin into the Italian vernacular.[87] This treatise likely horrified and embarrassed Leone, since it was filled with medical inaccuracies, which many might have assumed came from Leone's dissection. Leone subsequently published his own treatise later that year (1584), in which he explained what he had found during the autopsy.[88]

Leone corrected both what he saw as anatomical errors and misinterpretations in Botero's letter. In particular, he made it clear that Borromeo did not have an overly large heart, but rather one "of medium size."[89] Such a distinction was important since, according to Aristotle—who was one of several acknowledged classical authorities on anatomy—an overly large heart was a sign of cowardice.[90] Thus, popular and religious interpretations diverged from medical ones on the meaning of a large heart.

Regarding other anatomical features, Leone was less critical of Botero but more detailed in his description. He agreed that the lack of fat in Borromeo was extraordinary, but pointed out how extremely unusual it was by comparing it to other bodies he had seen, which always had some trace of fat.[91] Sometimes, Leone noted, he had during a dissection seen fat that was "four fingers deep" in the human body.[92] In addition to emphasizing his expertise, this contextualization of the meaning of fat from an anatomical standpoint transformed Borromeo's asceticism from a merely impressive feat into a true wonder that bordered on the supernatural.[93] On the other hand, Leone rated Borromeo's spleen as being well within the spectrum of the natural for the human body, despite being unusual.[94] Each of these examples, though not necessarily hindering Borromeo's canonization, worked more to illustrate Leone's knowledge and experience than to affirm Borromeo's sanctity.

Although apparently a devotee to Borromeo, Leone was writing to preserve and perhaps improve his reputation. This goal contrasted with Botero's, whose hagiography was designed to demonstrate the "truth" of Borromeo's spiritual status, rather than to provide the exact details of his anatomy. Leone was more successful in his aim since a public dissection he performed the following year was attended by a large audience, including a number of Milanese nobles. This led to an additional publication for the surgeon.[95] This suggests that there was great interest in saintly anatomy and writing about it was a way for an anatomist to augment his reputation.

Nevertheless, even though Leone and Botero's treatises attempt to demonstrate Borromeo's sanctity, no evidence of the autopsy appears in the remaining canonization records for Carlo Borromeo.[96] This was despite the fact that Borromeo's asceticism was listed as a virtue in his canonization proceeding and Francisco Peña's vita for Borromeo focuses heavily on the holy man's bodily asceticism.[97] Clearly his asceticism mattered for his canonization, but the anatomical evidence in favor of it was disregarded. Why?

Given the popularity of both Botero and Leone's accounts, it is likely that canonization officials—who paid attention to hagiography— were aware of these narratives.[98] Their decision to avoid discussion of the autopsy may have been deliberate, perhaps because the process of making Borromeo a saint involved a very careful reworking of his image to cast him as the perfect exemplar of the reforming bishop and saint.[99] Thus, the debate over what the anatomy of Borromeo's corpse meant and the ways of establishing the evidence through empirical techniques, which were still gaining status, rendered his anatomy too controversial to be included in the canonization process. Everything about Borromeo's canonization had to appear perfect and beyond debate. This rejection of anatomical demonstration echoes Loyola's case, in which Colombo and Polanco's disagreement over the meaning of his anatomy and their reliance on empirical evidence possibly rendered it invalid for canonization officials. Anatomy was too polyvalent to be useful for canonization at this point.

It was not until the decade following Borromeo's postmortem that canonization officials in Rome finally saw anatomy as an important piece of evidence to be used in verifying sanctity. Although attitudes toward empiricism and its role in anatomy were shifting throughout Europe at this moment, for canonization officials, two cases of unusual anatomy clearly brought the importance of anatomy in discerning sanctity to the fore.[100] These autopsies, like those of Borromeo and Loyola, had been ordered by local promoters of sanctity, but the eventual verification of the evidence would be directed by Roman officials. Through the canonizations of Filippo Neri and Teresa of Avila, canonization officials came to recognize anatomy as both a way to demonstrate sanctity and to centralize the canonization process.

TOWARD OFFICIAL RECOGNITION OF ANATOMY: FILIPPO NERI AND TERESA OF AVILA

After their deaths in 1582 and 1595, respectively, Teresa of Avila and Filippo Neri were subjected to postmortem examinations in which their bodies were opened. In each case the medical investigation yielded unanimous evidence in support of holiness. The expert testimony then came to be incorporated into the apostolic—or Roman-directed—phase of canonization. During this phase, the evidence was put to further scrutiny but was ultimately accepted as part of the miracles approved for each saint. Its approval signals a change of stance toward anatomical evidence among canonization officials. After these cases, anatomical investigations ordered by Rome became the method to verify bodily sanctity. In this way, the medicalization of holiness became part of the centralization of canonization.

The medical examination of Teresa of Avila was the first in which Roman officials accepted anatomy as part of the demonstration of sanctity. Although she died before Borromeo, Teresa of Avila's canonization took longer and was achieved only with great difficulty. The process began shortly after her death in 1582, but it did not result in a canonization until 1622. At numerous points, officials in Spain and abroad expressed doubt about Teresa's holiness and the veracity of her miracles.[101] Historian Romeo de Maio convincingly argues that the skepticism officials brought to her canonization raised the level of scrutiny applied to all saints thereafter.[102]

Part of the skepticism and scrutiny applied to Teresa's canonization also entailed a very careful consideration of the miracles attributed to her. This included one of the miracles most important to contemporaries: the incorruption of Teresa's corpse.[103] To help promote the acceptance of this miracle, local officials organized a medical examination of Teresa's body the year after she died. Over the next decade her body was exhumed and examined repeatedly and with increasing rigor as her canonization progressed. Ultimately, the Tribunal of the Rota, headed by Francisco Peña, took charge of this procedure and directed the chair of medicine from the University of Salamanca to inspect Teresa's body in the presence of the bishop. Roman officials subsequently accepted the medical evidence and incorporated it into her canonization process. Thus, the intense scrutiny applied to Teresa's canonization brought medical expertise to the forefront.

Even the nature of the sources that document Teresa's multiple postmortems signal the Church's increasing acceptance of anatomical evidence for holiness. The ongoing examination of Teresa's body was described in detail in the formal canonization process. The survival of these documents means that it was both submitted as part of her ordinary process of canonization and accepted as evidence during the apostolic phase. This contrasted with earlier anatomical evidence, such as that for Loyola and Borromeo, in which the postmortem medical examination appears only in materials printed either by the attending physicians or a zealous hagiographer. Anatomy now became part of the official examination of a candidate's bid for canonization.

According to the Registry of the Acts for Teresa's canonization, the first examination of her body occurred nine months after her death, when local church officials in the town of Alba exhumed her corpse in 1583. Upon opening the tomb, they discovered that the wooden casket that held her body had been "broken in the front part" and was "nearly rotten." Despite being surrounded by such decay, Teresa's body remained completely "incorrupt." The notary recorded that her body maintained "a certain wondrous integrity, [remaining] so flexible and pleasing to the touch, that it seemed as if she were alive." Several medical practitioners and other eminent observers affirmed that such a high level of preservation could only be caused by a miracle.[104] The medical professionals were, however, not named in this instance and did not testify in their own words. Possibly, this omission stems from an attempt on the part of the notary and his superiors to unify the medical opinions into one cohesive narrative. It may also be that these practitioners were not particularly eminent, as local authorities rather than the central Roman canonization officials deputed these *medici*. In fact, they were described simply as *peritissimis medicis* (skilled medical practitioners), not *medici fisici* (physicians).[105] In successive evaluations of her corpse this laconic medical approval would extend into much more thorough examinations, carried out by university physicians, and eventually ordered by Rome. Indeed, the trials of Teresa's body provides one of the first indications that Catholic officials preferred physician testimony to that of non-university trained practitioners, however skilled they might be.

Next to examine Teresa's body was Ludovico Vasquez, a *medicus* from Alba, who scrutinized the corpse a number of times in the years following her death. He confirmed, as had the earlier practitioners, that the body had not been embalmed, yet still resisted the forces of decay in a way that "could not be due to natural [causes], but must depend on miraculous ones."[106] However, Vasquez did not stop at this simple examination; according to the canonization process, "for the greater confirmation of the aforementioned [Teresa's incorruption] he [Vasquez] entered the monastery on different occasions and other times of the day to visit the infirm and attempted, and obtained the showing to him of the body without the intervention of the nuns[.] He especially visited the body on very hot days and always he saw it in the same way as he did in the beginning [i.e., it remained incorrupt]. And it [the body] was truly light, indicating that [it had] the weight of saintly flesh."[107] Vazquez, then, applied an empirical test to Teresa's body. He visited it on the hottest days of the year, when corpses would most be prone to rot, and even viewed it without nuns as witnesses. Presumably, their absence gave him greater freedom to be skeptical about the remains and also to test the body. He sought natural explanations for Teresa's unusual failure to rot, including temperature, moisture, and even perhaps the undue influence of outside observers. Unable to find a reason for the body's preservation, he ruled that it could only be a miracle.

The fact that Vasquez's examination appears in the canonization record implies that Church officials were beginning to consider the possibility of using empirical techniques from the medical field as part of the demonstration of bodily holiness. His examination was submitted by the promoters of Teresa's sanctity as part of the Ordinary Process. Clearly both Vasquez and the promoters of Teresa's canonization thought such empirical testing could be of great use in demonstrating Teresa's holiness. Canonization officials in Rome, in turn, had their interest piqued by this examination, since it appears in the Registry of Acts for Teresa's canonization and, for the first time, they ordered a follow-up. Roman officials, however, must ultimately have been unconvinced by the demonstrations of this non-elite, local practitioner, since Vasquez was not asked to be part of the examining team assessing Teresa's corpse during the apostolic process.

During the Rome-ordered apostolic process in 1592, an additional examination of Teresa's body was undertaken. The bishop of Salamanca, along with several eminent physicians, disinterred her yet again and, this time, the apostolic letters demanded that the corpse be opened to confirm the incorruption of its interior.[108] Cristoforo Medrano, chair of medicine at the University of Salamanca, recorded in the canonization process that "he diligently considered and inspected the aforementioned body, finding it to be complete, soft, and tractable, with the uterus, stomach, nipples, and breasts—the parts of the body which most readily rot and are consumed in dead bodies—whole and full as if the servant of God were alive [.] Thus, he judged it [the state of her body] to be an evident miracle."[109] Medrano, presumably relying on classical authority, identified the parts of the body that were the first to decay. He then performed at least a partial autopsy of her body, examining the several critical pieces of anatomy both by sight and by touch to make sure they met the standard of a miracle. Medrano thus employed knowledge of theoretical medicine, experience with dissection, and the ability to read signs in the human body to come to a conclusion about Teresa's incorruption. He therefore combined the empirical techniques that Vasquez had used along with a much deeper understanding of medical theory and human anatomy to develop an epistemology of the holy body.

In applying his expertise to understanding Teresa's corpse, Medrano followed not his own or local initiative, but a papal request. Canonization officials now recognized the utility of anatomy in examining claims of the miraculous in human bodies. Medical testimony could turn incorruption from a matter of popular acclamation into something determined by experts directed by central authority.

The Rota Tribunal must have deemed Medrano's examination sufficient and exemplary evidence, as he is the only medical testator about her corpse to appear in the final apostolic process.[110] The push to use anatomy in Teresa's case began with local enthusiasts, but their role was erased from the final verification of her incorruption. This miracle was now confirmed by an elite medical professional from outside her local community who had been directed by Roman officials to examine her body. That this was an act of centralization is demonstrated by the fact that even Medrano's testimony only counted as evidence after it gained approval from the most eminent members of the Roman Curia, including Francisco Peña, whose name appears on the process.[111] Her case, then, represents the moment in which canonization officials adopted anatomy as a tool for centralizing and universalizing the criteria for canonization. The agent who allowed this centralization was the elite physician who was versed in modern empirical techniques and anatomical knowledge. Catholic officials, therefore, not only endorsed a new way of making knowledge about the holy body, but also a new sort of medical practitioner—the Vesalian style anatomist-physician. Of course, Roman authorities did not fail to publicize their embrace of the new anatomical criteria for holiness, as Teresa's medically verified holy body was listed as her first postmortem miracle and it appeared in the saint's printed vitae.[112]

Nevertheless, Teresa of Avila's case might have ended up as the exception rather than the rule had not another sixteenth-century saint, Filippo Neri, the founder of the Oratorians, been subject to a high-profile autopsy at about the same time. Upon his death Neri was one of the most prominent holy figures in the city of Rome. He enjoyed a large following, even among the upper ranks of the Curia. Thus, there was a great deal of interest in the saint and his remains following his death.[113]

Additionally, Neri had suffered from unusual medical ailments for most of his adult life, including a strong and erratic heartbeat. His fame meant that his unusual medical condition received the attention of some of the most eminent medical practitioners in Rome during his lifetime. In particular, Andrea Cesalpino, a former papal physician, professor of medicine, and early pioneer of cardiac anatomy, evaluated the holy man several times.[114] At one point, when Neri was said to be experiencing strong and irregular heartbeats, Cesalpino examined him. He noted that in "examining where this palpitation came from, searching the chest, I found it [Neri's unusual anatomy] very extensive, with a tumor at the base of the ribs, on the left hand side, near the heart; and upon touching it one realized that the ribs had risen in that place, and, during the palpitation, it raised and lowered like a bellows."[115] By the time of Neri's death on May 25, 1595, the medical community had not yet identified where such palpitations came from, and there was some speculation that they were a further sign of his sanctity. Hence, there were multiple reasons to open the holy man upon his death including funerary, forensic, and devotional concerns.[116]

The night following his death, Neri's corpse was opened at the behest of his fellow Oratorians in the central church of his order, Santa Maria in Vallicella. Neri's brothers seem to have ordered the autopsy in the belief that it would yield hidden signs of sanctity.[117] By virtue of the fact that they were in Rome and given Neri's status, the Oratorians were able to assemble a medical team that included some of the finest physicians in Catholic Europe.[118] Four former papal physicians—including Angelo Vittori,[119] Andrea Cesalpino,[120] Angelo Porto,[121] and Ridolfo Silvestri,[122] as well as the surgeon Giuseppe Zerla and the barber-surgeon Marco Antonio del Bello—testified numerous times during the canonization process about the autopsy, though not all were present at the time.

The medical practitioners considered what they found in Neri's body to be extremely anomalous: his fourth and fifth ribs were broken to make room for his large and extraordinary heart. The praecordia, or front tissue of his heart, was strangely large and muscular; the pulmonary artery was twice as large as normal; the pericardium, which surrounds the heart like a wrapper, was devoid of fluid; and finally there was no blood in the ventricles.[123] In interpreting this wondrous evidence, the physicians unanimously proclaimed that what they had seen in Neri's anatomy was a miracle: his heart had been supernaturally inflamed by divine love and so his heart, lungs, and ribs had all been altered to make room for the intense heat.

Curiously, the barber-surgeon, Marco Antonio del Bello, who was present for the autopsy and who appears to have done much of the actual cutting of the corpse, did not testify to the wondrousness of Neri's anatomy. Instead, he stated that "in opening [the body] one found the whole interior clean, without any flaw[.] And looking carefully at the liver, the lung and the heart and all the other interior [organs] [were] without flaw."[124] The language del Bello uses is reminiscent of contemporary forensic autopsies undertaken to determine cause of death, especially in poisonings.[125] Del Bello then recounted at length the methods he used to embalm the body.[126] He therefore had in mind practices that were normal for elites—such as forensic and funerary reasons for opening the body—but not specific for uncovering sanctity. Del Bello's failure even to mention Neri's wondrous anatomy suggests either he was not aware of what the promoters of Neri's sanctity were looking for or he was not well enough versed in pulmonary anatomy to perceive the irregularity in Neri's organs. Whatever the reasons for the omissions in del Bello's testimony, it points to a central reason why canonization officials might have preferred physician to other medical testimony in canonization proceedings: learned physicians were considered better able to read the signs found in a human body and interpret them into a framework of understanding the natural world.[127]

Despite the unanimity of Neri's physicians about the miracle displayed in his anatomy, this case still represented a moment of transition during which the Church slowly came to accept anatomy as a demonstration of sanctity. Indeed, the numerous types of sources that document Neri's unusual anatomy illustrate that the meaning and use of such autopsies had not yet been set by Rome. Details of the autopsy appear in his canonization process, medical case studies, and works of hagiography. The published medical reports and hagiographies suggest earlier techniques of writing about the holy body, in which physicians and hagiographers sought to publicize the anatomy either to further a canonization cause or advertise a physician's skill. However, that Neri's anatomy eventually appeared as a miracle in the canonization process points to the acceptance by Rome of medical reports as valid evidence for saintliness. In later canonizations such anatomical descriptions would appear only in the canonization documents, indicating that the Curia both recognized the utility of such bodily evidence and wanted to control the meaning attached to it.

In the early hagiography produced by the Oratorians for the saint's canonization, the account of Neri's autopsy spanned several pages and seems to have been intended to convince readers of Neri's holiness through wealth of detail. His friend and biographer, Antonio Gallonio, described the autopsy itself at length, employing technical language.[128] Even a well-educated reader of the time might not have been able to follow all the details of this account since some of the anatomical features depended on recent discoveries in the field.[129] Thus, Gallonio was using anatomical innovation to demonstrate sanctity. Although Gallonio's vita for Neri was not censored, canonization officials might have been concerned about this apparent attempt to stir up devotion for the saint by using as of yet unproven miracles and contested medical knowledge. Further support for this interpretation of events is suggested by the fact that in 1605 Gallonio was forbidden to hold meetings in which he promoted devotion to the saint.[130]

Just as Gallonio used Neri's anatomy to spread enthusiasm for the saint's cult, several physicians involved in this case used it to further their own careers. Antonio Porto and Angelo Vittori, two of the physicians who initially testified for Neri, produced works that treated the saint's unusual anatomy at length.[131] Each of their discussions of anatomy was intricate and demonstrated that these men were on the forefront of understanding cardiac anatomy. Thus, Vittori's and Porto's treatises had much in common with Leone's autopsy of Borromeo, which both lauded the saint and demonstrated the anatomist's skill. Neri's case appears to have been particularly fertile as Vittori continued to publish on Neri throughout his lifetime, culminating with a much larger 1613 treatise on the saint.[132]

Neri's case resembled those of Loyola and Borromeo in that it could hold different meanings for anatomists and hagiographers. However, it also differed from those because, despite the fact that it relied on new discoveries in anatomy, the report of Neri's miraculous body was included in his canonization process and put forward as a miracle for the saint.[133] This difference may in part be due to the fact that in Neri's case the dissectors were unanimous about the supernatural origin of his unusual deformities. In addition, it signals an increased acceptance of the role of anatomy in determining sanctity. Such a change in attitude makes sense because the canonization officials who vetted the evidence for Neri largely included the same people—such as Francisco Peña, who was still deacon of the Rota and who oversaw Neri's canonization process—who had by now witnessed several earlier attempts to make anatomy count for sanctity. They were finally, it seems, convinced of the ability of physicians to understand the boundaries of the natural in the human body.

The cases of Neri and Teresa of Avila are indisputably the beginning of the requirement that anatomy must be used to discern sanctity. Due to irregularities in each of their cases—Teresa's body was considered somewhat suspect and Neri's anatomy was highly unusual—promoters of their canonizations ordered autopsies of each prospective saint. However, it was canonization officials in Rome who eventually accepted this medical evidence as part of the demonstration of the saint's sanctity. One reason for such acceptance was likely the increased familiarity with the type of knowledge made by anatomy and its rising prestige as a field. Anatomical case studies expanded greatly in numbers in this period and used empirical evidence as part of their epistemology. This, in turn, led to rising prestige of anatomical study in general.

The changes affecting the field of anatomy can be seen clearly in the cases of physicians testifying in canonization processes. In Teresa of Avila's case, medical practitioners used an array of empirical methods to test the incorruption of her body and relied on a combination of practical and theoretical expertise. In Neri's case, eminent physicians found and explained anomalies in his body that did not seem worthy of comment to less elite practitioners. In short, these were cases where the expert saw more in the human body than did the layman. It was through this anatomical lens that canonization officials would henceforth understand bodily holiness.

The examples of the two other saints canonized in 1622, Isidore the Laborer and Francis Xavier, demonstrate that by the early seventeenth century the new medical and anatomical criteria for bodily sanctity had become the norm, rather than the exception, to the rule.

THE CULMINATION OF THE PROCESS: FRANCIS XAVIER AND ISIDORE THE LABORER

By the early seventeenth century, innovating physicians and promoters of a saint's cult ceased being the ones who sought to use anatomy as a demonstration of sanctity; rather, canonization officials in Rome now incorporated such medical evidence into their attempt to centralize and standardize veneration. The cases of Francis Xavier and Isidore the Laborer illustrate how exacting and rigorous Roman criteria had become. Xavier, one of the first Jesuit missionaries, had died far away from Europe on the island of Sancian, off the coast of China. Nevertheless, a medical professional in the East conducted a postmortem on his body and a Roman physician in the employ of the Rota later reinterpreted that evidence so that it could count as part of his canonization. Similarly, Isidore the Laborer had been in the ground for nearly five hundred years when officials, following commands from Rome, unearthed his body. Eminent physicians examined him and the evidence counted for his canonization. In neither case did independent hagiographical or anatomical case studies precede the official consideration of the anatomy in the canonization process. That is, the papacy now dictated how anatomy should be employed in canonization cases and how that evidence was to be understood and circulated. Anatomy mattered for sanctity.

The report on the missionary Francis Xavier's life, produced in the final stage of his canonization and then printed, listed his incorrupt corpse as his first postmortem miracle.[134] Xavier's body seems to have merited much esteem: it resisted corrosive materials designed to part his flesh from his bones for transport, remained lifelike despite multiple reinterments and exhumations, and bled fresh blood when a relic-hungry woman bit off one of its toes.[135] Since such incredible preservation "exceeded belief," Xavier's body was "inspected and tested" while still in the Indies so that its miraculous nature could be verified.[136] The word used here, *pertentatum*, is significant and means both "to test" and "to feel all over."[137] This indicated both that the state of the body was ascertained through a careful empirical survey and that it was not at all based on theoretical deductions. This echoes contemporary ideas surrounding the meaning of the term *experimentum*, which meant not the formal testing of a hypothesis as "experiment" does now, but rather knowledge gained solely from experience.[138] Thus, the medical practitioner examining Xavier's corpse ascertained that its state exceeded the realm of the natural through careful inspection and manipulation. This inspection likely included opening the corpse since the intestines were also declared incorrupt.[139]

To add greater prestige and a theoretical element to the investigation carried out in the Indies, the Tribunal of the Rota asked Angelo Vittori (1547–after 1633), a former papal physician, to reevaluate much of the evidence about Xavier's body in the early 1600s.[140] Vittori was regularly employed to verify saintly anatomies for the Church in the early seventeenth century, testifying both for Neri and Loyola's canonizations as well as for that of Xavier.[141] His employment by the Rota and involvement with numerous cases would seem to imply that Peña and his successors in the Rota were working with Roman physicians in an attempt to establish a standard set of medical criteria for incorruption and other bodily phenomena.[142]

Although Vittori appears not to have seen Xavier's body firsthand, it was commonplace at the time for physicians to make judgments based only on reports and descriptions.[143] In his thorough analysis, Vittori relied on classical authority—he regularly cited Galen and Hippocrates—as well as his experience with dissections to argue that what had occurred to Xavier's body "was in every way wondrous and exceeded the possibilities of nature."[144] To contemporaries, this language represented an unambiguous statement that a miracle had occurred.[145]

Vittori must have been an especially persuasive witness since the various details he provided about Xavier's wondrous body counted as several distinct miracles for the latter's canonization.[146] Thus, Xavier provides an example of the solidification in attitudes on the part of the Church: it demonstrates a commitment to increased rigor, as even the body of a person who died thousands of miles from Europe was required to be analyzed by a physician who was trusted by the Holy See. Furthermore, even though the body had been thoroughly tested in the East, this was not considered sufficient evidence. The Church preferred a physician's testimony, which could marry empirical evidence with a theoretical framework.

In a similar example of the new rigor in canonization and the importance of medical expertise, on June 9, 1612, Isidore the Laborer, who had died in 1130, was unearthed. Remissorial letters from Rome, which opened the apostolic process of canonization, demanded that the body be "visited."[147] This demand seems to have implied that a medical inspection was required, since the local judges in charge of the canonization proceeding subsequently ordered three medical professionals—the physicians Juan de Atiensa and Juan de Negrete, and the surgeon Ludovico de Orseon—to examine the corpse.[148] The notary deputed to go with them recorded that they observed, first, that the body had not been embalmed, nor had any other attempt at preservation been made.[149] They then surveyed the corpse and found that it was still totally covered with skin and the hair was in place. The only flaws in the prospective saint's body were the caving in of the ears and nose, which were normal signs even in the best preserved bodies. The physicians, by comparing the body both with previous corpses they had seen and with what they knew about decay, declared that what had occurred to the corpse was totally "beyond nature" and therefore a miracle.[150] At this time, the examination seems almost routine; medical inspection of a purportedly holy body had now become a regular part of papal canonizations. Indeed, given the unambiguous medical verdict, Isidore's incorrupt body was quickly approved as a miracle for his canonization.[151]

The canonizations of Isidore and Xavier thus mark the regularization of the requirement that medical testimony be used to confirm a miraculous body. Even though each corpse adhered to traditional modes of sanctity—each was incorrupt and appeared lifelike—and had what might be called extenuating circumstances of distance and time, both underwent posthumous medical examination and verification of their miraculous nature. More importantly, though, this verification was ordered not by a mere local bishop, but by the Tribunal of the Rota in Rome and then approved by the pope himself. Moreover, the medical practitioners called in these cases were experts who were trusted by Rome: in both cases, university-trained physicians provided the evidence. The physicians, in turn, relied on a combination of empirical testing and theoretical interpretation to declare the body incorrupt. The Church, in asserting the usefulness of anatomy for determining sanctity, was also declaring the importance of physicians trained in practical anatomy. Medical expertise and Church authority now cooperated to define the operations of the divine in the human body.

CONCLUSION

What emerges from tracing the increasingly important role of medical examination in canonization proceedings is how, during the sixteenth century, both the understanding of medicine and the articulation of the Catholic religion underwent significant, and to some extent interwoven, development. In medicine, anatomy began to feature heavily in diagnosis and knowledge of how the body functioned. This led to the development of the medical case study, which came into wide use for religious, political, and polemical purposes. Indeed, as Gianna Pomata has argued, a new genre even appeared at the time to convey this important information.[152] At the same time, canonization officials experimented with new ways to prove the sanctity of those whom they canonized. In particular, Francisco Peña, who was first auditor and then deacon of the Tribunal of the Rota, clearly began with the first canonization after Trent—that of Diego of Alcalá—looking for methods whereby sanctity could be established. The fact that so many physicians testified for the miracles occurring during Diego's canonization seems to have led Peña to medicine for proving sanctity.

Nevertheless, anatomy remained problematic at times. The cases of Carlo Borromeo and Ignatius of Loyola show that anatomical evidence was controversial and polyvalent. Different writers could draw very different conclusions from similar evidence. In particular, anatomists used saintly anatomy to promote their own careers, whereas hagiographers sought ways to evangelize and bolster enthusiasm for a saint through his or her anatomy. Furthermore, each drew upon empirical evidence, which, though gaining in prestige, was in itself considered a somewhat less sure means of making knowledge.

Over the course of several decades, though, Peña and his contemporaries incorporated anatomical evidence more and more prominently into the examination of the body of the saint. The watershed case was the examination of Teresa of Avila. Her entire canonization process was put to intense scrutiny, as was the claim that her body was supernaturally incorrupt. A series of medical professionals were tasked with examining her corpse, culminating with the request in the remissorial letters that her body be examined by an eminent physician from a nearby university. His careful examination of her body, which included at least a partial autopsy, was the only evidence that counted, formally, as a demonstration of her incorruption. Thus, anatomical expertise was married to papal authority. Papal authority, in turn, gave approval to physicians' views of themselves as being at the top of the medical pyramid.

Teresa's case might have been anomalous were it not for the fact that around the same time, Filippo Neri died in Rome. His body, which was considered a wonder both according to medical and traditional religious criteria, became a subject of careful scrutiny: hagiographers, anatomists, and canonization officials all focused on the details found within his cadaver. The evidence of Neri's and Teresa's bodies convinced canonization officials—including Peña, who was still deacon of the Rota and who oversaw each of these canonizations—of the importance of anatomy for sanctity. In the cases that followed—those of Isidore and Xavier—the Rota had reached a point at which they demanded a medical examination be used to confirm bodily holiness. Thus, by the time five saints were canonized in 1622, it had become a standard practice of canonizations for a holy body to be examined by a medical expert, preferably a physician. This group canonization along with the accompanying hagiography proclaimed the importance of this new standard.[153] But, significantly, these canonizations also proclaimed a recognition on the part of the Church of the usefulness of physicians and their growing knowledge about the human body.

In the years following 1622, physicians who worked closely with the Curia increasingly defined standards for bodily holiness. In particular, several different types of bodily sanctity came to be subjects of inquiry. The following chapters analyze in detail the meanings of incorruption, asceticism, and unusual anatomy and how they fit into Catholic medical and theological understanding of the body. The chapters also explore the ways in which the physicians began to see their relationship with the Church as something more complicated than just employer and employee or judge and expert.

CHAPTER 3

Negotiating Incorruption

In 1625, the apostolic phase of the canonization process for Pope Gregory X, who had been dead nearly 350 years, opened in Arezzo, Italy. Among the purported miracles to be considered was that his body was said to have lain, since 1276, "incorrupt and whole . . . [and] emitting a sweet odor."[1] The Church had recognized such bodily incorruption as a conventional sign of sanctity since medieval times. Prior to the seventeenth century, however, popular acclamation decided whether the body of the deceased had miraculously resisted rot.[2] Now, when it came to determining whether Gregory's body was incorrupt, the judges called not on popular but on expert opinion: they summoned several physicians to testify about the state of Gregory's corpse.[3]

The examination of Gregory was part of a shift explored in the last chapter: the increasing reliance by canonization officials on medical professionals when trying to vet the potentially holy. Yet the medical professionals summoned to examine Gregory's corpse had trouble carrying out their task. In particular, they were unsure whether his body's level of incorruption exceeded the realm of the natural.[4] Each medical witness asserted that Gregory's corpse had been known at one time to have been incorrupt, but that the body had decayed in recent years. One of these physicians, Francesco di Santi Rosari, expressed the generally held opinion that "for some time the body has not seemed to me to be as complete as I remembered it to be."[5] Another physician, Gaspare Maltachini, stated that he had seen the body many times in the last fifty years, but that "it is no longer at present as whole and solid as it was before." Reasoning further, Maltachini suggested that the rotting of the body in recent years might be due to the decaying of the wooden casket that held Gregory's corpse and to the heat emitted by the numerous lamps lit near his tomb.[6]

Gregory was, in fact, never canonized. However, this failure was not due to the medical testimony alone. As Simon Ditchfield notes in his study of saint-making, Gregory's candidacy was hindered by a lack of patronage and was really only promoted by one eager Piacentine hagiographer, Pietro Maria Campi.[7] These additional factors, such as a lack of patronage, also affected how the medical practitioners in Arezzo interpreted the state of Gregory's corpse. Campi cajoled testimony for the canonization process in Arezzo, where Gregory was buried, but he was unable to engineer an official medical inspection of the body.[8] As such an inspection had become commonplace in cases involving bodily incorruption, its absence is noteworthy.[9] In judging Gregory's body, medically trained witnesses were forced to rely on memory or casual visits to the tomb. In addition, Campi—perhaps seen as a meddlesome outsider—likely pressured these medical professionals to testify favorably about Gregory's corpse. The medical testimony should therefore be understood as a reaction to these circumstances. Simply put, Gregory's body no longer seemed so miraculous after Campi began to interfere with local veneration of the deceased pontiff.

As this case suggests, the incorruption of a corpse was not unambiguous: local opinion, ecclesiastical authority, political pressures, medical expertise, and theological concerns all contributed to the attempt to define the boundary of the natural when it came to a rotting human body. As Aviad Kleinberg has noted for the cases of medieval saints, "The status of saint was conferred upon a person in a gradual process that involved disagreement and negotiation, as well as collaboration and even collusion."[10] This is equally true for miracles in the early modern period. When it came to sanctity, even medical knowledge of a human body was negotiated. When a physician looked into a potentially holy cadaver, he understood it both as a possible locus for sanctity and as a subject for medical knowledge. Both of these viewpoints conditioned how he understood—and perhaps to some extent even what he saw in—the interior of holy bodies.

This chapter follows the discussion begun in Chapter 2 by looking at how medical knowledge was used in the seventeenth century to establish a specific type of bodily holiness: incorruption. Incorruption, or the failure to rot, could be ambiguous and difficult to measure since both the theory and practice of its identification left a great deal to the discretion of the individual physician. Judgments of incorruption, therefore, present excellent case studies for understanding how medical and theological "truths" about the natural world were negotiated via the bodies of holy men and women.

THE IMPORTANCE OF BEING INCORRUPT

Although incorruption was an important and popular miracle in the Middle Ages, it became even more crucial to the Catholic faith after the Reformation.[11] Early Protestants rejected the possibility of this miracle and had mocked the idea that the human body could act as a conduit for the divine.[12] Therefore, belief in the possibility of incorruption became a badge of Catholic identity and a miracle that was thought to demonstrate the veracity of the faith.

Multiple examples illustrate the particular importance of miraculous incorruption after Trent. Incorruption was one of the miracles that counted toward the canonization of the first saint following the long hiatus after the Reformation—Diego of Alcalá.[13] The incorruption of Catherine of Bologna's body was considered one of her key miracles and therefore also one that was hotly debated.[14] The Jesuit Théophile Raynaud penned an entire treatise on incorruption when one of his secular patrons discovered and then unearthed a wondrously preserved body on his grounds.[15] In this work Raynaud made clear the importance of incorruption: it served to demonstrate the promise of resurrection for all good Catholics as it provided a "prelude of immortality."[16]

Incorruption as a sign of God's promise of salvation was a contemporary theme in a number of other works as well. The popular seventeenth-century Jesuit preacher Francesco Zuccarone told his audience that incorruption was a sign of what was to come for all believers. It signaled the promise of salvation, since, at the Last Judgment, all the saved would be like the saints and would exchange "for a cadaver, a living body, for rot the gifts of glory."[17]

In contrast, those who did not believe or act rightly could exhibit signs of their immorality after death. Raynaldus, for example, described how Martin Luther's body had rotted after death despite extensive efforts to embalm it.[18] A series of witchcraft trials in Venice accepted the premise that especially rapid corruption of a body could be a sign that the devil or one of his agents was at work.[19] Hence, those who were considered traitors to God's will rotted rapidly on Earth as a sign of their damnation. In this way, after the Reformation the imputation of rapid corruption or lasting incorruption to an individual's corpse signified for Catholics that they had been either particularly good or evil.

A final indication that incorruption was an especially potent Catholic miracle comes from the fact that later Protestant authors explicitly sought to refute specific accounts of miraculous incorruption. Shortly after the canonization of Mary Magdalene de' Pazzi (can. 1669), for example, an English edition of the vita printed for her was issued. In this new edition the anonymous translator and editor claimed that the "miracle" of her incorrupt body was actually due to her "humors being spent and wholly dryed up by her immoderate fasting."[20] Of course, the publication date of 1687 marks this work as being part of the polemics aimed against the Catholic James II and his attempts to achieve toleration for Catholics. The need to refute dei' Pazzi's miracle of incorruption in England, then, stemmed from a profound moment of religious and political crisis in the British Isles.[21] Nevertheless, that this miracle in particular was contested points to the evocative power that incorruption had for both Catholics and Protestants.

Indeed, incorruption was so powerful a theme that Protestant writers even occasionally appropriated it, despite their initial hostility to this miracle. The Genevan theologian Theodore Beza (1519–1605), looking at the cases of several Protestant martyrs, concluded that it was possible for bodies to remain incorrupt as a manifestation of the righteousness of the deceased. Similarly, the French martyrologist Jean Crespin (1520–1572) claimed that especially evil people might suffer their bodies' malfunctioning in graphic and gruesome ways.[22] Catholics, in turn, became increasingly concerned with ensuring that incorruption was defensible and demonstrable in the bodies of their saints. They turned to medical professionals to help them identify and substantiate this key miracle.

The importance of the miracle of incorruption and the role that medicine played in its confirmation became codified in the 1630s. Felice Contelori, a principal legal advisor to Pope Urban VIII (1623–1644), stressed its importance in his authoritative 1634 manual on canonization, *Tractatus et praxis de canonizatione*.[23] That Contelori cited the corpse being incorrupt and exuding a sweet-smelling odor as the first miracles which he said could count for canonization suggests that he gave these two signs of sanctity precedence over others.[24] Furthermore, he specifically asserted that physicians and surgeons held authority as expert witnesses and claimed that they were allowed to interpret evidence—even if they had not been present when the supposed miracle had occurred.[25] Thus, by the early seventeenth century, medical verification had become the standard way of verifying miraculous incorruption during canonization proceedings.

What Contelori left unsaid, though, was exactly what standards medical professionals should apply when determining whether the body of a deceased holy person could be considered incorrupt. It was, in fact, extremely difficult in practice to say whether a miracle had occurred because Catholic theology on incorruption as well as medical understanding of symptoms and signs left much room for interpretation.

The idea that a body might not rot was based on two central tenets of the Catholic faith: the doctrine of original sin and the belief in bodily resurrection at the end of time. In his treatise, Contelori maintained that the reason a body rotted after death was "due to the penalty of the first sins of the ancestors."[26] That is, in the Garden of Eden there would have been no decay, but owing to the sins of Adam and Eve, humans were henceforth condemned to rot after death. Yet through the sacrifice of Christ, God had chosen to offer man another chance at salvation. Following from this idea, the incorrupt body of the saint demonstrated the promise of eventual resurrection through its imitation of Christ's resurrection after crucifixion.[27]

These clear theological grounds for incorruption also allowed for a gray area in judging whether a body was incorrupt. Catholic theology stated that during the Last Judgment the entire flesh of a deceased individual would be brought together and reanimated.[28] The person was to be, quite literally, resurrected. Before that event, the bodies of deceased saints, which were thought to enjoy a direct connection with God, might demonstrate signs of their election by foreshadowing this reanimation. The incorrupt corpse provided a glimpse of the resurrection and the victory over death and decay that the elect would enjoy.[29] But even incorrupt corpses, by virtue of existing in this transient world, could show some sign of the passage of time—that is, they could rot a little bit.[30]

Furthermore, it was believed that holy bodies might begin to show some signs of rot in this world as an indication of their status in heaven. Resurrection of the body implied a scheme of punishments and rewards. The body that had either sinned or worked great piety on Earth would be brought back together to answer for its actions. The elect would be sorted based on moral acts, gender, and ecclesiastical status.[31] The bodily remains that bore evidence of a saint's elect status here on Earth also signified their position in heaven. From a theological point of view the resistance of a human body to rot—or lack of resistance—could be explained as a metric for determining the degree of excellence of the deceased in life.[32] Theology, however, left open specifics such as exactly how much rot was allowed for a body to still be considered miraculously incorrupt. It was partially owing to this difficulty that canonization officials turned to the experts in the body, medical professionals, in an attempt to identify where the boundary of the miraculous lay in the human body.

MEASURING MEDICAL INCORRUPTION

". . . so as to pursue full and undoubted truth, in examining some miracles the [Tribunal of the] Sacred Roman Rota sometimes orders medical professionals [*medicos*] to be sent for. . . . Since we, who incessantly pursue the works of nature, can recognize easily those things, which deviate from its normal operation, and those which excel the power of its operations."[33]

This statement, made by papal physician Paolo Zacchia (1584–1659), illustrates how medical practitioners were useful to the Church in determining whether a body had miraculously resisted rot.[34] Drawing on divisions made in the thirteenth century by Thomas Aquinas, early modern theologians and philosophers had established three general categories of phenomena that might occur in the terrestrial world: natural, preternatural, and supernatural.[35] Physicians were expected to be able to determine into which category events within the human body fell.[36] In doing so, they combined their philosophical knowledge of nature with an increasingly complex array of methods for reading the signs and symptoms presented by the human body.

The various categories of phenomena appearing in the world were well known in general to both physicians and other learned individuals, even if they were difficult to identify in practice.[37] Natural occurrences were brought about by the normal workings of nature. Preternatural events were unusual but were created through natural means. They were therefore definitely not divine and could potentially be demonic. Magic operated in the realm of the preternatural.

Monstrous births also counted as signs of the preternatural, as were many of the signs exhibited by those who were considered to be counterfeiting holiness.[38] Such events were believed to happen through some secret workings of nature. Hence, they were still part of the natural world, but it required an expert—a physician, for instance—to discover how nature brought about a preternatural phenomenon. In contrast to both of these categories, a supernatural event was divinely inspired and impossible without divine aid. It either occurred entirely outside of or completely reversed the ways in which nature operated.[39]

The failure of a body to rot after a lengthy period in the ground was categorized as a "supernatural" event since it was a reversal of the normal process of nature.[40] Yet embalming, desiccation, or perhaps some other unusual, preternatural phenomenon could make a body appear miraculously incorrupt. Indeed, the theologian Raynaud listed a wide range of techniques that embalmers used to preserve bodies for extended periods of time, including the application of salt, cedar oils, alkali sands, fragrant oils, myrrh, wax, and honey.[41] He furthermore claimed that the devil can alter the senses so that a rotting body would smell sweet and appear incorrupt.[42] Thus, there were many pitfalls in determining whether incorruption could truly count as a miracle. Only a thorough investigation, of the sort performed by a medical professional, could establish that incorruption had indeed exceeded the possibilities of nature.

In determining whether the level of rot found in a human body was natural, preternatural, or supernatural, seventeenth-century physicians drew heavily on their new practical experience with human anatomy.[43] With increasing frequency, this involved an empirical testing of the corpse, sometimes including an autopsy. The physicians who examined potential saints Giacomo della Marca and Andrea Corsini, for example, opened the chest cavity of each of the deceased to inspect the effects of previous embalming efforts on the body. In della Marca's case, one physician even noted that he and his colleagues had checked "by hand" the interior of the holy man's corpse. This detail underlines the importance of careful, firsthand examination that medical professionals undertook in verifying the incorruption of a body.[44] A physician who examined Elizabeth of Portugal in 1612 was careful to point out that he tested her flesh in multiple places to make sure that her bodily integrity stretched throughout her frame. He stated that he "did not only look but also touched by hand from the right shoulder down the whole arm to the hand."[45] In another case, that of Teresa of Avila, the medical practitioner Ludovico Vazquez felt her abdomen in several locations to check for rot. Finding that the skin seemed smooth and lifelike, he repeated this tactile examination on numerous occasions, returning at different times of day and in different weather conditions in order to see if the flesh had changed.[46] Vasquez relied on firsthand experience and testing of the corpse at different times and in different atmospheric conditions to help him determine whether the preservation of Teresa's body should be counted as supernatural.

As these examples indicate, by the late sixteenth century empirical methods—including careful observation, repeated probing in varying circumstances, and physical testing of the body—had become central to the demonstration of bodily sanctity. In an especially telling case, physicians repeatedly manipulated the body of Luis Bertrán to determine its level of preservation. In the words of the notary, they looked "at every part [of his body], touching it frequently."[47] The notary uses the word *inspexerunt* to describe the physicians' activities. Although the word might mean "they inspected," a contemporary dictionary indicated that it was a synonym with "probare," meaning "to test."[48] Thus, the word choice suggests that the physicians actively manipulated and tested the body in an attempt to determine its level of incorruption. Furthermore, this examination included a partial autopsy, after which examiners noted that they found the body to be without any previous signs of corruption, "not just in the internal parts and extremities, but also in the head, chest, and abdomen."[49] Thus, when physicians examined the bodies of potentially holy individuals, they engaged in firsthand observation, testing, and even opening of the corpse in an attempt to isolate signs that would indicate whether miraculous incorruption was present. The increasing status of empiricism as a route to knowledge thus also changed the ways in which holiness was now understood.[50]

Despite the increased prestige of empiricism in anatomical study, one should not overstate the ability of medical professionals to pronounce with absolute certainty in this period. Medical practitioners relied on a variety of signs and symptoms when trying to determine the causes for a disease.[51] The same was true for understanding the meaning of anatomy. Both diagnosing a disease and judging a bodily miracle involved reading and interpreting a number of discrete signs and then using them to determine the cause of the phenomenon witnessed.[52] Although physicians examining corpses could use autopsy to see into the interior of the body, even this additional information could be problematic. After all, debate persisted over what certain anatomical structures meant, how far the realm of natural variation extended, and the extent to which abnormal deaths or illnesses affected the interior anatomy of a body.[53] Every diagnosis of disease and judgment on the state of a supposedly holy body required interpretation by the medical practitioner involved. As Ian Maclean determined, when discussing medical history, "knowledge and meaning are negotiated by the communities in which they arise."[54]

In attempting to read the signs they found in a human body that might indicate supernatural incorruption, early modern medical practitioners relied on several accepted authorities. Until the early part of the seventeenth century, the main text employed was Aristotle's *Meteorology*, which presented a theoretical framework for understanding how quickly and why things decay.[55] By the 1630s, though, Paolo Zacchia had produced an authoritative guide, *Quaestiones Medico-Legales*, for doctors who would be called upon to testify before Church authorities. Zacchia enjoyed a close relationship with the Tribunal of the Rota, which regularly asked him to testify about a number of matters, including whether or not the bodies of prospective saints should be considered holy. Eighty-five of his expert testimonies before the Rota survive.[56] During the papacy of Urban VIII— that is, the 1620s through the 1640s—Zacchia outlined the lessons from his experiences in his *Quaestiones*.[57] In this work, he explained in careful detail the differences between natural, preternatural, and supernatural phenomena when found in the body. In short, Zacchia provided an epistemology through which to make sense of the empirical data recorded during the investigation of holy bodies.

In the portion of his guide in which he deals with incorruption, Zacchia notes that bodies can become corrupt in one of two ways: they can either dry out or they can rot.[58] He reminds his readers that the Egyptians routinely desiccated bodies to make mummies and this should not, therefore, be considered incorruption.[59] Similarly, he cautions medical experts to be aware that embalming can preserve a body for a long time and the investigator of incorruption must take into account any such effort and discount embalming during his evaluation of the body.[60]

Zacchia further advises potential testators that a body can only truly be considered miraculously incorrupt if it is preserved not just in the "harder and drier" parts of the body but also those which are "softer and wetter."[61] That is, Zacchia encouraged investigators to focus on fatty tissue as the true measure of how much rot the body has endured. He noted that the amount of this fatty tissue remaining in the body as well as the climactic conditions in which the body is kept should also be taken into consideration, as they affect rates of decay. Thus, fatter bodies subjected to moisture decay more rapidly.[62]

Zacchia additionally warns his readers against reading too much into a number of signs that have long been considered miraculous but which were, in fact, natural phenomena. A body might move after death, and bleed, convulse, feel warm, grow fingernails, or even have erections.[63] These events should not, Zacchia stressed, be thought of as anything out of the ordinary. Blood and humors might continue to flow or pool in the body for some time after death and could cause these phenomena.[64] However, after the body had cooled it should begin to smell foul rapidly unless some effort at embalming had been made. If, instead, it starts to smell sweet, then there is cause to think of this as a sign of sanctity.[65] In discussing these various details, Zacchia established that he was very familiar with the boundaries between preternatural and supernatural phenomena and thereby advertised his authority and expertise.

Throughout his manual, then, Zacchia guided his readers through the signs that he indicated were key to judging incorruption, where to find these signs, and how to test them. Physicians who sought to demarcate the boundaries of the supernatural for the Church were thus provided with a practical guide to accompany their broader theological understanding of incorruption.[66] His wide citation in subsequent canonization proceedings is a clear indication that his work was thought of as eminently authoritative and practical.[67] Zacchia's *Quaestiones* provided the epistemology for empirical understanding of holy bodies.

Nevertheless, despite his specificity, Zacchia warned his readers that a physician must also consider more than the evidence found at the tomb. Circumstances and personal history mattered because factors such as weight, sex, and cause of death all affected how long a body remained without rot.[68] Thus, even as a standard guide and set of techniques began to be employed by medical professionals, incorruption was still considered something that required the interpretation of specific details that had to be sorted out for each individual case. In short, incorruption required negotiation.

NEGOTIATING INCORRUPTION

By the early seventeenth century, the demand for and the skills to turn a popular element of sanctity—the incorrupt corpse—into a matter of expert opinion were in place. Medical professionals had developed a set of empirical tools and even had a practical guide to aid in reading signs in the human body. This allowed these experts to determine whether a body's level of rot fell into the category of natural, preternatural, or supernatural. Still, the establishment of miraculous incorruption depended on local knowledge and details particular to the individual holy person. The miracle of the incorrupt body was a negotiation in which personal belief, local opinion, professional obligations, and Church authority all affected how the evidence was interpreted. A few examples will illustrate how all these factors interacted when it came to judging the bodies of the holy dead.

The failed canonization process of Francesco Girolamo Simon, a parish priest from Valencia, demonstrates how the understanding of a holy body, even in the eyes of medical experts, was conditioned by various competing local interests. Shortly after Simon died in April 1612, many of the faithful from within his parish of Sant'Andrea began venerating him and declared his corpse to be miraculously incorrupt.[69] This local enthusiasm was soon accompanied by wider support throughout the city. During his sermons, a famous Franciscan preacher, Antonio Sobrino, lauded Simon's asceticism and works of piety. Stirred up by Sobrino, large sections of Valencia's populace began to venerate the dead priest. Sick individuals experienced healings and other miracles at Simon's tomb.[70] Several eminent personages, including Cardinal Gaspar Borja, and King Philip III's favorite, the Duke of Lerma, began to support Simon's canonization.[71] An ambitious priest and metropolitan canon, Balthazar Borja, opened the cause for Simon's canonization.[72] Borja, although ordinarily without such authority, was allowed to proceed because the archbishop's seat was temporarily empty.[73]

As had become commonplace in canonization proceedings, Borja solicited medical practitioners in the city of Valencia to attest to the miraculous incorruption of Simon's body. One physician, José Perez, claimed that Simon's body exuded an "odor of sanctity" and that after his death "the Divine Goodness began to show hidden [signs of] sanctity" via the cadaver, including his failure to rot.[74] Two other medical experts further testified, unambiguously, that the corpse displayed a range of wondrous abnormalities that could only be divinely inspired.[75]

Yet within the space of a few years, the same experts reversed their statements. After the canonization process had been sent to Rome, a Spanish priest, Pedro Cabezas, journeyed to the Holy City to denounce Simon.[76] Among his accusations, Cabezas claimed that Simon's "holy" body had been faked, with saint-like qualities produced by washing the corpse in sweet-smelling water and displaying it in favorable lighting.[77] Pope Paul V immediately called upon the Spanish Inquisition to investigate these charges.[78] The Inquisition had, in fact, already taken some interest in the case due to denunciations that the veneration surrounding the body was excessive and unapproved.[79] With instructions from Rome, inquisitors reinterviewed many testators, including some physicians involved in the case. Miguel Tudela, a medical expert who had testified about Simon's saintly corpse, changed his statement and asserted that he had never seen holy signs in the man's body.[80] He was subsequently accused of having lied in the earlier process so as to "please the people" of the city of Valencia.[81]

Although in Simon's case it might appear that medical opinions swayed with the changing political and religious winds, the situation was in fact more complex. In the years between 1612, when the process was opened, and 1619, when the process was initially halted, a number of conflicts broke out in the city over Simon's canonization and a competing canonization attempt for the previous archbishop had even been started.[82] The conflict that his canonization had sparked possibly conditioned examiners to interpret the evidence of Simon's corpse less favorably than before. Furthermore, no truly detailed medical testimony survives in the documents for Simon's canonization, so it is impossible to say how definitive the bodily evidence was. In such a context, it is easy to see how evidence that might at first have seemed convincing slowly began to appear somewhat less so to the medical testators.

The pressures exerted by the local community in Simon's example were not unique. In another case, when the Theatine monk Andrea Castaldi died on May 16, 1629, the citizens of Naples immediately hailed his corpse as miraculously incorrupt. However, a month later the father general of the Theatines in Naples denounced the veneration to the Roman Inquisition, claiming that there were those who were manufacturing "false miracles" to increase devotion to Castaldi.[83] Members of the Roman Inquisition ordered a local agent to remove the body from its exalted position in a church to a group tomb. A Neapolitan mob responded, threatening to stone anyone who attempted to do this. Given the danger presented to his person, the Inquisition's agent decided not to move the body.[84] Such enthusiasm was certainly not unique to Castaldi's case. Thus, medical practitioners who testified about the holiness of certain prominent figures did so in a setting characterized by violent public opinion and possible threats to their lives.

It was perhaps due to such pressure that medical professionals declared the body of Thomas of Villanova in 1611 "complete and incorrupt without any sort of bad odor,"[85] despite the fact that their examination also showed that all the skin of his body had decayed and several of his bones were missing.[86] This decay had occurred even though the body had been partially embalmed.[87] That the medical witnesses may have felt the weight of popular opinion in this case is indicated by the fact that the ecclesiastical officials ordering the examination required that the visit be done "in secret" to "avoid a rush of people."[88] The need for secrecy suggests that many eager believers were waiting outside the building to hear the verdict on Villanova's corpse.

Yet many of the physicians who testified likely held beliefs similar to those of the crowds that waited outside the church, and they may not have needed additional encouragement to believe in the miracles of the saints for whom they testified. The famous papal physician Giovanni Maria Lancisi (1654–1720), for example, took a relic from the body of Pope Innocent XI while performing an autopsy on him.[89] Similarly, another medical practitioner, Bernardino Romano, testified in the 1596 proceeding for Raymund of Penafort that the saint had cured him of terrible pain in his head.[90] When questioned about it, another physician, Emanuel Lopez, confessed that he became a devotee of Giuliana Falconieri, a candidate for whom he was testifying as an expert witness, after he observed her healing miracles.[91] Thus, medical professionals may very well have been devotees of those for whom they were testifying. Such admiration doubtless predisposed some to testify favorably about the "incorruptness" of corpses, when evidence might have been ambiguous.

Nevertheless, despite their personal beliefs, medical professionals at other times issued verdicts on the holiness of the body that opposed local enthusiasm and ecclesiastical wishes. During the apostolic phase of the canonization of Lorenzo Giustiniani, a physician and a surgeon refused to give a positive verdict about the state of the holy man's corpse. Indeed, when the fifteenth-century Venetian Patriarch's corpse was exhumed in 1624, the two medical practitioners stated that they found a "very decayed skeleton."[92] The physician performing the examination, Alberto Colombo, claimed that an earlier embalming effort had actually made the corpse worse as it was now "totally put together with silver threads, and in part with cloth and glue, but with little knowledge of the art [of anatomy]. Due to this [manipulation], there was created in the skeleton a rather large deformity."[93]

The negative judgment of these medical practitioners about Giustiniani's body is somewhat surprising, given the immense desire of powerful individuals to produce a positive verdict. The Doge of Venice had specifically called upon the papacy to open the process of canonization for the holy man.[94] The Venetian ambassador in Rome and the bishop of Cremona repeatedly requested that the papacy move the process forward.[95] The patriarch of Venice at the time, Giovanni Tiepolo, was also involved with the promotion of Giustiniani's sanctity.[96] Finally, the church in which the examination of Giustiniani's cadaver took place was ordered closed during the procedure, to avoid a crowd of people.[97] That a crowd might form implied that there was widespread popular devotion to the deceased patriarch. So when Colombo and the surgeon, Antonio Molinetti, came to look at the body, they were already undoubtedly aware of what high-ranking religious officials as well as local believers wanted to hear. How, then, did they produce a negative verdict?

A growing sense of professionalism among physicians might be one reason why Colombo in particular chose to pronounce a negative verdict in this case. Medical testators were usually paid by the promoters of an individual's sanctity during a canonization proceeding, and a normal payment might be about ten scudi, a respectable sum.[98] However, as Gianna Pomata has argued in her study of medical practice in Bologna, already by the first half of the seventeenth century physicians were beginning to see themselves as an elite professional group. With increasing frequency, they were not paid for specific cures and successful outcomes. In this way, they distinguished themselves from lesser practitioners, such as surgeons and apothecaries.[99] For professional reasons, then, Colombo may not have wanted it to appear as though his opinion was purchased, by merely telling the canonization officials what they wanted to hear.

Colombo and the surgeon, Antonio Molinetti, may also have been making a statement about their practical knowledge of anatomy when they issued a negative judgment about Giustiniani's corpse. In the earlier embalming effort, whoever had embalmed the corpse had failed not only to preserve the body but also to make the body fit together properly. In pointing this out, Colombo and Molinetti highlighted the difference between a trained medical professional with practical experience of anatomy and other, less trained practitioners who had originally sought to preserve the corpse.

That Colombo and Molinetti might have been particularly sensitive about their professional status is suggested by their location in Venice. Venetian physicians tended to enjoy connections with the nearby prestigious medical school at the University of Padua. Indeed, Molinetti himself would become professor of anatomy at Pauda in 1649.[100] This connection with the medical school would have exerted additional pressure on both doctors to testify according to how a strict medical evaluation would have judged Giustiniani's corpse, as succumbing to decay. After all, given the enthusiasm for Giustiniani's canonization, many Venetians—including other medical practitioners—knew the circumstances surrounding the medical testimony. In this case, safeguarding professional reputation may have outweighed communal or religious pressures for both Colombo and Molinetti.

Giustiniani's case was not unique; in other examples, from very different geographical areas, medical practitioners seem similarly aware of professional obligations when testifying about the bodies of saints. At times, this might lead them to be reluctant to testify at all. In 1632, during the apostolic phase of the canonization of Rose of Lima (d. 1617), two of the four medical practitioners who were supposed to examine her body were conveniently unavailable on the appointed day.[101] Melchor Amusco, the long-serving protomedico for the viceroyalty of Lima, fell sick on the day of the actual exhumation, and the canonization judges had to name a substitute.[102] On the same day, the surgeon Pedro de Villareal could not be found.[103] No additional information survives that might explain this coincidence, so of course it is simply possible that Villareal was otherwise engaged and Amusco was ill.[104]

Another and perhaps more plausible reason for their absence may lie in these medical professionals' concerns about Rose's body and their desire to maintain their integrity within the medical community. From the time of her death, a community of faithful devoted to her had asserted that Rose's body had lain incorrupt.[105] Thus, when the medical practitioners were called to testify in this case they likely knew very well what the community wanted to hear. Yet what the substitute medical team found upon opening the tomb was a somewhat decayed body and scattered bones. According to the presiding physician, Juan de Vega, "all the principal bones and the head of the aforementioned blessed Rose were divided and separated from each other, and some with dried and rotten [*consumata*] flesh." He conceded, however, that her body exuded "a sweet odor similar to that of dried roses and very different from that which dead bodies in a similar state usually have."[106] In saying this, Vega may have been attempting to offer something to the promoters of Rose's sanctity. Additional evidence that Vega may have carefully planned what he said is suggested by the fact that the only other medical witness to testify about Rose's body in the apostolic process, the surgeon Aloisius de Molina, made a statement using almost the same words as Vega to describe the state of the corpse.[107] It seems likely that these two agreed upon a story they thought would uphold their medical reputations yet placate the local canonization judges and believers.

Even in faraway Lima in the 1630s, emerging ideas about medical professionalism affected how the body of a saint might be interpreted. The current protomedico, Melchor Amusco, had made clear efforts to establish rigorous professional standards in his jurisdiction. Trained at the University of Seville in Spain before emigrating to the Americas in the late sixteenth century, Amusco was appalled by the diversity of people claiming to be physicians in colonial Peru and by the general fluidity of boundaries between medical professions.[108] Therefore, upon becoming protomedico, he empaneled a special judicial agent to seek out and prosecute those who infringed on correct medical practice.[109] Thus, the atmosphere in Lima in 1632 was one in which rigorous standards of professionalism were encouraged, if perhaps not always observed, among the elite. Amusco and Villareal very likely avoided testifying because they had trouble squaring both their professional and religious convictions when it came to the body of the saint. The substitute medical team of de Molina and Vega were under great pressure, but their efforts to make both sides happy apparently paid off: Rose was canonized and Vega was appointed protomedico for Lima the following year.[110] Testifying about the bodies of holy individuals was part of local politics.

The examination of the corpse of Gregorio Barbarigo by two eminent Italian physicians, Antonio Vallisneri and Giovan Battista

Morgagni, provides a striking, albeit late, case that demonstrates most clearly the conflict between local opinion, ecclesiastical authority, and medical professionalism when it came to understanding the holy body.[111] Vallisneri was the chair of practical and then of theoretical medicine at the University of Padua from 1700 until his death in 1730.[112] Morgagni was an equally famous physician. Dubbed the father of modern anatomical pathology, Morgagni helped explain the effect of disease on human organs.[113] Thus, the team sent to look at Barbarigo's body represented the finest medical minds in the Italian peninsula.

On December 18, 1727, Vallinsneri, Morgagni, and the surgeons Antonio Masieri and Agostin Danieli examined Barbarigo's cadaver, which had been exhumed as part of the apostolic process of his canonization.[114] When interviewed as to their opinion of the corpse's state, all four medical practitioners asked for time to reflect over what they had seen.[115] Canonization officials gave them two days to submit a written report in which they were specifically required to declare whether or not Barbarigo's physical state was miraculous.[116]

On December 19, 1727, the day after the exhumation of the corpse, Vallisneri wrote his friend and regular correspondent, the priest Ludovico Antonio Muratori. In this letter, Vallisneri declared, "To tell the truth, we did not find him [Barbarigo] in such a good state." This placed Vallisneri in an awkward situation since, as he went on to say, he did not feel that he was able to lie, having sworn on the sacred scriptures. However, at the same time, Vallisneri indicated that he could not describe the body as it really was, presumably because that would dash the prospective saint's canonization hopes.[117] In his response, Muratori observed that Vallisneri was stuck in a "bad situation . . . for it is necessary to say the truth, but the already printed *avvisi* from Mantua state that you and Signor Morgagni were authentic testators to [Barbarigo's] supernatural incorruptibility, and to say otherwise would be terrible." In this instance, public opinion had strongly asserted already how Vallisneri and Morgagni were supposed to testify. As Muratori observed, Vallisneri and his colleagues were stuck in a "labyrinth" out of which they would have to guide themselves.[118]

In his report to the Congregation of Rites, submitted two days after the initial survey of the body, on December 20, 1727, Vallisneri recounted in thorough detail the exhumation of the corpse and his careful examination of it. He then addressed six points in particular in discussing whether the body was miraculously incorrupt, employing a combination of observations and empirical testing of the corpse.[119] From these details, Vallisneri concluded that the body was a "wondrous" thing. However, he declined to comment on whether or not a miracle had actually occurred, stating that "whether this thing qualifies as a miracle intervening above the order of nature it is not in my talents or in my ability to define."[120]

In his final letter to Muratori on the subject, Vallisneri added, "in the end, it seems to me that I succeeded in liberating myself from the difficulty with dexterity. His eminence [Cardinal Giovan Francesco Barbarigo, Gregorio's nephew] was satisfied, and that is enough for me."[121] He then reflected that neither he nor Morgagni actually said the body was miraculously incorrupt, but rather "wondrous, which is within the confines of a miracle, but not actually a miracle."[122] Vallisneri exploited the fact that his expert knowledge allowed him to argue subtly that the body's state was just below the line of miracle. He used the murky boundary between preternatural and supernatural to give the most diplomatic answer possible.

Vallisneri's reasons for equivocating are fairly clear. Both ecclesiastical authority and popular opinion—reaching all the way to the *avvisi* issued in Mantua—strongly dictated how he should view the body. Yet Vallisneri's own personal and professional beliefs refused to allow him to be unambiguously positive in his verdict. In another letter to Muratori, he stated that he was bothered by those who enthusiastically advertised Barbarigo's incorruption without sufficient proof of it because it "gives cause to the heretics, who make fun of and joke about the lives and miracles of our saints."[123] Furthermore, Vallisneri was deeply concerned about the reputation of Italian intellectual culture and he had worried in another, much earlier letter to the Roman physician Giovanni Maria Lancisi, that the French in particular "little esteem us Italians."[124] Vallisneri was concerned both with defending the faith and with defending the reputation of Italian intellectuals—including himself—when testifying about the wondrous body of Gregorio Barbarigo. He therefore had walked a tightrope between declaring outright that the body was saintly and sticking to his professional opinion that the body had somewhat decayed.

Vallisneri's attempts to please all parties may have somewhat backfired on him, though, as the niceties of his argument were lost on local believers. Many believed him to have flatly affirmed that Barbarigo's corpse was miraculous. In a later letter to Muratori, Vallisneri expressed exasperation over "the fables being told by the mob. They say that I took blood from the body, that it jumped out of the veins, as if he were living. . . . Others say that he was incorrupt and seemed to be sleeping when he was really all black and nearly made me afraid."[125] Although there is no record of Vallisneri saying all that he was reputed to have said, the Rites testimony provides evidence that these rumors were not invented out of whole cloth. Vallisneri, for example, stated that given how light and flexible Barbarigo's arm was, he "seemed recently dead."[126] Thus, Vallisneri, in his attempt to hold true to his professional obligations, while also pleasing the Church and the local populace, allowed his testimony to remain vague enough that favorable interpretations could be read into it.

CONCLUDING REMARKS: INCORRUPTION AS MEDICAL AND RELIGIOUS TRUTH

In his *Quaestiones Medico-Legales*, Paolo Zacchia himself claimed that the truth in certain cases was not merely based on the facts at hand. He concludes, when discussing honor, a key trait for a reliable witness, "that honor is the exhibition of respect in the witnessing of virtue: or we say that honor is a certain outward sign of excellent virtue through civic action."[127] Such a notion of honor might include testifying favorably about the evidence of a prospective saint's miracles if such testimony could either support or quash the beliefs of his local community. After all, incorruption was a matter not absolute but of degrees. It was therefore subjective. Faith, honor, and concern for his community might lead a medical witness to interpret physical evidence liberally. Furthermore, such favorable testimony may not have even been a conscious choice, but rather an outcome of a physician's cultural milieu that conditioned how he even experienced the viewing of holy cadavers. We may speculate that the dilemma experienced by Vallisneri was actually unusual and many medical testators saw no division between their professional, communal, and religious obligations. In this way, then, the medical examination of saintly cadavers mirrors Steven Harris's characterization of Jesuit science, which sought "to spread and strengthen the Catholic faith wherever it was found to be weak, unknown, or under attack."[128] Testifying in favor of saintly bodies was therefore an act of a good Catholic, an upstanding citizen, and a well-respected physician. All three roles went together, reinforced one another, and helped define what it was to be an honorable medical professional.

Zacchia's definition of honor contrasts with that of the Royal Society in England, which Steven Shapin has studied and whose work has been taken up by other scholars. Shapin argues that the entire basis for knowledge production in Restoration England was the idea that gentlemen were honorable and would therefore tell the truth about what they observed in nature. The status of a gentleman in early modern England was achieved by economic, social, and biological circumstances that allowed the individual to not be so easily influenced by monetary or patronage inducements.[129] Zacchia's definition, in contrast, highlighted civic virtue and respect toward one's community as marks of honor. These very different criteria necessarily affected what could be considered fact and truth in two contemporaneous societies. In the view of early modern Catholic intellectuals, the interpretation of natural phenomena could not be disinterested because such conclusions deeply affected communal bonds and the strength of the renewed Catholic faith after the Reformation

Thus, in the body of Catholic saints medical practitioners found what we might say was a double knowledge.[130] On the one hand, there was the physical evidence, which could be read and understood within an evolving epistemological framework due to the growing prestige of anatomy. Yet, on the other hand, the body was not at any point in this period viewed solely as a medical specimen. It was, especially for Catholics, connected intimately with the divine. Thus, judging a prospective corpse during a canonization proceeding was not a simple act where the evidence at hand was easily reduced to a comprehensible category. Rather, it was a process of negotiation in which the various demands of the community, the faith, and the profession of medicine conditioned the ways in which the truth of the saintly body was understood. The next chapter turns to how such negotiations played out in the medical investigation of another sign of sanctity: the extremely ascetic body.

CHAPTER 4

Medicine and Authority

Creating Elite Asceticism

Shortly after Pope Pius V died on May 1, 1572, the physicians and surgeons who attended him during his final hours performed an autopsy on the pontiff. To some extent, this was expected: from at least the fourteenth century onward attendants had opened the papal cadaver in order to embalm it.[1] Yet Pius's case differed from those of earlier pontiffs because there were also forensic and spiritual motives for the autopsy. According to one of the physicians who attended Pius in his final hours, Gian Francesco Marengo, for years the Pope had "suffered exceeding pain in the pubic region and the whole of the penis while urinating . . . and not only while he was urinating was he tortured in this way, but also after he was done."[2] Pius's physicians could not determine the source of this pain.[3] Then, during his final illness, several attending physicians suggested surgery as a means to alleviate this discomfort and perhaps save the patient. Marengo, however, was steadfastly against surgery due to the potential danger.[4] Pius's subsequent death called Marengo's decision into question.

The autopsy vindicated Marengo, since the anatomists found three stones in Pius's bladder that were "the size of a circle made with the forefinger and the thumb, blackish in color, smooth on the surface . . . and as hard as marble."[5] Trying to excise them almost certainly would have killed the pope. Through writing and then circulating his treatise about Pius's final illness and autopsy, Marengo defended his reputation. Since the treatise was addressed to Cardinal Giulio Antonio Santori, a high-ranking member of the Curia who many believed might be the next pope, Marengo might also have been seeking to secure a future position through his authorship.[6]

Yet, perhaps unintentionally, Marengo's treatise also served another purpose: it was one of the first works to document via autopsy that a spiritual leader had privately undertaken extreme acts of asceticism. As the previous chapters have demonstrated, during the later sixteenth century medical examination became a standard way to verify the bodily holiness of prospective saints. Among the sorts of holiness that medical professionals verified were signs of incorruption and that an individual had rigorously disciplined his or her body as part of their faith.[7] In Pius's case, the size and severity of his bladder stones, which had gone undiagnosed while he lived, signaled that he had borne his agony with incredible—and perhaps supernatural—patience and endurance. Indeed, Marengo concluded, based on Pius's case history, the pontiff had suffered from these stones for nearly twenty years and they had been brought on by his exertions in ecclesiastical office.[8] Thus, through Marengo's treatise, Pius's autopsy revealed him to be a rigorous ascetic.

The trope of the ascetic prelate was a long-standing one within the Church. As André Vauchez has shown, the figure of the outwardly impressive bishop who secretly disciplined his body at night was well known by the late Middle Ages.[9] This model endured and became, in some respects, even more prevalent in the period after the Council of Trent.[10] However, with the innovations in medicine in the sixteenth century and the new confidence in postmortem examinations as a means to create knowledge about the lifestyle and habits of the deceased, anatomy now became a tool that could be used to verify wondrous acts of asceticism.[11] Indeed, the vita printed for Pope Pius V's canonization in 1712 even cited the results of the 1572 autopsy as a clear demonstration of Pius's self-control and heroic endurance for the faith.[12]

This chapter therefore follows the previous one in demonstrating the ways in which bodily holiness was constructed through a negotiation between medical expertise, ecclesiastical authority, and local belief. In asceticism, as with incorruption, anatomy was often ambiguous. Gender and social class in particular conditioned the ways in which anatomy could be used to provide evidence of an abstemious and rigorous lifestyle. Anatomical demonstration most frequently bolstered the long-standing association between asceticism and male ecclesiastical authority. Although late medieval female piety had been characterized by ascetic practices and bodily rigor, such avenues to saintliness and its associated authority were viewed with concern from the start and became increasingly restricted after Trent. Medical evaluation of the human body appears only to have amplified such restriction. Indeed, medicine played a dual role when it came to asceticism and sanctity: for holy women, anatomy became a way to challenge their appearance of sanctity, whereas for elite male prelates it served to reinforce traditional signs of holiness.

ASCETICISM AND AUTHORITY

From almost the beginning of Christianity, asceticism lent power to the practitioner and drew people to the faith, but at the same time was problematic for the Church. According to early Christian theologians, through asceticism one could achieve a near pre-Lapsarian or angelic state. That is, in the Garden of Eden—just as in heaven— man was not assaulted by bodily desires such as hunger, lust, and thirst. It was believed that individuals who could master their bodies to the extent that they could almost completely overcome these bodily needs, as ascetics, became something more than men—they became like Adam or like angels.[13]

In the early Church, then, individuals who pursued a rigorously ascetic lifestyle became imbued with spiritual authority.[14] Their proximity to God, achieved through denial of fleshly desires, made them fit leaders for the Church. Eventually, especially in the writings of Saint Jerome and early hagiographers, asceticism and spiritual purity came to be seen as a necessary component for ecclesiastical office.[15] Asceticism implied purity and the right to lead—and the right to lead, in turn, came to demand asceticism.

Such claims about asceticism and authority provoked debate and dissension even in antiquity. Skeptics asked: if the authority to minister came from a person's individual asceticism and not from the office, then what need was there for the office? Indeed, what need was there for the Church? Furthermore, if spiritual authority came from the virtues of the individual priest, what happened to the sacraments that he had performed if it was revealed that the priest had actually succumbed to sin? Finally, the belief that asceticism made one nearly like Adam veered dangerously close to a claim that man could achieve salvation through his own efforts and without faith. Such problems besieged the Church in Late Antiquity and were discussed at length, in particular, by Saint Augustine. His solution, which most ecclesiastical leaders adopted, claimed that authority resided in the office and in the Church, not in the man.[16] Pope Gregory I expanded on Augustine's line of reasoning and managed to fuse asceticism and authority again, without making it about individual virtue. Gregory asserted that the burden of leadership was heavy enough that office holding acted as a sort of penance.[17] Therefore, any office holder deserved his office, if he exercised his duties.

New challenges to the role of asceticism in establishing authority arose most prominently during the late Middle Ages, when its connection with authority bifurcated along gender lines. As Donald Weinstein and Rudolph Bell noted in their survey of medieval and early modern sanctity, "Nothing so clearly divided the ranks of the saints as gender," and this division was especially apparent when it came to the articulation of authority in this period.[18] Although men might continue to practice asceticism, in general, it was not a key focus of male reputations for holiness.[19]

For women, in contrast, their bodily suffering and asceticism became a key identifier of sanctity. Barred from leadership positions within the Church due to their sex, women's authority as holy figures could not be based primarily on their status as societal or ecclesiastical elites. Rather, they returned to the older idea from antiquity, in which asceticism led to authority. Late medieval holy women founded their authority on bodily denial, discipline, and sacrifice—especially of food. Their suffering recalled the sacrifice of Christ and thereby lent them authority as leaders within the Church.[20]

Yet the number of women who achieved such spiritual authority was small, and even those who managed to practice incredible acts of sacrifice were watched with skepticism and concern. In general, male churchmen viewed women as inherently more lustful and morally weaker than males, and therefore much more open to the machinations of the devil.[21] Women who achieved a public profile due to extraordinary feats of self-denial, prophecy, or other apparently saintly behavior were viewed with particular concern. Contemporaries worried that such signs were not manifestations of the divine, but a product of pride or even demonic influence. A body of literature offering guidelines for separating the holy from the hellish—known as the discernment of spirits—arose in the fourteenth century to address this concern.[22] Although men could be and were charged with being false saints, theologians were most concerned about deceitful women.[23] Autopsies of several fourteenth-century holy females, but not males, demonstrate this heightened and gendered concern. The basis for these postmortems was embalming and forensic, as local adherents to the saint's cult attempted to prepare the body for burial and determine where the unusual bodily signs of holiness that these women exhibited came from.[24] Even though these autopsies were undertaken by promoters of a holy person's sanctity, such scrutiny of the body implied deep concern over the most suspect saints, a concern that would become even more pronounced in the period following the Reformation.

The Reformation presented the most severe challenge to Catholic ideas about the role of bodily discipline in establishing holiness. Indeed, at the center of the Reformation was an attack on the ideal of asceticism and its connection with authority. Martin Luther, who himself had practiced rigorous asceticism for years in an attempt to merit salvation, decried such practices.[25] Although Luther did believe that people should discipline their bodies, he rejected the notion that any such sacrifice could lead to salvation.[26] Only faith could achieve salvation and disciplining the body did not necessarily imply any spiritual merit.

In the wake of such attacks, the Catholic Church responded at the Council of Trent by asserting the spiritual merit of asceticism. Nevertheless, canonization officials sounded a note of caution and stressed that judges must be vigilant in assessing claims of extraordinary acts of self-mortification.[27] They recognized the dangerous connection between asceticism and authority, which could easily be misused by those who did not put the Church's interests first. Theologians and canon lawyers renewed their interest in the literature on the discernment of spirits, and inquisitors actively sought "false" or "affected" saints.[28] In addition, canonization officials pursued new means for deciding whether or not an individual was worthy of canonization. In this reconception of sainthood, asceticism actually took on new importance in the fundamental requirement of "heroic virtue."

The important ideal of heroic virtue put asceticism again at the center of sanctity, but now it was a concept that supported the Church establishment rather than the individual ascetic. Heroic virtue was a term first used by the college of theology at Salamanca to describe Teresa of Avila during her canonization process, in 1602.[29] Saintliness, according to this new ideal, involved a life lived according to the cardinal virtues and in voluntary suffering for the betterment of the Church.[30] Men and women who sought to use their mortification as part of a campaign not merely to fight their own desires, but as part of a battle against the enemies of the Church in general—including the devil, heretics, and infidels—exemplified this new ideal. Obedience was also a hallmark of this new ideal, as the hero of the faith recognized that the fight against evil could not be waged without the power of the Church and the ecclesiastical hierarchy.[31] Thus, asceticism was co-opted more firmly than previously into supporting the hierarchical structure of the Church. Asceticism was wedded to the authority not of an individual, but of the Church as a whole.

Although the ideal of heroic virtue allowed asceticism to become a tool for supporting the Church hierarchy, it remained difficult to discern who was practicing such virtue. Numerous cases abound during both the medieval and early modern periods in which individuals who had been reputed to live on the Eucharist alone were found to be sneaking food.[32] Similarly, there were several instances in the sixteenth century when pious and ascetic Christians—including Martin Luther—converted to the Protestant faith.[33] The Catholic canon lawyer Felice Contelori (1588–1652) echoed the concerns of many when he expressed deep reservations about the ability of canonization judges to establish the holy life of an individual. He argued that the human testimony upon which canonization judges relied was "fallible."[34] He then acknowledged the widely held concern that some of those venerated on Earth actually were burning in Hell.[35] In answering such objections, Contelori defended canonization officials by observing that the Church did not rely just on human testimony but also "on divine promises."[36]

Such divine promises might include wondrous alteration to the body of the true believer. That is, God made the holy individual physically different from other men or women as a sign of His favor. In line with such ideas, a number of theologians and inquisitors began to assert the utility of medicine in discerning spirits.[37] Recognizing an opening for their services, several medical professionals in turn began to produce works purporting to help differentiate between divine or normal signs in the human body.[38] Theologians and physicians, at least in theory, now cooperated in the discernment of spirits.

MEDICINE AND THE DISCERNMENT OF SPIRITS

At the same time that canonization officials doubted their ability to identify a true ascetic, medical practitioners produced a number of treatises that dealt with precisely these issues. For the most part, these appeared as collected case histories that detailed unusual patients and the outcomes of their ailments. In this respect, these works participated in the epistemic genre of *Observationes* that Gianna Pomata has discussed and which was expanding in the sixteenth and seventeenth centuries.[39] Such works relied on specific observations and empirical details as an attempt to guide future practice. Especially for wondrously unusual abnormalities that might be related to sanctity, Marcello Donato, Paulo Lentulo, and Fortunio Liceti penned treatises in the late sixteenth and early seventeenth centuries that documented a number of specific cases.[40] Many of their examples straddled the boundary between the natural, preternatural, and supernatural, and so were of interest to theologians and expert medical witnesses involved in canonizations.

In the middle of the seventeenth century, Paolo Zacchia went further than these earlier writers and attempted to fuse such citation of case history with medical theory in creating an epistemology for understanding unusual physical ailments and anatomies. As in the case of incorruption, discussed in the last chapter, Zacchia's *Quaestiones* acted as a guidebook on asceticism, instructing a practitioner in what to look for when dealing with stigmata, extended fasts, ecstasies, raptures, and even unusual diseases.[41] However, in guiding physicians through the practice of judging ascetic behavior, Zacchia's text—perhaps unintentionally—gave medical support to long-standing concerns about female sanctity.

In discussing extreme fasts—a key element of any rigorous ascetic routine—Zacchia cautioned the examining physician to be skeptical and remain cognizant of the wide variety of potential natural variations a body could exhibit.[42] His cautionary tone on this matter extended to his other discussions of other signs of holiness as well. In each case he relied on classical Galenic theory, which viewed the body as consisting of a series of systems that, if balanced, brought good health. First there was complexion, or temperament, which denoted the balance of the fundamental qualities—hot, cold, wet, and dry—in the body. In addition to an individual having an overall complexion, specific body parts had their own complexion. Thus, a man might have a hot and dry temperament—as was considered normal—but have a hotter or colder than normal heart, depending on the blood flow in the body and the anatomy of this organ. Complexion was complemented and in part determined by the flow of the four humors in the body: blood, phlegm, yellow bile, and black bile. In addition to these two systems, depending on what school one subscribed to, the body was also pervaded by several types of *spiritus*, which provided the body with the impetus to move, digest food, grow, and perform other physical actions.[43] Then, a variety of additional factors, including a person's stage in the life cycle, his pulse, his spiritual state, and the astrological conditions could affect one's health.[44] Although there were certainly challenges to this humoral-based system in the sixteenth and seventeenth centuries—most notably by Paracelsus and the iatrochemists—Zacchia's advice was based on a long-standing and accepted medical system, which he then combined with evidence gleaned from specific cases.[45]

Zacchia considered these various factors as well as his previous experience when assessing whether unusual bodily ailments fell within the realm of the natural.[46] In the case of extended fasts, for example, an individual with a particularly hot temperament might appear emaciated and ascetic, although in reality he was gluttonous—his hot complexion merely burned off all the excess. Similarly, an individual with a cold temperament might eat very little yet remain overweight. Marcello Donato, a sixteenth-century Italian physician from Mantua and compiler of a popular collection of unusual case histories that Zacchia regularly cited, explicitly connected a cold heart to greater ease in fasting.[47] Here the allusion is to vital heat, which derived from the heart and which both consumed food and was powered by that consumption. Donato pointed to the elderly as an example in which their diminished vital heat allowed them to subsist on much less: "The [internal] heat has become smaller and weaker and so one hungers little and can get by with little or no food."[48]

This ease of fasting due to diminished heat also affected women, as Zacchia observed in his *Quaestiones*. He further explained that, on account of their colder nature, "many more women than men have been seen who can naturally put up with much longer fasts."[49] This argument was employed in a number of actual cases in which a woman's lengthy fast was declared to be of natural and not divine origin, based largely on conclusions about her natural heat.[50] Thus, the use of medical reasoning gave justification to those who were skeptical of female ascetics known for their ability to endure long fasts. As survival on the Eucharist alone was, for example, a central aspect of late medieval female sanctity, such medical skepticism opened the door for natural explanations that could be used to hinder female spiritual expression.[51]

In other cases of unusual physical ailments, Zacchia was similarly circumspect, advising the physician to consider the patient's overall health before drawing conclusions. Zacchia further concluded that natural raptures and ecstasies can occur when a person—especially a woman—focuses and fixes the imagination intensely on something like the saints or angels. The imagination causes a physiological reaction: the animal spirits, which were responsible for sensory appreciation and animation, flood the brain.[52] This then leads the person to be "completely alienated from his or her senses" and to believe that he or she is conversing with these spiritual beings that are only imagined.[53] Zacchia classified this sort of physiological reaction as a type of disease and so definitely not of divine origin.[54] Thus, Zacchia made it clear that the physician should be aware of the case history of the person experiencing an ecstasy or rapture as there are natural ways that such a state can arise. Again, although expressed in a manner that emphasized caution and the ability of medicine, Zacchia provided explanations that called into doubt another primary aspect of female holiness.[55]

On the other hand, Zacchia acknowledged that supernatural or preternatural forces can be responsible for some apparently natural diseases or other ailments.[56] However, he advised physicians, even if they could not find a cure for the disease, to consider an illness natural until they had fully exhausted the possibilities. After all, there were many reasons why someone might fake a malady.[57] Zacchia therefore advised ascertaining whether the pattern of the illness could be explained by the natural heat, age, social status, and lifestyle of the sick or deceased person. Only if the course of the disease was totally at odds with all these aspects of the patient's life should the possibility of a supernatural cause be considered.[58]

In this way, Zacchia offered an epistemology and a practical guide of bodily signs to categorize various supposed ascetics. Throughout his text, he stressed the range of possibilities within the natural and the importance of correctly interpreting the various signs that were found in the body.[59] He recommended that theologians rely on medical professionals who alone understood how to read the human body.

As a consequence of his argument for increased medicine in the evaluation of holiness, he naturalized many aspects of sanctity, especially those practiced by women, and so potentially narrowed the range of possibilities available for them.

Even in an anecdote, in which he advertised his own skills as a discerner of spirits, Zacchia struck a misogynist tone. When discussing signs of deception, he recounted the tale of a woman everyone believed to be a holy person and subject to divinely inspired raptures. Zacchia alone recognized her as a fraud and "laughed at" her. Without explaining what signs in particular betrayed her as a fraud, Zacchia stated that he knew her "inside and under her skin" and that was how he could be so sure.[60] That is, his medical skills and knowledge of the human body made him an expert in the discernment of spirits. This tone, though, in which masculine medical expertise is established through uncovering feminine deception, is explored in greater detail in the next chapter, in which the relationship between female sanctity and masculine medical authority is expanded on.

Despite Zacchia's well-known expertise and the existence of other medical treatises on the subject, the Roman Inquisition never employed his skills or those of other physicians when assessing claims of extreme asceticism.[61] The previously mentioned case studies all detail incidents in which local officials asked for medical evaluation.[62] In the surviving records of the Roman Inquisition, which are admittedly not numerous, there are only a few cases in which a physician was called in.[63] In each of those cases it was merely to confirm that the individual's health was not in immediate danger.[64] Thus, although medical scrutiny did provide an apparatus whereby bodily, and particularly female, sanctity could be viewed with a skeptical eye, it was not used by the office of the Inquisition, which was tasked especially with rooting out unapproved veneration.

The failure of the Inquisition to use medical expertise is especially striking, since both religious and medical writers advocated cooperation. Anne Schutte, in her work on saints charged with pretense of holiness by the Venetian Inquisition, asserts that one reason for the failure of the Inquisition to consult medical professionals "is tunnel vision: inquisitors simply had not bothered to acquaint themselves with parallel and potentially complementary developments in medicine. As learned and widely read as they were, their mental universe did not extend beyond their own disciplines of theology and canon law."[65] Although that is likely true for many individual inquisitors, in several instances inquisitors took over cases in which a large amount of medical details were already known.[66] In addition, the Tribunal of the Rota frequently employed physicians and it, like the Inquisition, was composed of theologians and canon lawyers.[67] Yet, unlike the office of the Inquisition, this group routinely made use of medical expertise in its evaluation of physical evidence. Furthermore, some men who consulted for the Inquisition—such as Francisco Peña—were judges on the Tribunal of the Rota.[68] Certain inquisitors, then, were likely aware of medical theories about the discernment of spirits but consciously chose to not employ experts in the field when investigating cases of unapproved veneration.

The most likely reason for the Inquisition's failure to use medical expertise in its evaluation of saintly bodies is that, by the time a case reached the Inquisition, there were already other factors that had disqualified the body from being holy. Indeed, to have a trial opened before the Holy Office meant that either someone had denounced the person or cult in question to the Inquisition or an inquisitor felt that the case was suspect enough to invite inquiry.[69] Given these circumstances, the Inquisition did not want to encourage unapproved veneration of an unusual body by seeking testimony from physicians. Involving a high profile medical figure would almost certainly have been noticed by individuals in the local community and hence would lend credence to claims that the body in question was actually that of the saint.[70] Furthermore, it was expensive and many branches of the Inquisition were fairly poor.[71]

The trial of Sister Maria Christina Rovoles of Sicily in 1680 clearly illustrates how the Inquisition dealt with unusual physical ailments, especially those attributed to women. A copy of the process against her states that numerous witnesses observed red marks on her hands, feet, and left side, which seemed to mirror the stigmata.[72] Even more impressive, though, was the crown of thorns, "the points of which were coming out [of her skin], and were touched by her Confessor."[73] The preponderance of well-documented and unusual physical details in this case should have invited medical evaluation. Furthermore, Paolo Zacchia's *Quaestiones* had been widely published by this point and included sections that could easily have been used to interpret Rovoles's wounds.[74] However, the local inquisitors dismissed the case without a medical investigation. The inquisitors stated their reasons for denying the possibility of her sanctity and the superfluity of a medical examination: the tribunal thought that "a woman of so few years, and without the precedence of a long period of penance and a continual exercise of the most heroic virtues is prevented from enjoying the privileges of the great saints Francis of Assisi and Catherine of Siena."[75] That is, bodily evidence only counted if the person experiencing the somatic signs already enjoyed an approved fame of sanctity, which had been attested to by long years of holy behavior. Anatomical evidence depended on context when it came to defining the boundaries of the supernatural.

Unusual physical signs did not stand on their own merit. Corporeal evidence of sanctity was constructed in a web of authority and expertise. Once the Church had determined, through an evaluation of the potential saint's virtues, that it was possible for this person to work miracles, only then could his or her body be considered holy. Thus the cases in which medicine was used to confirm ascetic practices overwhelmingly came from the canonization trials of elite, male prelates.

ESTABLISHING ASCETICISM: AUTOPSY
AND THE CASE HISTORY

In multiple cases from the sixteenth and seventeenth centuries, medical evidence obtained via autopsy promoted an image of a saintly prelate who practiced secret asceticism. In two already cited sixteenth-century cases the secret asceticism of both Carlo Borromeo—the model Counter-Reformation bishop—and Ignatius of Loyola, the founder of the Jesuits, was confirmed in a postmortem examination.[76] The surgeon examining Borromeo saw "no sign of fat" in his body and took this to be a sign of his extreme asceticism. To have fasted so much that absolutely no fat could be found in his body was interpreted as a wondrous and potentially miraculous phenomenon.[77] Similarly, the Roman physician Realdo Colombo removed from the founder of the Jesuits, Ignatius of Loyola (1491–1556), "innumerable stones from his penis and found stones of various colors in his lungs, liver, and in the vena porta. . . . I saw moreover pebbles in the urinary duct in the bladder, in the colon, in the hemorrhoidal vein and in his navel area."[78] The image Colombo gives of Loyola mirrors that of Marengo's depiction of Pius V and casts him as a man quietly and patiently living in continual agony.

In the agonies that they bore, Loyola and Pius V were not alone: patience in bearing kidney or bladder stones was the most frequent sign of asceticism found in the bodies of reputedly holy individuals.

Francis de Sales (1567–1622), the bishop of Geneva and an active missionary against Protestantism, was posthumously opened and found to have "many small stones of various colors and shapes" in his gall bladder. These affected him to such an extent that there was not left "a drop of humor in the gall bladder."[79] Such an ailment would have been painful and possibly life-threatening. Similarly, the Archbishop of Reggio Calabria, Annibale d'Afflitto (1560–1638), was found during his autopsy to have "a stone the size of a walnut" in his kidney.[80] In these cases, the anatomical details contributed to an image of a saintly, male prelate who secretly endured excruciating pain for years prior to his death.

At least one elite holy woman was also depicted as enduring painful stones as part of the image of her sanctity. Caterina Ricci (1522–1590), a patrician Florentine who became a Dominican tertiary and then prioress of a convent in Prato, amazed the physicians who cared for her during life with her incredible and patient suffering. In her canonization process, a group of unnamed medical professionals stated that she suffered for over a year from "hydropsy, great inflammation of her body, fever, and the stone."[81] Then suddenly, she passed "thirty or thirty-two stones" from her body. This, the medical practitioners concluded, could not have occurred through "natural virtue or power" but must have been caused by "superior and divine power and virtue." She passed these stones, furthermore, without any pain.[82] In short, her endurance and then liberation from the stone was deemed a medical miracle. Ricci's is the only case for which records could be found in which a woman was determined to be a divinely inspired ascetic due to the suffering from the stone. Ricci's elite position—both coming from a prominent family and acting as prioress of a convent— helps explain why she enjoyed expert medical verification. She exercised authority in a way similar to elite male prelates and also had better access to medical professionals than other holy women, given her position. Yet even Ricci's bodily miracle was not confirmed by a postmortem autopsy—an issue that is explored below.

Kidney or bladder stones thus appear regularly in medical evaluations of prospective saints and function on several levels to demonstrate the holiness, and hence authority, of the deceased. First, as kidney and bladder stones were a widespread and excruciatingly painful ailment in early modern Europe, many people experienced directly the sort of pain the saints endured and so would have been awed by these stories.[83] Second, contemporary theories on how stones formed in the human body also helped establish the virtuous life of the deceased. Although even in the sixteenth century physicians recognized that the kidneys functioned as filters for the urine, there were various theories to explain the appearance of stones.[84] The surgeon Ambroise Paré (1510–1590) laid out one of the most widely read and comprehensive explanations for how stones formed. His work enjoyed broad circulation and was translated into Latin, despite his status as a surgeon and not a physician.[85] His explanation of kidney or bladder stones was that they resulted from "heavy, sticky humors, thick and viscid, formed from crudities caused by poorly regulated temperature and immoderate exercises."[86] In particular, "too much staying awake, working, and fasting" could bring on such coagulation of humors in the kidneys or bladder.[87] That is, asceticism combined with overwork caused kidney or bladder stones. Thus, they were the perfect physical evidence of asceticism.

It was perhaps because dissection of the kidneys could so clearly demonstrate hidden sanctity that the prominent physician and later priest Levinus Lemnius (1505–1568) wrote that "God scrutinizes both the heart and the kidneys."[88] Lemnius's writings enjoyed wide readership in early modern Europe, going through several Italian editions, and influencing even Vesalius.[89] Lemnius reasoned that the heart held the secrets of the soul whereas the kidneys revealed the ways in which a person suffered for God.[90] Thus, Lemnius and Paré provide medical justification for seeing long endurance of painful stones as a clear sign of ascetic virtue. Anatomy helped physicians and theologians in their attempts to discern spirits.

The eminent Roman physician Giovanni Maria Lancisi's (1654–1720) postmortem examination of Pope Innocent XI in 1689 most clearly articulated the link between kidney ailments and secret, elite asceticism. Because Innocent was regarded as saintly even during life, his canonization process began shortly after his death, though he was not beatified until the twentieth century.[91] Given his rank and sex, Innocent met the conventional profile of someone whose asceticism might be secret and connected to office. Medical expertise, deployed during his canonization process and in posthumous vitae, demonstrated the extent of his ascetic practices, which had largely been kept hidden from his parishioners.

Lancisi, Innocent's personal doctor, was the main medical witness to the pope's medically confirmed asceticism. Lancisi was an important figure in the medical world. He achieved his doctorate from the

University of Rome "La Sapienza" in 1672 before serving as assistant at the large Santo Spirito Hospital, where he gained greater knowledge of human anatomy.[92] Afterward, he served as chief physician, or *archiater*, to both Innocent XI and Clement XI and was a member in several international scientific societies, including the Royal Society of London.[93] However, at the time of his postmortem of Innocent in 1689, he had not yet garnered most of these accolades. He stepped into his role as chief physician to Innocent only in 1688, when his instructor at the Santo Spirito, Giovanni Tiracorda, put him forward for the open position.[94] For both pious and professional reasons, then, Lancisi was very devoted to Innocent, even admitting to having taken a relic from the deceased pontiff's body after dissecting him.[95]

Lancisi's most extensive and explicit testimony for his former employer's canonization centered on Innocent's final illness. He stated that during this time, the pope endured for fifty-eight days a mix of "fever, inflammation, foot abscesses, gout, which together with the sores and the fistulae in the joints of his feet made him suffer an incredible martyrdom[.] Adding to these severe pains was his kidney illness, which he had suffered continuously for thirty-three years."[96] Lancisi was explicit that Innocent's patient bearing of these illnesses signaled his sanctity: "He was very saintly because other than his great acts and the heroic virtue that he exercised in life he added to this an incomparable suffering" leading up to his death, which he bore with incredible patience. Indeed, Lancisi stated that even just one of the illnesses that Innocent suffered would have "brought any other patient to unending agitation and anxiety [whereas] in the holy pontiff I never saw the least sign of impatience."[97] Calm bearing of illness was a clear sign of asceticism, and Lancisi here makes this into not just a matter of faith, but a medical detail in a case history.

Shortly following Innocent's death, Lancisi and another colleague were asked to open the body. Although reasons are not explicitly given for the postmortem, as in the case for Marengo's autopsy of Pius V, the mix of motives likely included embalming, forensic analysis, and a search for sanctity. A later letter to Pope Clement XI about this event, which can be read as an attempt to curry favor from a future patron or employer, further supports the idea that Lancisi had personal and professional reasons to want to open Innocent's corpse.[98]

Upon opening Innocent's cadaver, Lancisi found clear confirmation of Innocent's sanctity. Inspecting in particular Innocent's kidneys, which had pained the pontiff for more than three decades,

Lancisi found "two stones of immense size."[99] Interpreting the significance of these stones, Lancisi stated that "the marvel that I saw was beyond belief: the stones had totally consumed the substance of the kidneys and there only remained in each one a thick membrane, like a bag which enclosed and squeezed the stone."[100] That is, Innocent's kidneys were entirely given over to the stone. Lancisi concluded that it was a "supernatural" thing for a man to survive for so long with this condition.[101] His continued ability to live was a daily miracle. Lancisi's analysis was also taken up by more popular writers, who circulated pamphlets highlighting the dramatic size of Innocent's stone.[102] Thus, medically confirmed kidney stones were both an effective and popular sign of Innocent's sanctity. They cast him as the elite prelate who secretly bore incredible pain with the utmost patience.

Although stones were perhaps the most effective demonstration of extreme asceticism—likely because they were both common and yielded a tangible piece of evidence—other ongoing and patiently borne illnesses could also be harnessed as part of an image of a secretly suffering prelate, even if no postmortem was undertaken. The physicians who attended Luis Bertrán (1526–1581), a successful Dominican missionary, noted that throughout his life he frequently suffered patiently from illnesses that lacked a clear cause.[103] Although not stated explicitly, the implication seems to be that the lack of a cause made these diseases seem divinely inspired as a way to test the prospective saint.

The most controversial and prominent case in which ongoing illness contributed to an image of a saintly sufferer was that of Maria Maddalena de' Pazzi (1566–1607). Although not subjected to a full posthumous autopsy, her body became a site of medical debate between Catholics and Protestants. A Carmelite nun from an elite Florentine family, de' Pazzi suffered from a wide range of physical ailments throughout her life. According to her main hagiographer, Vincenzo Puccini, several physicians visited her on numerous occasions and determined that there was no natural cure for her many diseases.[104] De' Pazzi was, in fact, in so much pain that these medical men were at a loss to explain how she was able to survive so long in such torment.[105] Such endurance was typical of the trope of unknown illnesses accepted patiently by a saintly individual and cast her survival as miraculous. It was also exactly the sort of medical miracle that Paolo Zacchia had cautioned against trusting.[106]

Despite the rather meager medical support for de' Pazzi's asceticism, an anonymous English editor of her vita reinterpreted de' Pazzi's ailments to cast her as a very ill and confused woman. This recharacterization of de' Pazzi functioned well in the anti-Catholic atmosphere that James II inspired in England since it appeared to be a vita for the saint, but worked to blacken the Catholic Church as indulging or perhaps exploiting a weak woman.[107] The editor described de' Pazzi as experiencing a sort of spiritual bi-polarism: he explained that de' Pazzi went into raptures by focusing overly long on saints and the crucifixion. Such fixation caused a physiological reaction in her body in which her "heart is dilated, and the spirits are exalted and become more vigorous in their motion." This excitation of the spirits in her body—that is, the animal spirits discussed by Zacchia, and not her soul—led her to enter into a sort of mania in which she felt full of energy and ardor for the lord. However, when it ended "the spirits are quite tired, they grow dull and stupid, the mind is affected with the contrary passion, despair and despondency take place." That is, de' Pazzi became depressed and quite low after such passions. Furthermore, such drastic physiological changes in her body frequently made de' Pazzi sick—thus explaining her repeated and numerous illnesses.[108] Her problems, according to the editor, "should have been corrected by medicine and sober counsel."[109] By indulging de' Pazzi's exalted view of herself, the editor alleged that Catholic officials were just making her sicker. In his polemic, de' Pazzi required medication, not veneration.

Why did de' Pazzi's body arouse such controversy? A long-standing belief among elite theologians held that "little women" might lead overly credulous confessors astray.[110] The English author exploited this idea as a way to accuse the entire ecclesiastical hierarchy of being misled when Church officials proceeded with canonizing de' Pazzi in 1671. The editor, furthermore, used medicine to buoy his claims by attempting to reinterpret de' Pazzi's illnesses and raptures as natural, rather than supernatural events. Such medical arguments in an anti-Catholic treatise suggest that authors as far away as England were aware of the medical demonstrations that Catholic officials had engaged in and now had begun to employ them for their own ends. This seems especially likely since the editor's naturalization of this miracle echoes, and perhaps borrows from, Paolo Zacchia's advice to inquisitors on how to judge raptures.

De' Pazzi's body thus became a site of knowledge that both Catholics and Protestants filled with meaning. For Catholics, her ongoing illnesses without clear causes were a demonstration of her asceticism and calm acceptance of divine will. For Protestants, the illnesses signified that the Catholic Church both manipulated and was manipulated by those who experienced unusual physical ailments. Medical understanding of disease and the interaction of the supernatural with the human were key to the elaboration of both arguments.

CONCLUSION

Kidney stones, a lack of fat, and unknown diseases—all of which could be verified by a medical examination or autopsy—were employed to perpetuate and expand the long-standing trope of the ascetic prelate after the Reformation. Medicine helped breathe fresh life into the old connection between asceticism and authority, both individual and ecclesiastical. The preference for the stone in these narratives demonstrates that the meaning of disease was embedded in a cultural moment. The commonplace nature of this ailment combined with the connection between kidney or bladder stones and asceticism endowed them with spiritual meaning. But for such meaning to be achieved the individual first had to already enjoy an excellent reputation for sanctity and be attended by educated physicians who could undertake an autopsy. This largely restricted the field to elite men. In addition to these societal issues that barred women from receiving anatomical verification of their holiness, both medical and theological literature on the discernment of spirits tended to be severely skeptical of women who experienced somatic signs of holiness. Thus, it was overwhelmingly males who were the subjects of forensic postmortems that sought signs of asceticism. In this way, then, a medical link was forged between asceticism and authority, relying especially upon the common ailment of kidney stones.

Occasionally, as in the cases of Maria Maddalena de' Pazzi and Caterina Ricci, medical testimony confirmed signs of asceticism in female bodies. Yet in neither case were the bodies opened posthumously as part of a forensic investigation into their asceticism or their ailments. Such an omission is especially noteworthy in de' Pazzi's case, as her body did undergo a postmortem examination on more than one occasion by a medical team.[111] Why did they not also check her body for signs of the agony that she bore so patiently during life? Although there were numerous female saints who were known for their asceticism in the sixteenth and seventeenth centuries, almost none of them were opened as part of an attempt to confirm their

suffering as miraculous.[112] This was despite the fact that many prospective female saints were examined after death to confirm the
miraculous incorruption of their bodies.[113] The next chapter explores
this conundrum: although women had been opened in the late Middle
Ages to search for anatomical signs of holiness, this practice seems
nearly to have disappeared in the seventeenth century. Instead, it was
predominantly men who underwent medico-spiritual autopsy. The
reasons lie in the ambivalent status of the female body as medical
specimen, saintly relic, and sexual object.

CHAPTER 5

Engendering Sanctity

On October 20, 1618, Orsola Benincasa, the founder of the Oblates of the Immaculate Conception, died in the city of Naples. Although many in the city already hailed her as a holy person, very shortly after Benincasa's death her body began to provide further evidence of her sanctity. Witnesses noted that a great deal of heat emanated from her chest. Exploring more closely, they discovered that "her chest had swollen in such a way that it seemed almost as if the area around her heart was boiling." The swelling was so great that it burst the seams of her clothing and then blood began to pour from her nose.[1]

Curious as to the cause for such wondrous abnormalities, Antonio Carmignano, a member of a prestigious and powerful local family, suggested that Benincasa's body be opened.[2] Her sisters and other religious officials agreed, with the caveat that it be done immediately and secretly, "so as not to be oppressed by devoted individuals."[3] That is, they wanted to avoid the crowd that would undoubtedly attend such a spectacle.[4]

Given their haste, Benincasa's devotees did not wait for a medical expert but had her opened by those present, using an assortment of tools that included an awl and various knives.[5] As her hagiographer notes, it was "more the work of a slaughterhouse, than the observations of doctors [medici] and anatomists."[6] In the grisly scene that unfolded, the dissectors reported that they did not find a heart in Benincasa's body because it had been "totally consumed by fire."[7] The interior of her chest had been scorched by the heat of divine love and it had completely destroyed her heart, making the fact that she had lived so long a miracle. In addition, the makeshift anatomists found her body to be "fat in all of its parts" despite the fact that everyone knew that Benincasa had almost completely abstained from any sort of food except for the Eucharist.[8] This was taken as another sign of divine intervention. God had allowed the Eucharistic wafer to nourish Benincasa so completely that she actually grew fat from it.

The opening of Benincasa's body formed part of the growing trend, discussed in the previous four chapters, in which theologians, physicians, and the public more generally came to believe that saints' holiness could be verified through anatomical investigation. Yet there was something fundamentally different about Benincasa's case. First, no medical professionals were noted as having been in attendance at Benincasa's autopsy. By the early seventeenth century it had become standard for at least one and normally several medical experts, including university-trained physicians, to examine the body of a prospective saint during a postmortem. Second, by the seventeenth century Church officials in Rome acting during the apostolic process had taken over the postmortem evaluation of saintly cadavers. In Benincasa's case, though, it was local enthusiasts acting quickly who ordered the autopsy. Third, the evidence provided by Benincasa's body was interpreted in a way that was contrary to what were accepted medical signs of holiness. A fat body almost always denoted gluttony, and no other extant records or reports of cases from the period indicate that excess fat might be interpreted as a sign of sanctity. Normally, emaciation, not obesity, hidden by the vestments of office revealed an individual's hidden sanctity, and such persons were almost always deceased male prelates.[9] Furthermore, a missing heart was an ambiguous sign that could be taken as a mark of holiness or interpreted to signify the cruel or miserly nature of an individual.[10] Finally, Benincasa's case is only one of two from the period after the Council of Trent in which women's bodies were opened to look for signs of sanctity other than incorruption. For all these reasons, despite the attempt to document Benincasa's holy anatomy, Benincasa was not made a saint.

The differences between Benincasa's case and those of other holy people opened to confirm sanctity stem from her sex and point to the fundamental role that gender had in the construction both of saints and of anatomical evidence of holiness in the sixteenth and seventeenth centuries. Prior to the Reformation, only prospective female saints had been subject to autopsy in an attempt to demonstrate their sanctity. In these cases it was always local supporters who opened the body under their own initiative.[11] By the seventeenth century, as we have seen, medical expertise and ecclesiastical authority began to work jointly in an attempt to define signs of holiness when they occurred in the human body. Postmortem analysis of saintly bodies became part of the canonization process, and this led to the opening of both male and female bodies. In examining bodies for canonization, though, Church officials and medical professionals drew stark lines in how they treated men's and women's corpses: only men could have their asceticism verified through autopsy, and whereas women's genitalia became focal points of the postmortem, in a man reproductive organs became notable primarily for their absence or diminutive appearance.

The different treatment of male and female saintly bodies stemmed from a vigorous reassertion of both Church and medical hierarchies in the sixteenth and seventeenth centuries. After the profound crisis of the Reformation, Church officials reasserted the authority of the exclusively male hierarchy in Church leadership.[12] This emphasis helped reify gender hierarchies, which were being reinforced generally in European culture after a period of flux.[13] Similarly, as the medical profession both underwent innovation and sought to professionalize during this period, its practitioners increasingly tried to define whose medical authority was legitimate. This, in particular, led to an emphasis on university-trained male knowledge of the body over that possessed by female healers.[14] These gender dynamics in different fields came together and played out in the creation of saints in the sixteenth and seventeenth centuries.

A survey of prospective female saints in the seventeenth century reveals almost a sort of gender confusion with contemporaries unsure of how to square the public role of famous holy women with increasingly rigorous gender hierarchies. Indeed, it seems that to have a public role in the Church women had to act manlike and even become physiologically like men. Only masculine authority was public authority. Yet after death, the posthumous medical examination reasserted a woman's feminine and sexual nature, thus drawing a clear line between male and female saints. Gender hierarchy was necessary to support ecclesiastical hierarchy, renewed Church power, and construct medical expertise. Therefore, boundaries that had become blurred in life were reasserted after death.

This fixing of gender boundaries not only supported hierarchies in the Church and the medical profession, but also was important for the establishment of miracles performed by female saints. Although sex was not considered a binary in the early modern period, but ranged over a spectrum with a number of grades, there were still ways in which one's gender could be unnatural.[15] Those who could change their sex or fall squarely between the male and the female presented a problem for religious and medical authorities concerned with the boundaries of the natural world.[16] Did such gender fluidity exceed the normal forces of nature? If so, were women who had to become like men during life to exercise religious authority guilty of subverting natural laws? If such gender transformation could be considered an aberration not inspired by God—that is, a preternatural event— then all of the saint's miracles could similarly be called into question. Gender was at the center of a saint's identity, and if it could be shown to be fluid in a non-natural way, it threw the individual's whole character into question. Male anatomists reestablished gender hierarchies through their postmortem investigations and thereby reestablished the boundaries of nature. Stable boundaries of the natural world were crucial for miracles to occur. Women's bodies had to be natural with respect to their gender so that the wonders performed by them could be considered supernatural.

OPENING WOMEN'S BODIES

As in the case for men, women's bodies had been opened for a variety of purposes—teaching, embalming, forensic inquiry—from the late Middle Ages. But even at this early moment, there was a difference in the way in which medical practitioners perceived the status of men's and women's bodies: anatomists assumed that the male body was the generic body. Therefore, women's corpses were most interesting for the ways in which they differed from the male—especially in their reproductive organs. In particular, since women's genitalia are mostly internal, the uterus came to hold special symbolic weight as the secretive organ that could only be understood through dissection.[17] Thus, even in the late Middle Ages the opening of female bodies tended to focus specifically on the reproductive organs.

By the fifteenth century, this reproductive focus allowed female autopsy to be seen as a sort of status symbol and a way to demonstrate the honor of a woman and her family. Although opening a woman's body in a public anatomy theater was and continued to be deeply shameful, postmortem examinations undertaken in private were acceptable. Italian patrician women—especially those who died in childbirth—were often opened at the behest of their widowed husbands. The motivation behind these autopsies was in some cases practical, to see if a fetus had survived and could be birthed via cesarean section or, otherwise, to determine the woman's cause of death.[18] This connection of autopsy with maternity and the identification of the mother's womb with the family lineage actually made the procedure not only acceptable, but even honorable. It served as final proof to the husband's family of the wife's virtue: the womb and body destroyed in childbirth demonstrated the wife's sacrifice for this family's honor. As Katharine Park maintains, "Good wives and mothers . . . opened themselves to scrutiny in the interests of their children and their husband's families, to whom those children by definition belonged."[19]

This conviction that the body could demonstrate the virtue of the deceased was likewise the motivation for the autopsies performed on female saints in the fourteenth century. The corpses of two late medieval holy women—Chiara of Montefalco (d. 1308) and Margherita of Città di Castello (d. 1320)—were opened both to embalm the bodies and to search for signs of their sanctity. In these instances, the autopsy focused not on the uterus, but on the woman's heart, which was considered to be the center of spiritual devotion.[20] The autopsies revealed that Chiara's heart held within it the instruments of the Passion, including a rod, sponge, cross, and tiny nails, whereas Margherita's had a tiny tube attached to it in which figured stones appeared. These stones were impressed with images of the Virgin Mary, the infant Jesus, Joseph, the Holy Spirit, and a kneeling penitent who was likely Margherita. In each of these cases, local believers as well as medical practitioners with only rudimentary anatomical knowledge confirmed the authenticity of the items as well as their supernatural and divine origins.[21]

Katharine Park and Dyan Elliott have argued that it was the embodied nature of female holiness that, at least in part, led to these autopsies.[22] Late medieval holy women experienced their sanctity in a real, physical sense much more frequently than men: they went into ecstasies, endured long fasts by surviving only on the Eucharist, produced stigmata, and experienced a range of other abnormalities that were considered divinely inspired.[23] Given the physical manifestations of female holiness, the body was thought to provide evidence of their sanctity. Anatomy could therefore be a useful tool in establishing holiness as it was in establishing honor for patrician women. However, neither Chiara nor Margherita were canonized in the Middle Ages, so the power of anatomy to demonstrate sanctity could be considered limited at best in this early period.

Although female saints continued to be popular and to exhibit physical signs of holiness from the fourteenth into the sixteenth century, no new prospective saints, either male or female, were subjected to an autopsy until about 1500.[24] Then, medical experts opened Colomba of Rieti (d. 1501) and Elena Dugioli (d. 1520) early in the sixteenth century. In these cases the examination seems to have been both religious and medical, with skilled medical practitioners curious to understand the physical abnormalities experienced by these women. The anatomists discovered evidence that Colomba had eaten almost nothing, implying she lived exclusively on the Eucharist. Furthermore, her heart was bathed in blood that seems to have miraculously sat on the organ without killing her.[25] Elena Dugioli, in contrast, was notable because her breasts had lactated for years before her death, producing a healing milk. After she died, the wondrous and unexplained nature of her breasts seems to have been the main motivation for her autopsy. This postmortem examination further revealed that her heart had been replaced by a strange lump—a detail used to support a claim that the organ had been taken by Jesus.[26]

These early sixteenth-century women's cases of autopsy are distinct from the fourteenth-century examples of female saints whose bodies had been opened. The bodies of Dugioli and Columba were opened and examined by prestigious medical experts, and the evidence consisted of medical signs instead of wondrous objects. This difference stemmed both from continuing skepticism about visionary women on the part of Church officials and the rising prestige of anatomy in Europe at the time.[27] After all, when Elena and Colomba were opened, the first anatomical case studies based on the burgeoning field of an empirically based study of human anatomy began to appear in Europe.[28]

This trend toward using medical experts to interpret recondite signs in the body continued with the next series of autopsies, which came after the Reformation. Now, however, male saints also began to come under the dissector's knife. The reasons why both male and female saints came to be autopsied at this time were twofold: medical practitioners had become interested in unusual cases, such as the wondrous anomalies found in holy bodies, and promoters of a saint's canonization sought to use any means possible to demonstrate a saint's election during a period of crisis. They therefore turned toward the medical techniques of verification that had been previously employed only for female saints.

These religious and medical motivations for performing a postmortem on a holy body clearly played out in the first case after Trent, when Ignatius Loyola, the founder of the Jesuits, was opened in 1556. As we have seen, the eminent physician Realdo Colombo initially opened the body for a mix of forensic and embalming purposes. However, he documented what he found in a printed treatise because Loyola's ailments were so unusual. Several ecclesiastical writers then sought to use Colombo's autopsy to promote Loyola's sanctity. Their treatises were ignored by canonization officials, and it seems that by the time Francisco Peña and his contemporaries on the Rota began to require postmortem examinations during canonizations, the types of evidence and meaning of saintly autopsies had departed from the earlier female cases.

One sign that Peña and other canon lawyers were not following medieval examples lies in the fact that overwhelmingly the examinations in the apostolic phase were used to confirm incorruption, not wondrous asceticism or unusual bodily organs. On the rarer occasions that postmortem evaluations sought to confirm anatomical wonders, the autopsy was generally undertaken at the behest of local promoters for sanctity and only ended up being considered as acceptable evidence during the apostolic phase if the prospective saint was male. The reason for the preference of type of miracle and gender of the miracle worker are evident: incorruption was a miracle that demonstrated the promise of eventual salvation through God and the Church. It also admitted hierarchies with different degrees of incorruption being possible.[29] It was therefore a miracle that could be applied to both sexes as it reaffirmed faith in the Church and the structure of Church hierarchies. On the other hand, signs of asceticism or miraculous alteration to bodily organs testified more to the prospective saint's practices during life. It indicated the holy person's personal virtue and connected the holy person with long-standing traditions of authority within the Church. It was therefore a miracle that was predominantly attached to men, as the office holders and wielders of authority within the Church.

In fact, in only two cases in the period after Trent have I found autopsies performed on women that sought to demonstrate their anatomical wonder. In each of these two cases, local adherents to the saint's cult undertook the autopsy shortly after the woman's death to investigate the claim that Jesus had touched her heart. Each autopsy was therefore a sort of forensic investigation in which the dissectors sought to verify the holy woman's spiritual claims through physical examination. One of those examined was the previously cited Orsola Benincasa, whose heart was reported missing. The other was Paola Napolitana (1572–1624), a Dominican tertiary, who, like Benincasa, was opened shortly after her death without a medical practitioner present. The unnamed dissectors cut open her heart and found inside "a network of branches of flesh forming reliefs, among which two were larger than the others[.] One of these clearly depicted a cross and a person kneeling before the side of that cross."[30]

These two cases have more in common with the early fourteenth-century examinations performed on Chiara of Montefalco and Margherita of Città di Castello than with postmortems of their contemporaries. Indeed, these two autopsies were carried out by non-experts, yielded objects instead of medical signs, and did not lead to evidence in favor of canonization. Paola, like Chiara, had an image of the cross in her heart. Although Benincasa, like Elena Dugioli, was said to lack a heart, in the latter's case physicians verified its absence and found another anatomical structure in its place. For Benincasa, her well-disposed hagiographer even admitted that her autopsy was more like the work of butchers than surgeons, and one might speculate that her dissectors could not find a heart in her body because they did not know where to look. These autopsies, therefore, were carried out by believers who sought to use anatomy because they recognized its ability to demonstrate sanctity. However, they failed to recognize that new standards were being developed for understanding the holy corpse via the alliance between medicine and Catholicism.

That a new standard was being applied to the interpretation of men's holy bodies, but not women's, is revealed by the profoundly different ways in which men's anatomically irregular hearts were treated during postmortem examinations into sanctity. At least four cases survive from the late sixteenth and early seventeenth centuries in which a holy man's heart was examined as part of the consideration of his holiness including Filippo Neri, Carlo Borromeo, Angelo del Pas, and Francis de Sales. Although only in the case of Neri was the evidence included in the apostolic process, the nature of the evidence and who testified to it marked a clear difference between the treatment of male and female hearts in this period.

As discussed in previous chapters, Neri had incredibly unusual cardiac anatomy, which could only be understood by those who were at the forefront of the anatomical understanding of the heart. Indeed, as Nancy Siraisi has observed, the demonstration that his heart was miraculously abnormal relied on an acceptance of the new theory of pulmonary transit, which was a crucial piece leading to William Harvey's discovery of blood circulation.[31] This, then, was an expert reading of recondite signs in the human body, which eventually counted toward Neri's canonization.

Even in cases in which the anatomy did not eventually count for canonization, the evidence was of a different sort and analyzed by more prominent medical experts than in the cases of Benincasa or Napolitana. When the Franciscan Friar Angelo del Pas died in 1596, many of his supporters believed that he had suffered the wounds of the stigmata on his heart. In fact, del Pas, like Neri and several female saints, experienced cardiac pain during life without a clear cause.[32] To search the source of this pain and to embalm the deceased friar, his fellow Franciscans called upon a Roman surgeon, Giovanni Battista Piceni. Testifying in the ordinary canonization process, Piceni recounted what he found upon opening del Pas's chest cavity: "I found the interior of the body to be most beautiful and without any infection. And when I removed the interior [organs] with everything else, I took out the heart separately, where I found in the heart a cut that seemed like a wound."[33] The surgeon did not speculate on the nature of this wound. This silence is significant because in other cases canonization officials asked examining medical experts explicitly to judge whether abnormalities found in the human body were beyond the realm of the natural.[34] In fact, Piceni gave equal weight in his description to the lack of any infection in del Pas's cadaver as he did to the wound he discovered in del Pas's heart. Piceni's judgment, then, was that del Pas's cardiac abnormality fell within the realm of the natural. Canonization officials sided with medical expertise instead of popular acclaim: del Pas's unusual heart was not counted as a miracle and he was never canonized. The lack of patronage in del Pas's case may have inspired Piceni to cautiously assert that his corpse lay within the realm of the natural.[35] Nevertheless, the nature of the evidence that he uncovered and the way it was treated differed significantly from that which was presented in the cases of contemporary females, in which it was dismissed outright.

In the forensic investigation into cardiac abnormalities as signs of sanctity as well as the attempt to identify wondrous asceticism by means of a postmortem, men were treated completely differently from women. By dismissing the wondrous anatomy of holy women, canonization officials reinscribed them into a specifically female sphere, just as women living as nuns in convents were subordinate to the priests who administered the Eucharist and other rites to them. Such subordination necessarily elevated the male ecclesiastics and saints and established a hierarchy based on gender. This hierarchy was further elaborated through the instances in which women's bodies were subjected to postmortem examinations, that is, when confirming claims of their wondrous incorruption.

INCORRUPTION, GENDER, AND AUTHORITY

In the period after the Reformation, postmortem examinations of saintly bodies generally served two purposes for the Church: they reinforced the long-standing right of the male office holder to lead the Church by demonstrating his rigorous and secret asceticism, and they verified the miracle of incorruption. Anatomy was now a force employed to legitimize claims of extraordinary human sanctity. But at the same time that anatomy established miracles, it also secondarily reinscribed sex onto male and female bodies in a way that supported a clear gender hierarchy.

At the center of both the Counter-Reformation and the Reformation was a reassessment of gender roles.[36] Several historians have even seen in the Counter-Reformation an attempt on the part of the male ecclesiastical elite to assert a newly implemented patriarchal and exclusionary brand of Christianity.[37] Although the evidence is more suggestive than conclusive, male saintly vitae support such a view. In these works male holiness is defined in opposition to feminine weakness, sexuality, and deception. In the vita published for Filippo Neri's canonization (1622), for example, his hagiographer recorded the saint's advice to a young man who was concerned that his sister might be possessed. After visiting the girl, Neri "saw at once that it was all willfulness, whereupon he called the girl's brother and said to him, 'if you wish to cure your sister, give her a sound beating whenever she begins her fooleries, and that will bring her round without any further trouble.'" The young man then followed up on Neri's advice and, after having been beaten, his sister admitted "that it was all imposture from beginning to end."[38] Neri's holy nature here was demonstrated in his ability to see past the deceptions of a woman and

his willingness to use violence to reassert the normal order. It therefore casts him as a clearly masculine and hierarchical leader of the
Church, on guard against feminine weakness and deception.

Even those women who maintained the traditional religious roles
might represent sources of danger and pollution for male ecclesiastics.
In another section of Neri's vita, the same author claimed that "when
he [Neri] first began to hear confessions he was more ready to hear
the sins of men than of women and as far as he could, avoided hearing the faults of the latter, cautious of any threat to his virginal purity.
I will add that he was so strict and vigilant in guarding his modesty
that if he was obliged to hear women's confessions, he would receive
them in church, speaking abruptly rather than gently, and from time
to time showing his annoyance in his looks."[39] That a hagiographical
vita, which should be putting forward a model of piety, casts Neri as
reluctant to listen to female parishioners and annoyed when he had to
hear their confessions suggests that male holiness was defined in part
through its exclusion of women. Although it might have been detrimental to the souls of the women in his parish, these women were
so dangerous that Neri strenuously avoided them. His holiness was
defined, at least in part, in opposition to women.

These unusual qualities pointed out by Neri's vita also appear in
hagiography of other men. The author of a vita for Antonio Colellis
(1586–1654), a Neapolitan priest, similarly stated that Colellis "was
an enemy of hearing women's confessions, and when by some grave
necessity he had to confess one, he did it with great caution[.] And he
continually exhorted his priests [he was rector of the Church of Saint
Gregory the Great] to comport themselves with great care when dealing
with women."[40] Women presented such a possibility of corruption that
priests who heard their confessions jeopardized their own salvation.

Part of the concern in these cases may also have been the perception that some priests used the confessional to solicit sexual favors.
This was, indeed, an issue that was serious enough to be the subject
of a number of papal decrees and a crime that the Inquisition prose-
cuted.[41] However, the concern in these vitae seems to be different: it is
not the priests who are immoral, but the women who are tempting the
men—perhaps even unintentionally. This reversal, which shifts the
blame for a major problem within the Counter-Reformation Church
from male clerics onto the female parishioners, in itself suggests the
ways in which male sanctity was created in opposition to perceived
female sinfulness.

That authority and holiness in the Counter-Reformation Church was constructed as masculine power against feminine weakness and deception is additionally suggested by the fact that many holy women reportedly became physiologically like men in life. During the canonization of Teresa of Avila, for example, one of her confessors answered a question put to him by stating, "Oh, you fooled me by saying that she was a woman; by faith she isn't, but rather a masculine man and of the most manly [breed]."[42] In another section of her canonization process, one of Teresa's promoters claimed that, through her contact with the burning fire of divine love, Teresa actually overcame the cold and wet complexion considered characteristic of female bodies.[43] Rather, divine love had made the proportion of humors in Teresa's body more characteristic of a man than a woman.[44] God had altered her gender. Medical practitioners examining Rose of Lima similarly described her body as having overcome the complexion natural to women through a heat provided by the divine.[45] She also became physiologically like a man. One of Teresa of Avila's confessors elaborated on this theme and even noted that it was not unheard of "for a woman to transform herself into a man, leaving behind her feminine being and weakness to be considered a robust man and given masculine attributes," something he asserted had happened in the case of Teresa.[46] Thus, in the eyes of their devotees, holy women became, not just in a figurative sense but in a medical sense as their humors changed, masculine, as they followed the road to spiritual perfection.

This gender switching of early modern female saints was actually in line with contemporary theories of the body, as noted earlier, in which gender definitions were incredibly fluid and open to change. Modern scholarship has shown that the boundaries between men and women in the early modern period were labile and that many believed that women could become men.[47] In fact, several popular authors reported cases of such sexual transformation in the sixteenth and seventeenth centuries. Michel de Montaigne (1533–1592) related the story of an old man who had been a woman, named Marie, until the age of twenty-two. Then one day she was exerting herself especially hard— that is, acting like a man and increasing her bodily heat—when suddenly male genitalia sprouted forth from her body. Montaigne even concluded the anecdote by noting that "it is not so great a marvel that this sort of accident is frequently met with," thereby implying that such gender transformation was almost commonplace.[48] The surgeon Ambroise Paré (1510–1590) devoted an entire chapter of his treatise

On Monsters and Marvels to "Memorable Stories about Women who have Degenerated into Men." In this section he recorded several cases drawn from classical and modern sources, including Montaigne's account of Marie.[49] He concluded with an explanation of why such transformation was possible: "The reason why women can degenerate into men is because women have as much hidden within the body as men have exposed outside; leaving aside, only that women don't have so much heat, nor the ability to push out what by coldness of their temperament is held as if bound to the interior."[50] That is, when some unusual event changed the natural heat of women's bodies, male genitalia could sprout and women could indeed turn into men. Paré explicitly denied that any transformation could happen in the other way, though, noting that men could not turn into women because "Nature tends always toward what is most perfect."[51]

These scholars opened the door to belief in the possibility that women saints became like men through their faith. Although becoming men allowed women's authority in the Church to be legitimate, it also created a new problem for canonization officials. When Paré described the possibilities of women becoming men, he was discussing preternatural phenomena—occurrences that were outside the normal operations of nature, but not divinely inspired. This classification of women turning into men as preternatural spelled a problem for prospective female saints. There was something sinister in events that veered away from the ordinary course of nature, especially in the sexual realm, as contemporary literature on hermaphrodites and sodomites made clear.[52] In fact, Paré included the activities of sorcerers and demons in creating monstrosities in the same book in which he discussed the transformation of women into men.[53] A conversion of women into men, then, might throw the saint's character and the origins for his or her miracles into question.

It was perhaps due to such concerns over crossing gender boundaries that medical professionals during postmortem investigations into the incorruption of saints' bodies also began looking at reproductive organs. If changing gender could be considered an aberration against nature and potentially something demonically inspired, a medical examination could secure the stability of the holy individual's sex. The posthumous examination of saintly bodies thereby solidified gender boundaries for holy people. At the same time, such an examination could also establish the celibacy of the deceased. Although celibacy was important after the Reformation for both male and female holy people, for women it was a bedrock of both their honor and any claim to spiritual purity.[54] That such purity could be checked via postmortem is revealed by the fact that some contemporary theorists even asserted that regular sexual activity could alter a woman's physiology, literally turning her into a loose woman, more open to the machinations of the devil.[55] A knowledgeable investigator could tell the difference between a sexual and a celibate woman. Checking a holy woman's reproductive organs during a postmortem was, therefore, both about confirming her virtue and that she had been fully a woman during life.

Nevertheless, both male and female reproductive organs were examined at times during postmortem examinations of saintly cadavers. In these examinations both the amount of evidence and the nature of it was heavily dependent on the sex of the deceased. Out of more than twenty cases of men subjected to posthumous autopsy, in only four cases was their genitalia mentioned, and then only to comment on its absence.[56] In contrast, most women had some aspect of their reproductive system checked during the postmortem. During these examinations, men were found to be almost totally devoid of sexual organs while women were, to a great extent, defined by theirs.

The cadavers of holy men examined by anatomists as part of canonization proceedings after the Reformation were deliberately portrayed as nonsexual. In the four cases in which genitalia did appear in a male postmortem, the purpose was to highlight its non-appearance: the physicians who opened Filippo Neri's body, for example, noted only that Neri supernaturally moved to cover his sexual organs after his death, a sign of his modesty and virginity.[57] Similarly, in a treatise in which he lauds the saint's holy anatomy, Giovanni Botero states that after Carlo Borromeo's death the surgeon performing the autopsy discovered that "there was not seen to be any penis, other than the skin and bone [in that place] which was rather hard."[58] The suggestion here was that the sexual organ had withered away from disuse. When anatomists were about to perform an autopsy on Antonio Colellis, they paused to note that his genitals were curiously small, "as if he were a baby three or four months old."[59] As in the case of Borromeo, the implication here is the Colellis's unused sexual organs had shrunk. Finally, when the medical professionals examined Francis de Sales, they confirmed that he was celibate, "like a baby shortly after birth," perhaps implying that he similarly had little or no genitalia.[60] The absence of male genitalia for these saints should not be taken as a sign that they were feminine—rather, from a spiritual point of view, they were hypermasculine. These bodies had been so purified of all lust that the offending organs had shrunk or disappeared.[61] As celibacy was connected with spiritual authority in the Catholic Church, these prelates were now the supremely qualified office holders and the idealized leaders of the Church.[62] Indeed, they became Christ-like in that they were no longer even physically blighted by the possibility of sinful sex.[63] Anatomy was used to affirm the right certain men had to wield authority within the Church.

Whereas genitalia were absent or not commented upon during the postmortems of prospective male saints, the search for women's holiness centered on their sexual organs. Physicians frequently and explicitly discussed and documented the state of women's breasts and their genitalia as part of the consideration of their holiness. The physicians who performed the autopsy of Teresa of Avila, for example, examined her breasts and uterus, declaring them to be incorrupt.[64] The medical investigators into Maria Maddalena de' Pazzi's incorruption probed her breasts and declared that they had preserved their natural color.[65]

One might be inclined to claim that these examinations were nonsexual in nature based on the fact that, consisting almost entirely of white, fatty tissue, breasts were key organs to look at for signs of decay. Furthermore, they perhaps connoted childbearing and motherhood more than sexuality. Finally, the words used by the physicians in these instances are formal and technical in nature and give no indication that the examiners had erotic ideas in mind when conducting the autopsy.

Nevertheless, one should not underestimate the sexual meaning associated with the breast in this period and the gendered nature of anatomical investigations in general. In late medieval England, male impotence could be checked in legal courts by testing whether the person in question became aroused by the exposed breasts of prostitutes.[66] Furthermore, when discussing Louis XI's entry into Paris in 1461, Jean de Roye noted that "there were also three very handsome girls dressed as mermaids, completely nude and one saw their beautiful upright, separate, round and hard breasts, which was a very pleasant sight."[67] Although these examples are early, they indicate that breasts were also seen as erotic in late medieval and early modern culture. Furthermore, both Kathryn Schwartz and Gianna Pomata have recently explored contemporary understanding of the breasts in the sixteenth and seventeenth centuries. They have concluded that erotic meanings attached to the breast just as frequently as maternal ones.[68] At the very least, therefore, sexual connotations would have been present alongside questions about bodily preservation or maternal duties when medical practitioners exposed and examined the breasts of holy women.

With this contemporary meaning of the breast in mind, the recounting of a few of the medical examinations on saintly bodies comes across as suggestively sexual. The medical team tasked with the postmortem on Queen Isabel of Portugal reported that when they came to her chest, they discovered "her breasts to be totally white and upright . . . and being touched by hand, they remained solid and firm."[69] The word choice here is significant since the physicians describe her breasts as *erectis*. The same word is used in contemporary medical manuals when discussing the arousal both of the penis and of the breasts. As Berengario da Carpi states in his sixteenth-century medical manual, which was reproduced frequently in the seventeenth century, "The breasts are also useful in providing a stimulus to coition when they are fondled, both in males and females, although in the females this is felt more strongly. . . . And it is very true that if the nipple is touched, it immediately raises [*erigitur*] like the penis; and thus because of the connection of uterus and penis with the breasts, these organs are aroused, especially in those who are already prepared and ready for coition."[70] Da Carpi here not only associates the breast quite clearly with arousal, but uses the same word to describe that arousal that the medical team investigating Isabel's holiness used to comment on the upright nature of her breasts. In short, the language these medical practitioners employed to describe Isabel's breasts implies that they saw her body, at least partially, as erotic.

There are additional indications that the examination of Isabel's body had a sexual component for at least some of the medical practitioners. One of the physicians involved in this examination further stated that he "did not only look but also touched by hand from the right shoulder down the whole arm to the hand," giving the impression of stroking the dead queen's arm.[71] He further claimed that the hair of the deceased queen, who had been in the ground for two hundred and seventy-five years, "was gold colored and so pretty that it seemed as though it had just been washed."[72] The act of the physician, to not just probe the dead queen's breast but also stroke her arm and comment on the beauty of her hair, suggests that his evaluation of her body was not strictly confined to the clinical sphere.

The details of this recounting demonstrate that the anatomist's gaze was sexual and gendered, even suggesting a prurient interest. Stroking arms and smelling hair are not acts that male physicians were recorded as having engaged in when examining male corpses, and this clearly shows that the anatomist/patient relationship was also a male/female one. Such a gendered relationship is additionally suggested by the cases in which male physicians surveyed a holy woman's uterus or vagina during a postmortem, such as during the examination of Teresa of Avila or the Blessed Elena Enselmini.[73] These were organs defined by sexual and reproductive connotations, which also had profound significance for anatomists as well. The uterus in particular was seen as an organ that could only be understood via autopsy and therefore represented both the difficulty of knowing women—including their nature to deceive—as well as the potential for anatomists to uncover hidden knowledge about women's bodies.[74] In short, through anatomy the male physician penetrated a woman's body and revealed her secrets, which implied both sexual and more mundane knowledge of her.

Other studies have also pointed to the sexual nature of the anatomist's gaze, since even prominent early modern anatomists frequently used poses taken from quasi-pornographic literature when depicting female anatomy in their printed anatomical models.[75] The male body, however, was never depicted suggestively in anatomical manuals. This disparity points to the persistent eroticism of the female body, which carried over even into the anatomical sphere. Thus, in these investigations of saintly female bodies, the medical teams were not just viewing the corpses as holy relics or medical specimens, but also transgressive objects that even in their decayed state represented the dangerous power of female sexuality that Filippo Neri had so feared. The anatomist, then, became not only the documenter of the spiritual, but also the investigator into the carnal.

The anatomist's sexualized view of the body arose not just because ecclesiastical authority was based on gender, but also because medical expertise was. By focusing on female reproductive organs, the male anatomist emphasized his skill. As Monica Green suggests, part of the delineation of a professional, masculine sphere of medical practice in the sixteenth and seventeenth centuries included their ability to have access to the intimate parts of female bodies. That is, parts of the body that were once inspected only by other women now came under the purview of the medical practitioner, as the ultimate expert of the human body.[76] Furthermore, through examining these organs the physician cemented his own expertise. The uterus was deemed to be one of the most poorly understood organs. Therefore, knowledge of its secrets also implied extensive knowledge of human anatomy.[77] In the case of Teresa of Avila, for example, the physician Christopher Medrano was therefore not just investigating her incorruption or documenting her sexuality when he examined her uterus, but also establishing his skill.

Anatomical investigations into saints reified gender hierarchies and power structures in both sanctity and in medicine. Such demonstrations cast ascetic male saints as nonsexual, idealized leaders. Women, by contrast, became sexualized even while they were virginal. Anatomical investigation recapitulated the gendered nature of early modern sanctity and medicine by assigning a sexual role even to women who had studiously attempted to purge lust and sexuality from their lives.

CONCLUSION

The Counter-Reformation, like other moments of crisis in Church history, was fundamentally both about gender and about who could wield authority in the Church.[78] In this case, though, a union of Church authority and medical expertise helped establish boundaries that had been in flux since the late Middle Ages. Late medieval female saints wielded immense authority and therefore were also considered incredibly suspect. Ecclesiastical officials in turn sought means to verify their holiness. Due to the somatic nature of their piety, the bodies of late medieval female saints were taken as evidence of their holiness—revealed in two cases via an autopsy. In the sixteenth century, the increasing prestige of anatomical experts and concern among churchmen led to the recording of two additional female anatomical investigations. The watershed came, however, with the Reformation, when Protestant polemicists cast the whole concept of sainthood into doubt. In response, canonization officials turned to medical practitioners to help establish the veracity of saints. But, by the very nature of who sought medical consultation, such intervention worked primarily to support the power of male ecclesiastical leaders.

In fact, these medical examinations functioned as a means to relegate women to a second tier of sanctity. Far fewer women than men were inspected for anatomical signs of holiness. Even when a medical examination might affirm that a woman's body was miraculously incorrupt, it also highlighted her feminine, and therefore sexual, nature. This feature alone marked women as being less perfect than the sexless men who attained the ranks of sainthood in the sixteenth and seventeenth centuries.

Such a gendered reading of holy bodies was based on the ways in which early modern churchmen reconstructed both the Church hierarchy and ideas of nature in the period after the Reformation. Part of the reaffirmation of the power of the ecclesiastical hierarchy was to make authority exclusively male. For this reason, then, female saints were described as becoming physiologically like men during life. Their public roles required them to be masculine. But by gender bending in this way Catholic officials introduced a new problem by opening the possibility that holy women might be preternaturally altering their sex during life. The medical examination of saintly bodies put such confusion to rest as it firmly assigned gender to the deceased saints and thereby reasserted the firm boundaries of both the Church hierarchy and of nature itself.

This construction of medical professionalism and knowledge about the natural world more generally also contributed to the sexualization of female saints after death during this period. In a classic, if controversial, thesis, Carolyn Merchant has claimed that during the sixteenth and seventeenth centuries, nature became gendered: the natural world was now cast as a passive, female subject that would be explored and examined by an exploitive, masculine gaze.[79] Even if Merchant's thesis is overstated, in the case of anatomy the examinations of saintly bodies support her claims. To be an expert the male anatomist had to be able to penetrate the inner workings of the subject's body and extend complete mastery over its operations. In short, it was a relationship of power that bifurcated along gender lines. In the establishment of their mastery, male anatomists gendered the subject body female.

These changes brought by the application of anatomy to sanctity may also provide some insight into the old debate over how the Reformation affected women and gender. In one interpretation, during the Reformation Protestant leaders removed the possibility of becoming a mystic or saint for Protestant women. The only virtuous path left was in becoming a wife and mother.[80] One might argue, therefore, that Catholicism left more options open to women, including that of remaining celibate through devotion to God in a convent. However, the posthumous medical examination to which most early modern female prospective saints were subjected inscribed sexuality into their bodies even as it confirmed their virginity and incorruption. Thus, in some ways, the Protestants and Czatholics converged in their treatment of the female body. Each of them refused to allow women's bodies a role that was not in part defined by their sexuality.

Conclusion

Then he said to Thomas, "Put your finger here, and see my hands; and put out your hand, and place it in my side; do not be faithless, but believing." Thomas answered him, "My Lord and my God!" Jesus said to him, "Have you believed because you have seen me? Blessed are those who have not seen and yet believe."
— John 20:27–29, Revised Standard Version, Catholic Edition

For Christ's apostle Thomas, Jesus' flesh was proof of his resurrection.[1] Thomas's story was meant to be a cautionary tale, intended to remind the faithful that they must believe in what they could not see. Yet in the period after the Reformation the Catholic Church assumed the guise of doubting Thomas: they looked to the flesh for proof of the spirit.

This study has examined the attempt on the part of the Catholic Church to use anatomy to demonstrate the possibility of the divine to become manifest in the bodies of its saints. I have argued that medicine and religion collaborated in their attempts to understand nature and the divine, and how to make knowledge that could gain universal acceptance. The rising prestige of medicine in the sixteenth century and a change in how knowledge was being produced in the medical field led to the first of these examinations in the period after the Council of Trent (1545–1563). Although a small number of female saints had been subjected to autopsy in the late medieval period, the initial impetus for the examination of saintly remains in the sixteenth century arose from medical interest in unusual case studies. During the early sixteenth century a number of fields of study placed an emphasis on the utility of firsthand empirical knowledge as a guide to practice. Medicine was among these fields and medical writers began circulating texts, generally under the title of *Observationes*, which drew on specific cases as a means to create techniques for understanding and treating different ailments.[2] Postmortem autopsies of unusual cases also featured in this genre as a way to understand the nature of an unusual illness.[3] The earliest cases of sixteenth-century saints who fell under the anatomist's knife—such as Ignatius Loyola—were featured in medical works that were part of this genre and which sought to document unusual anatomies.

Local promoters of an individual saint's canonization were quick to realize the potential of anatomy to demonstrate sanctity. The reason they were so ready to turn to medical experts is because there was a long-standing cooperation between the Church and medicine. In particular, anatomy had been connected to a number of religious functions from the late Middle Ages onward. Bodies of elite prelates had been opened for embalming purposes since the late Middle Ages, and both legal and ecclesiastical tribunals had and continued to employ medical professionals to conduct postmortem examinations in criminal cases.[4] Autopsy had been a recognized tool for knowing the body and was only gaining in prestige during the sixteenth century.[5] Therefore, sixteenth-century writers who sought to spread the fame of a saint penned treatises that combined anatomy with spirituality in an attempt to promote the individual for canonization. Carlo Borromeo and Ignatius of Loyola both had treatises of this sort written about them. Initially, canonization officials in Rome did not recognize the validity of anatomical examination in providing evidence of holiness, and these anatomical-spiritual treatises at first had little effect on canonization.

During the late sixteenth century, though, the Catholic Church reevaluated how it made saints. There had been a long hiatus in saint-making caused both by Protestant attacks on the cult of the saints and preexisting concerns within Catholicism. When saints began being made again in the 1580s, new methods and new rigor were applied to the criteria by which saints were evaluated. Several canon lawyers connected with the Roman Curia—in particular, the influential Deacon of the Tribunal of the Rota Francesco Peña—explored the possibilities of using anatomy to determine sanctity. By the early seventeenth century, the utility of the postmortem examination had been recognized by Rome. In the following decades nearly every canonized saint and many other prospective saints were subject to a postmortem examination, sometimes including a full autopsy, ordered by Rome.

That these examinations took place and were so widespread should profoundly affect how scholars view both the Church and the development of medicine in the early modern period. By allowing medical witnesses, especially physicians, such a prominent role in determining who was and was not a saint in the early modern period, the Catholic Church endorsed both the rising prestige of the medical profession and the new empirical techniques that were becoming characteristic of this and other fields.[6] In short, the Church was promoting innovation in how the natural world was understood.

Medical professionals such as Paolo Zacchia also created epistemologies for understanding the holy body. Rather than being a diversion from their main medical work, examining the bodies of those touched by God was a central preoccupation of many medical professionals. Numerous prominent physicians—including Readlo Colombo, Andrea Cesalpino, Marcello Malpighi, Paolo Manfredi, Giovanni Maria Lancisi, Antonio Vallisneri, and Giovan Battista Morgagni—all participated in the examination of saintly cadavers. The Church's explicit solicitation of expertise from physicians, rather than other types of early modern healers, in turn helped solidify the position of these practitioners as being at the top of an evolving medical hierarchy.

During the sixteenth and seventeenth centuries, then, medical expertise and Church authority not only worked together but also mutually reinforced one another. This is especially illustrated when the lens of gender is applied to the examination of saintly remains. Medical practitioners regularly found signs in the bodies of male saints that illustrated both their asceticism and their chastity. Such bodily discipline connected the deceased with long-standing traditions of authority within the Church. Women's bodies, in contrast, were sexualized and their reproductive organs, in particular, were subject to examination. The postmortem therefore diminished the authority holy women had exercised in life, which had been established through a deliberate suppression of their female, and therefore questionable, nature. By reinscribing their female nature in their bodies, the postmortem examination cemented gender hierarchies within the Church and subordinated even the female saint within a male ecclesiastical hierarchy. Furthermore, the postmortem established the expertise and exclusivity of the medical expert. Knowing the female reproductive organs—considered one of the most poorly understood anatomical systems—demonstrated the skill of the dissecting physician.[7] And, by demonstrating his skillful knowledge of female anatomy, the male physician also advertised his ability over those of other medical practitioners, especially midwives, who were more commonly associated with gynecology and obstetrics.

The medical examinations of saintly remains occurred at a critical juncture in both the history of medicine and the history of the Church, in which both sought ways to increase their prestige, understand God's interaction with the world, and define more clearly who could exercise power and expertise. Many of the factors that went into this alliance between medicine and religion and their cooperation in defining bodily sanctity seem unique to the sixteenth and seventeenth centuries. Did the posthumous examination of saints and the search for the divine in human cadavers come to an end after 1700?

EPILOGUE

"The etiology of Padre Pio's lesions cannot possibly be of natural origin. The agent that produced them must assuredly be sought in the realm of the supernatural."[8] This was the judgment of Luigi Romanelli, chief surgeon at the Barletta public hospital in southern Italy, after he inspected the stigmata appearing on the hands of Padre Pio in May 1919.[9] During Pio's beatification eighty years later in 1999, Pope John Paul II explained that through his stigmata, Pio's body "displayed the intimate link between death and resurrection that composes the mystery of Christ's return."[10] Such a link was additionally emphasized through Pio's incorruption, which was confirmed by a medical team as recently as 2008.[11] Thus, the medically examined body of this twentieth-century saint provided evidence of his connection with the divine and hence his sanctity.

The search for the holy in human bodies and the alliance between the Church and medicine did not expire at the end of the seventeenth century, but continues with modification to the current day. That said, the modern conception of the natural world, the roles in which both medical professionals and churchmen see themselves, and the ways in which scientific ideas are proven have all changed dramatically in the intervening three hundred years.

One of the most significant changes to the ways in which medicine was used to construct sanctity occurred in the middle of the eighteenth century. Katharine Park and Lorraine Daston have cited this century as the crucial moment in which the possibilities of preternatural phenomena began to be reconceptualized and ideas about the boundaries of the natural world changed.[12] Such changing attitudes can be seen in the Catholic Church, especially during the pontificate of Pope Benedict XIV, Prospero Lambertini (r. 1740–1758).[13] Benedict was strongly influenced by the Catholic Enlightenment, which sought to bring new scientific rigor to a general religious framework.[14] One of the central articulations of the Catholic Enlightenment during his tenure as pontiff emerged in a complete reevaluation of canonization proceedings.[15]

In his massive and authoritative opus on canonization, *De servorum Dei beatificationis et beatorum canonizatione*, Benedict changed many of the criteria though which saintly remains were evaluated. For example, he specifically stated that the abnormalities found in Neri's heart were not miraculous.[16] In general, he expressed skepticism about anatomical irregularities in the body as a sign of the supernatural and sought to align himself with the best of modern medicine in the evaluation of saintly remains.[17]

Benedict, in particular, warned canonization officials about the danger of excessive asceticism or other unusual signs of suffering. Although he recognized the importance of self-discipline and heroic virtue, Benedict worried about the ability of believers to delude themselves even to the point of altering their own bodies. Benedict asserted in *De Servorum Dei* that imagination could have a powerful effect on the perception that a miracle had occurred. He posited that the mind could alter the material in a way totally unconnected with the divine. Individuals could be so inflamed by passion that their mind could "divide their body," that is, put holes in their flesh to give themselves stigmata-like wounds.[18] These wounds, however, were not miraculous but psychological. According to Benedict, people could also make themselves believe that they were sick and then be miraculously cured, all through the faculty of their imagination.[19] Thus, Benedict invested the human mind with the power to change the body in ways that had previously been attributed only to God. In doing so, he removed the justification and therefore the merit of many ascetic practices that had long been associated with sainthood.

The one type of bodily miracle that Benedict did not question and that he thought still could benefit from postmortem confirmation was incorruption. For Benedict, incorruption could even be two miracles made up of both the initial incorruption when examined up to a few days after death and then the continuing incorruption of the body for years later.[20] Benedict's emphasis on this miracle followed trends already established in the seventeenth century, in which incorruption was preferred over other types of bodily miracles. Incorruption, by providing a glimpse of the resurrection, demonstrated the possibility of salvation through the Church. It also pointed believers back to the Church and the ecclesiastical hierarchy as the guides who could eventually lead one to heaven. In this respect, it stood in contrast to other types of bodily miracles that tended to demonstrate more the authority and endurance of the individual rather than the Church in general.

Benedict XIV was not the last pope to innovate on matters related to canonization, but his exhaustive tome has continued to provide guidance for how medical expertise should be used in establishing the miracles of the saints. In particular, it has pointed to the importance of continually updating standards of miracle verification according to contemporary medical ideas. As Jacalyn Duffin has emphasized in her survey of the role of medicine in modern canonizations, "Canonization officials strive to consider the latest in science; they do not want to be manipulated by the wiles of sensationalists or the aspirations of the gullible."[21] Hence, medical professionals investigating a case of incorruption in the early nineteenth century explored the possibility that electricity might have led to her unusual preservation.[22] Likewise, a case of stigmata from the turn of the twentieth century pondered whether animal magnetism might have been responsible.[23] That is, canonization officials have employed the most current medical and scientific theories available to them at the time. Early modern postmortems of saintly bodies share in this provenance.

Outside of the Church, some of the early modern investigations into holy anatomy have been used to argue for the gullibility of contemporary believers or the naiveté of early modern medical practitioners. The various ailments suffered by Maria Maddalena de' Pazzi, for example, are no longer seen as miraculous or even physical realities. Rather, she has been recast as suffering from various shades of mental illness. Several current books that deal with anorexia or self-mutilation cite de' Pazzi as an early example.[24] In a well-known twentieth-century study, E. J. Dingwall cast her as a sexual deviant, proclaiming de' Pazzi to have been a "masochistic exhibitionist with now and then, as might be expected, a slight sadistic streak."[25] All these texts either explicitly state or imply that de' Pazzi's contemporaries had totally misunderstood her and her ailments. Similarly, Filippo Neri's unusual heart has been reinterpreted as a combination of several grave ailments.[26] Such a reinterpretation implies a lack of medical sophistication and anatomical understanding on the part of early modern physicians. These studies, which seek to understand early modern saintly bodies in light of modern medicine, miss the importance of contemporary context not just for interpretation, but even for seeing the same things in the human body. In the sixteenth and seventeenth centuries human bodies were not understood mainly through the lens of medicine, but through a series of overlapping points of view with religion being perhaps the most important. This profoundly influenced the range of what was possible within the human body.

The legitimacy of the post-Reformation Catholic Church rested in the incorrupt and wondrous bodies of its saints. These bodies provided evidence of their connection with God and therefore the correctness of the Catholic faith. Saints made the transcendent idea of the Catholic faith manifest.

In a moment of crisis following the Reformation, canonization officials turned to the new experts in the body—anatomists—in an attempt to demonstrate the existence of the divine in the human. In so doing, Church officials endorsed certain ideas about how to make knowledge about the natural world, who was allowed to do it, and what appropriate topics of study were. Although early modern medicine was a long way from its current-day descendent, it relied on empirical evidence, acute observation, and logic to reach its conclusions. Thus, for about a century, from 1600 until 1700, the Church fully invested itself in the idea that medicine could help establish miracles. In the search for God they turned to the flesh of man in the guise of a scalpel-wielding Doubting Thomas.

Date of Postmortem	Name of Individual	Date of Death	Body Opened?	Type of Evidence Found	Location	Date of Canonization
1552	Francisco Xavier	1552	No	Incorruption	Goa, but reinterpreted in Rome.	1622
1556	Ignatius Loyola	1556	Yes	Kidney and bladder stones	Rome, Italy	1622
1572	Pius V	1572	Yes	Asceticism	Rome, Italy	1712
1583, 1592	Teresa of Avila	1582	Yes	Incorruption	Alba de Tormes, Spain	1622
1584	Carlo Borromeo	1584	Yes	Emaciated body and other signs of extreme asceticism	Milan, Italy	1610
1595	Filippo Neri	1595	Yes	Unusual cardiac anatomy	Rome, Italy	1622
1596	Angelo del Pas	1596	Yes	Unusual anatomy	Rome, Italy	Never canonized
1598	Diego of Alcalà	1463	No	In a much later account, Diego's hagiographer records that found days after his death a "Medico del Re dei Mori" examined the body and noted Diego's incorruption. I have therefore dated the postmortem to its recounting in this later vita	Alcalà de Hernares, Spain	1588
1606	Andrea Corsini	1373	Yes	Incorruption. Rudimentary embalming attempt uncovered	Florence, Italy	1629

Date of Postmortem	Name of Individual	Date of Death	Body Opened?	Type of Evidence Found	Location	Date of Canonization
1611	Thomas of Villanova	1555	No	Incorruption. Mostly skeletal remains	Valencia, Spain	1658
1611	Pasquale Baylon	1592	No	Incorruption	Villareal, Spain	
1612	Isabel of Portugal	1336	No	Incorruption	Coimbra, Portugal	1625
1612	Isidore the Laborer	1130	Maybe. The intestines are reported as still being in the body, but this might have been ascertained without opening the corpse.	Incorruption	Madrid, Spain	1622
1612	Francesco Girolamo Simon	1612	No	Contested Incorruption, asceticism	Valencia, Spain	Never canonized
1618	Peter of Alcantara	1562	No	Incorruption. Mostly skeletal remains	Arenas de San Pedro, Spain	1669
1618	Orsola Benincasa	1618	Yes	Unusual anatomy	Naples, Italy	Never canonized

Date of Postmortem	Name of Individual	Date of Death	Body Opened?	Type of Evidence Found	Location	Date of Canonization
1621	Roberto Bellarmine	1621	Yes	Opened for embalming, no evidence of sanctity reported	Rome, Italy	1930
1622	Francis de Sales	1622	Yes	Asceticism and unusual anatomy	Lyon, France	1665
1624, 1663	Maria Maddalena de' Pazzi	1607	No	Incorruption	Florence, Italy	1669
1624	Lorenzo Giustiniani	1456	Yes, but much of the flesh was missing	Incorruption	Venice, Italy	1690
1624	Paola Napolitana	1624	Yes	Unusual anatomy	Naples, Italy	Never canonized
1625	Gregory X	1276	No	Contested incorruption	Arezzo, Italy	Beatified 1713, Not yet canonized
1628	Ferdinand III of Castile	1252	No	Incorruption	Seville, Spain	1671
1632	Rose of Lima	1617	No	Incorruption	Lima, Peru	1671
1638	Annibale d'Aflitto	1638	Yes	Asceticism	Reggio Calabria, Italy	Never canonized
1654	Antonio Colellis	1654	No	Incorruption	Naples, Italy	Never canonized

Date of Postmortem	Name of Individual	Date of Death	Body Opened?	Type of Evidence Found	Location	Date of Canonization
1663	Luis Bertrán	1581	Yes	Incorruption	Valencia, Spain	1671
1671	Catherine of Bologna	1463	No	Contested incorruption	Bologna, Italy	1712
1689	Innocent XI	1689	Yes	Asceticism	Rome, Italy	Beatified 1956
1690	Elena Enselmini	1242	No	Incorruption	Padua, Italy	Beatified 1695
1700	Giacomo della Marca	1476	Yes	Incorruption	Naples, Italy	1726
1727	Gregorio Barbarigo	1697	Yes	Incorruption	Padua, Italy	1960
1806	Domenica del Paradiso	1553	No	Incorruption	Florence, Italy	Never canonized

INTRODUCTION

1. Archivio Segreto Vaticano (ASV), Rites Process (RP) 501, 43v–44r: "corpus B[eatae] Reginae ex capite usqe ad pectora, quod repterum fuit valde sanum, integrum, et sine ulla corruptione impositiu ad modum odoriferum."

2. André Vauchez, *Sainthood in the Later Middle Ages*, trans. Jean Birrell (New York: Cambridge University Press, 1997), 24, observes that a good smelling, incorrupt body was a key element of sanctity in the Middle Ages. For a broader work on bodily incorruption in popular culture see Piero Camporesi, *The Incorruptible Flesh: Bodily Mutation and Mortification in Religion and Folklore*, trans. Tania Croft-Murray (New York: Cambridge University Press, 1988). See also Chapter 3 of the present work.

3. The term "Counter-Reformation" is, of course, full of meaning. I use it here only to signify that in this aspect of the late sixteenth-century Church's agenda, Catholic officials were to a great extent responding to Protestant attacks on the faith. See also the discussion in Chapter 1 of this book. For a consideration of the meaning of these terms see John W. O'Malley, *Trent and All That: Renaming Catholicism in the Early Modern Era* (Cambridge, MA: Harvard University Press, 2000).

4. ASV, RP 501, 41r.

5. Ibid., 43v–44r, 596r.

6. Ibid., 596r. Testimony of Doctor Antonius Sebastianus: "et per certo habeo esse extra naturam, et extraordinarium, quodque fieri non potest, nisi miraculose."

7. Lorraine Daston and Katharine Park, *Wonders and the Order of Nature, 1150–1750* (New York: Zone Books, 1998), 120–128; Lorraine Daston, "Marvelous Facts and Miraculous Evidence in Early Modern Europe," *Critical Inquiry* 18, no. 1 (Autumn 1991): 93–124.

8. On the role of physicians as experts in the natural world see Harold J. Cook, "Physicians and Natural History," in *Cultures of Natural History*, ed. N. Jardine, J. A. Secord, and E. C. Spary (New York: Cambridge University Press, 1996), 91–105.

9. See, for example, Jacalyn Duffin, *Medical Miracles: Doctors, Saints, and Healing in the Modern World* (New York: Oxford University Press,

2009); David Gentilcore, *Healers and Healing in Early Modern Italy* (New York: Manchester University Press, 1998); Fernando Vidal, "Miracles, Science, and Testimony in Post-Tridentine Saint-Making," *Science in Context* 20, no. 3 (2007): 481–508.

10. Katharine Park, "The Criminal and the Saintly Body: Autopsy and Dissection in Renaissance Italy," *Renaissance Quarterly* 47 (1994): 1–33; idem, *Secrets of Women: Gender, Generation, and the Origins of Human Dissection* (New York: Zone Books, 2006); Nancy Siraisi, "Signs and Evidence: Autopsy and Sanctity in Late Sixteenth-Century Italy," in *Medicine and the Italian Universities, 1250–1600* (Boston: Brill, 2001), 356–380; Elisa Andretta, "Anatomie du Vénérable dans la Rome de la Contre-réforme. Les autopsies d'Ignace de Loyola et de Philippe Neri," in *Conflicting Duties: Science, Medicine and Religion in Rome, 1550–1750*, ed. Maria Pia Donato and Jill Kraye (London: Warburg Institute, 2009), 255–280; Gianna Pomata, "Malpighi and the Holy Body: Medical Experts and Miraculous Evidence in Seventeenth-Century Italy," *Renaissance Studies* 21, no. 4 (2007): 568–586.

11. From my examination of records at the Archivio Segreto Vaticano, where most of the apostolic canonization processes from this period are housed, I have found that at least eighteen of twenty-six saints canonized between 1588 and 1700 were examined by a medical practitioner. These include Diego of Alcalá, Carlo Borromeo, Filippo Neri, Ignatius of Loyola, Isidro Labrador, Teresa of Avila, Francis Xavier, Isabel of Portugal, Andrea Corsini, Thomas of Villanuova, Francis de Sales, Maria Magdalene de Pazzis, Pedro de' Alcantara, Rose of Lima, Luis Bertrán, Ferdinando III of Castile, Lorenzo Giustiniani, and Paschal Baylon. In the eight cases of canonized saints from this period who were not subjected to a posthumous medical examination, three were early and so declared incorrupt prior to the routinization of medical examination (Hyancith, Francisca Romana, and Raymond Penafort), two lacked sufficient remains for there to be an examination that would confirm or deny incorruption (Filippo Benizzi and Gaetano Thiene), one did not enjoy a reputation of being incorrupt (Francisco Borgia), and the last two (John of God and John of Sahagun) seem likely to have been examined given a few references that I have found, but I was unable to find a medical report. Thus I did not include them in my tally. In addition to these saints canonized in this period, many other prospective saints were similarly examined but not elected. See the appendix for a tabulation of all the saintly examinations occurring in this period.

12. ASV, RP 3192, 655r–655v.

13. *Relatio facta in Consistorio Secreto coram S.D.N. Gregorio Papa XV . . . die XIX Ianuarii MDCXXII super vita, sanctitate, actis canonizationis, & miraculis Beati Francisci Xavier e Societate Iesu* (Rome: apud Haeredes Bartholomaei Zannetti, 1622), 48–49. Rose of Lima and Toribio de Mogrovejo were also each examined posthumously in the Spanish colonies and had the details of their body communicated to Roman officials. These officials, in turn, asked medical professionals to reexamine some or all of the evidence. See discussion in Chapters 1 and 3 below for these two saints.

14. For this older view of the relationship between science and religion see John W. Draper, *History of the Conflict Between Religion and Science* (New York: D. Appleton and Company, 1875); Andrew D. White, *A History of the Warfare of Science with Theology in Christendom* (New York: D. Appleton and Company, 1896). More recently, Richard J. Blackwell has portrayed Counter-Reformation Catholicism and especially Rome as developing a mind-set that was "monolithic, centralized, esoteric, resistant to change, and self-protective," which caused it to censor ideas, such as scientific ones, that had competing truth claims. Richard J. Blackwell, "Could There be Another Galileo Case?," in *The Cambridge Companion to Galileo,* ed. Peter Machamer (Cambridge: Cambridge University Press, 1998), 359. For a discussion of the evolution of the idea that there is a conflict between science and religion see John Hedley Brooke, *Science and Religion: Some Historical Perspectives* (New York: Cambridge University Press, 1991), 1–116.

15. Rivka Feldhay, "Religion," in *The Cambridge History of Science, Vol. 3: Early Modern Science,* ed. Katharine Park and Lorraine Daston (New York: Cambridge University Press, 2006), 727–755; David C. Lindberg and Ronald L. Numbers, eds., *When Science & Christianity Meet* (Chicago: University of Chicago Press, 2003); Ole Peter Grell and Andrew Cunningham, eds., *Medicine and the Reformation* (New York: Routledge, 1993).

16. J. L. Heilbron, *The Sun in the Church: Cathedrals as Solar Observatories* (Cambridge, MA: Harvard University Press, 1999); Marcus Hellyer, *Catholic Physics: Jesuit Natural Philosophy in Early Modern Germany* (Notre Dame, IN: University of Notre Dame Press, 2005); Sachiko Kusukawa, *The Transformation of Natural Philosophy: The Case of Philip Melanchthon* (New York: Cambridge University Press, 1995); Rivka Feldhay, *Galileo and the Church: Political Inquisition or Critical Dialogue?* (New York: Cambridge University Press, 1995).

17. Maria Pia Donato, "Medicina e Religione: Percorsi di Lettura," in *Médecine et religion: Collaborations, competitions, conflits (XIIe-XXe siècle),* ed. Maria Pia Donato et al. (Rome: École Française de Rome, 2013), 27.

18. On the importance of saints for Catholic identity see Simon Ditchfield, "Thinking with Saints: Sanctity and Society in the Early Modern World," *Critical Inquiry* 35, no. 3 (Spring 2009): 552–584; Philip M. Soergel, *Wondrous in His Saints: Counter-Reformation Propaganda in Bavaria* (Berkeley: University of California Press, 1993).

19. Siraisi, "Signs and Evidence," 358–361.

20. Gian Luca d'Errico, "La Chiesa, l'Inquisizione, l'anatomia: storia di un tabù," in *Anatome: Sezione, scomposizione, raffigurazione del corpo nell'Età Moderna,* ed. Giueseppe Olmi and Claudia Pancino (Bologna: Bononia University Press, 2012), 247.

21. There are numerous works that treat the diversity of medical and healing practice in the early modern world. For brief overviews see Gentilcore, *Healers and Healing,* 1–28; Mary Lindemann, *Medicine and Society in Early Modern Europe* (New York: Cambridge University Press, 2010), 235–280; Gianna Pomata, *Contracting a Cure: Patients, Healers, and the*

Law in Early Modern Bologna (Baltimore: Johns Hopkins University Press, 1998), 56–94.

22. Gentilcore, *Healers and Healing*, 58–64; Pomata, *Contracting a Cure*, 1–24; Harold Cook, *The Decline of the Old Medical Regime in Stuart London* (Ithaca, NY: Cornell University Press, 1986).

23. Gentilcore, *Healers and Healing*, 3; Roy Porter, "The Patient's View: Doing Medical History From Below," *Theory and Society* 14, no. 2 (March 1985): 175–198.

24. *Relatio facta in Consistorio Secreto coram S.D.N. Gregorio Papa XV*, 48–49. See also discussion of this episode in Chapter 2 of this book.

25. ASV, RP 3156, unfoliated, estimated ff. 268–269, 712–713, 715. See Chapter 2 for a discussion of these successive postmortems.

26. ASV, RP 2009, 491r–491v.

27. All witnesses in canonization proceedings were routinely asked if they knew the difference between grace and a miracle. Aside from theologically trained churchmen, physicians routinely gave the most rigorous and educated responses to such questions. See, for example, physician testimonies about grace and miracles in the canonization of Maria Maddalena dei Pazzis, ASV, RP 771, 492r; and in the failed canonization and eventual Inquisition inquest into the life of Francesco Girolamo Simon Archivio della Congregazione per la Dottrina della Fede (ACDF), Stanza Storica (St. St.) C-1-C, 1472 v–1474r. See also Gentilcore, *Healers and Healing*, 188–189.

28. Pamela O. Long, *Artisan/Practitioners and the Rise of the New Sciences, 1400–1600* (Corvallis: Oregon State University Press, 2011), 1–9, 30–62; Gianna Pomata and Nancy Siraisi, "Introduction," in *Historia: Empiricism and Erudition in Early Modern Europe*, ed. Gianna Pomata and Nancy Siraisi (Cambridge, MA: MIT Press, 2005), 1–38; Gianna Pomata, "Observation Rising: Birth of an Epistemic Genre, 1500–1650," in *Histories of Scientific Observation*, ed. Lorraine Daston and Elizabeth Lunbeck (Chicago: University of Chicago Press, 2011), 45–47; Alisha Rankin, *Panaceia's Daughters: Noblewomen as Healers in Early Modern Germany* (Chicago: University of Chicago Press, 2013), 25–60.

29. Chiara Crisciani, "Fatti, teorie, 'narration' e malati a corte. Note su empirismo in medicine nel tardo-medioevo," *Quaderni storici*, 108, 36, no. 3 (December 2001): 695–718; Michael McVaugh, "The Experimenta of Arnald of Villanova," *Journal of Medieval and Renaissance Studies* 1 (1971): 107–118; idem, "Two Montpellier Recipe Collections," *Manuscripta* 20, no. 3 (1976): 175–180; Katharine Park, "Natural Particulars: Medical Epistemology, Practice, and the Literature of Healing Springs," in *Natural Particulars: Nature and the Disciplines in Renaissance Europe*, ed. Anthony Grafton and Nancy Siraisi (Cambridge, MA: MIT Press, 1999), 347–367.

30. Pomata, "Observation Rising," 45–80.

31. Rankin, *Panaceia's Daughters*, 59.

32. ASV, RP 3156, unfoliated, estimated ff. 268–269, 712–713, 715.

33. See discussions of these bodies in Chapters 2–4.

34. ASV, RP 762, 149r–150v.

35. ASV, RP 3638, 117v–119v.

36. On these techniques of establishing knowledge in the early experimental setting see Peter Dear, "*Totius in verba*: Rhetoric and Authority in the Early Royal Society," in *The Scientific Enterprise in Early Modern Europe: Readings from Isis*, ed. Peter Dear (Chicago: University of Chicago Press, 1997), 263–265; idem, *Discipline and Experience*, 21–26; Steven Shapin and Simon Schaffer, *Leviathan and the Air-Pump: Hobbes, Boyle, and the Experimental Life* (Princeton, NJ: Princeton University Press, 1985), 22–79; Steven Shapin, "Pump and Circumstance: Robert Boyle's Literary Technology," *Social Studies of Science* 14, no. 4 (November 1984): 481–520.

37. Michael Goodich, *Vita Perfecta: The Ideal of Sainthood in the Thirteenth Century* (Stuttgart: Anton Hiersemann, 1982); André Vauchez, *Sainthood in the Later Middle Ages*, trans. Jean Birrell (New York: Cambridge University Press, 1997); Ronald Weinstein and Rudolph M. Bell, *Saints and Society: The Two Worlds of Western Christendom, 1000–1700* (Chicago: University of Chicago Press, 1982).

38. Pomata, "Observation Rising," 45–80.

39. On the role of signs in creating medical knowledge see Ian Maclean, *Logic, Signs, and Nature in the Renaissance: The Case of Learned Medicine* (New York: Cambridge University Press, 2002). See also Chapter 3 of the present volume.

40. On the role of place in producing knowledge in early modern Europe see Jan Golinski, *Making Natural Knowledge: Constructivism and the History of Science* (Chicago: University of Chicago Press, 2005), 79–102; David Livingstone, *Putting Science in Its Place: Geographies of Scientific Knowledge* (Chicago: University of Chicago Press, 2003); Shapin and Schaffer, *Leviathan and the Air-Pump*.

41. Tessa Storey, *Carnal Commerce in Counter-Reformation Rome* (New York: Cambridge University Press, 2008), 234; Merry E. Wiesner, *Women and Gender in Early Modern Europe* (New York: Cambridge University Press, 1993), 179–217, 255.

42. Dyan Elliott, *Proving Woman: Female Spirituality and Inquisitional Culture in the Later Middle Ages* (Princeton, NJ: Princeton University Press, 2004), 127–141.

43. The most famous examples of studies which have used inquisition sources to get at non-elite viewpoints are Carlo Ginzburg, *The Cheese and the Worms*, trans. John and Anne Tedeschi (Baltimore: Johns Hopkins University Press, 1992); Emmanuel LeRoy Ladurie, *Montaillou: The Promised Land of Error*, trans. Barbara Bray (New York: Vintage Books, 1979)

44. Ginzburg most clearly puts this argument forward in Carlo Ginzburg, "Witchcraft and Popular Piety: Notes on a Modenese Trial of 1519," in *Clues, Myths and the Historical Method*, trans. John and Anne C. Tedeschi (Baltimore: Johns Hopkins University Press, 1989), 1–16; see also John Tedeschi, "Inquisitorial Sources and Their Uses," in *The Prosecution of Heresy: Collected Studies on the Inquisition in Early Modern Italy* (Binghamton, NY: Center for Medieval and Early Renaissance Studies, 1991), 47–88.

45. See Chapter 1 for a discussion of the questions posed by canonization judges during a process.

46. ASV, RP 797, 218r–229r, 258r–268v, the testimonies of "S[uor] Modesta" and "S[uor] Maria," respectively.

47. ASV, RP 2584, 109v–127v.

48. Ginzburg, *The Cheese and the Worms*. Ginzburg notes a similar phenomenon when his miller, Menocchio, testified before inquisition officials.

49. Fra Giovanni da Bergamo,"Testimony for San Felice of Cantalice," unnamed interviewer (Rome, June 13, 1587), in *I Frati Cappuccini Documenti e Testimonianze del Primo Secolo, Vol III, pt 2*., 4668: "Questo è stato un gran miracolo della vita di fra Felice. Lui ha studiato in queste tre cose, cioè: il dispreggio di se stesso, nell'ubedienza e nell'orazione."

CHAPTER 1

1. Giovanni Paolo Mucanzio, Clement's master of ceremonies, records the agenda of this meeting and what was discussed. See Biblioteca Apostolica Vaticana (BAV), Barberini Latini (Barb. Lat.) 2810, 315: "Dubia De Beatis non Canonizatis Sa[nctis]s[i]mo D[omino]N[ostro] formata." As Miguel Gotor makes clear in his monograph on the subject, this was the first meeting of the Congregation of the Blessed which was tasked by Clement with finding a way to approve some veneration of saints prior to canonization. See Miguel Gotor, *Chiesa e santità nell'Italia moderna* (Rome: Laterza, 2004); idem, *I beati del Papa: Santità, inquisizione e obbedienza in età moderna* (Florence: Leo S. Olschki, 2002), 127–134.

2. BAV, Barb. Lat. 2819, 315–318.

3. Peter Burke, "How to Be a Counter Reformation Saint," in *Religion and Society in Early Modern Europe 1500–1800*, ed. Kaspar von Greyerz (London: German Historical Institute, 1984): 46; Gotor, *Chiesa e santità*, 26; Philip M. Soergel, *Wondrous in His Saints: Counter-Reformation Propaganda in Bavaria* (Berkeley: University of California Press, 1993), 146–151, 159.

4. Gotor, *I beati del papa*, 1–9; Jean Claude Schmitt, *The Holy Greyhoud: Guinefort, Healer of Children Since the Thirteenth Century*, trans. Martin Thom (New York: Cambridge University Press, 1982).

5. For recent surveys on the Reformation attack on the cult of the saints see Carlos M.N. Eire, *War Against the Idols* (New York: Cambridge University Press, 1986); Carol Piper Heming, *Protestants and the Cult of the Saints in German-Speaking Europe, 1517–1531* (Kirksville, MO: Truman State University Press, 2003); Robert Kolb, *For All the Saints: Changing Perceptions of Martyrdom and Sainthood in the Lutheran Reformation* (Macon, GA: Mercer University Press, 1987); Helen Parish, *Monks, Miracles, and Magic: Reformation Representations of the Medieval Church* (New York: Routledge, 2005), 46–70; Lee Palmer Wandel, *Voracious Idols and Violent Hands: Iconoclasm in Reformation Zurich, Strabourg and Basel* (New York: Cambridge University Press, 1999). For a particularly damning passage from Luther see, for example, Martin Luther, *Luther's Works, vol 3* ed. Jaroslav Pelikan (Philadelphia: Fortress Press, 1955), 109.

6. Burke, "How to Be a Counter Reformation Saint," 47.

7. André Vauchez, *Sainthood in the Later Middle Ages*, trans. Jean Birrell (New York: Cambridge University Press, 1997), 33–57; Laura Smoller, *The Saint and the Chopped-Up Baby* (Ithaca, NY: Cornell University Press, 2014), 49–84.

8. Burke, "How to Be a Counter Reformation Saint," 45–55; Simon Ditchfield, "How Not to Be a Counter-Reformation Saint: The Attempted Canonization of Pope Gregory X, 1622–45," *Papers of the British School at Rome* 60 (1992): 379–422; idem, "Tridentine Worship and the Cult of the Saints," in *The Cambridge History of Christianity, vol. 6*, ed. R. Po-Chia Hsia (New York: Cambridge University Press, 2007): 201–224; Gotor, *Chiesa e santità*; idem, *I beati del Papa;* Giovanni Papa, *Le cause di canonizzazione nel primo periodo della congregazione dei Riti (1588–1634)* (Rome: Urbaniana University Press, 2001).

9. Both Aviad Kleinberg and Peter Burke have called canonization a "negotiation." It is a concept, I think, that accurately describes the act of papal canonization and is one I use frequently in this book. Burke, "How to Be a Counter Reformation Saint," 53; Aviad M. Kleinberg, *Prophets in Their Own Country* (Chicago: University of Chicago Press, 1992), 4.

10. Peter Brown, *The Cult of the Saints: Its Rise and Function in Latin Christianity* (Chicago: University of Chicago Press, 1981); Patrick J. Geary, *Furta Sacra: Thefts of Relics in the Central Middle Ages* (Princeton, NJ: Princeton University Press, 1978), 6–9; Vauchez, *Sainthood*, 13–21.

11. Vauchez, *Sainthood*, 30–32; "Canons of the Fourth Lateran Council," in *Readings in Medieval History,* ed. Patrick J. Geary (Orchard Park, NY: Broadview Press, 2003), no. 62, 464: "As for newly discovered relics, let no one venture to venerate them publicly without their having first been approved by the authority of the Roman pontiff."

12. Kleinberg, *Prophets*, 21.

13. Vauchez, *Sainthood*, 74–84.

14. Ibid., 6–7.

15. Ibid., 139–140; Ditchfield, "Tridentine Worship," 206–207, has highlighted the continuation of local cults even throughout the sixteenth century.

16. See note 5 above for the Protestant reaction against the saints in central Europe. For reactions during the English Reformation, see also Peter Marshall, "Forgery and Miracles in the Reign of Henry VIII," *Past & Present*, No. 178 (February 2003): 39–73. For particularly vehement attacks by Luther and Calvin in particular, see John Calvin, *Institutes of the Christian Religion, vol. 2*, ed. John T. McNeill (Louisville: Westminster John Knox Press, 1960), III.22, 880; Luther, *Luther's Works, vol. 3*, 109.

17. Burke, "How to Be a Counter Reformation Saint," 46; Ronald C. Finucane, *Contested Canonizations: The Last Medieval Saints, 1482–1523* (Washington, DC: Catholic University of America Press, 2011), 207; Robert Scribner, *Popular Culture and Popular Movements in Reformation Germany* (London: Hambledon Press, 1987), 74–75.

18. For some of the post-1520s vicissitudes of Benno's cult, see Ditchfield, "Tridentine Worship," 219; Trevor Johnson, "Holy Dynasts and Sacred Soil," in *Europa sacra: raccolte agiografie e identità politiche in Europa fra*

Medioevo ed età moderna, ed. Sofia Boesch Gajano and Raimondo Michetti (Rome: Carocci, 2002), 92.

19. Burke, "How to Be a Counter Reformation Saint," 46.

20. Finucane, *Contested Canonizations,* 252–253; Gotor, *Chiesa e santità,* 24–26.

21. Gotor, *Chiesa,* 70–72.

22. J. Waterworth, ed. and trans., *The Canons and Decrees of the Sacred and Oecumenical Council of Trent* (London: Dolman, 1848), 236: "And that these things may be the more faithfully observed, the holy Synod ordains, that no one be allowed to place, or cause to be placed, any unusual image, in any place, or church, howsoever exempted, except that image have been approved of by the bishop: also, that no new miracles are to be acknowledged, or new relics recognized, unless the said bishop has taken cognizance and approved thereof."

23. Thomas F. Mayer, *The Roman Inquisition: A Papal Bureaucracy and Its Laws in the Age of Galileo* (Philadelphia: University of Pennsylvania Press, 2013); Adriano Prosperi, *Tribunali della coscienza: inquisitori, confessor, missionary* (Turin: Einaudi, 1996), 135–153

24. Gotor, *I beati del Papa,* 206. See also Ruth S. Noyes, "On the Fringes of the Center: Disputed Hagiographic Imagery and the Crisis over the *Beati moderni* in Rome ca. 1600," *Renaissance Quarterly* 64 (2011): 800–846. In this article Noyes discusses the difficulty in general that the Church had in regulating the cult of the saints.

25. Archivio della Congregazione per la Dottrina della Fede (ACDF), Stanza Storica (St. St.) B-4-F, B-4-P. These two manuscripts are collections of inquisition trials begun over cases of false sanctity or unapproved veneration. Each contains numerous cases of this sort.

26. Papa, *Le cause di canonizzazione,* 20.

27. Gotor, *Chiesa,* 39.

28. On the Rota see Gotor, *Chiesa,* 39–40; idem, "La canonizzazione dei santi spagnoli nella Roma barocca," in *Roma y España: un crisol de la cultura europea en la edad moderna,* ed. Carlos José and Hernando Sánchez (Madrid: Sociedad Estatal para la Acción Cultural Exterior, 2007), 623–625; Charles Lefebvre, "La procedure du tribunal de la Rote romaine au XVIIe siècle d'apres d'un manuscript inédit," *L'Année Canonique* 5 (1957): 143–155; Niccolò del Re, *La Curia Romana: Lineamenti storico-giuridici* (Rome: Sussidi eruditi, 1970), 243–259.

29. Vauchez, *Sainthood,* 33–57; Gotor, *Chiesa,* 16–18; Dyan Elliott, *Proving Woman: Female Spirituality and Inquisitional Culture in the Later Middle Ages* (Princeton, NJ: Princeton University Press, 2004), 127–141. Elliott makes an interesting and fruitful comparison between canonization and inquisitorial investigations, pointing out that the procedures were quite similar in each case.

30. For a good summary of the early modern process of canonization see Ditchfield, *Tridentine Worship,* 208–212; Gotor, *Chiesa e santità,* 17–21, 41–43.

31. Ditchfield, "Tridentine Worship," 208–209.

32. Ibid., 212.

33. Ibid., "Tridentine Worship," 208–209. On this topic, and canonization procedures in general, the main seventeenth-century manual on canonization by Felice Contelori also gives clear instruction. See Felice Contelori, *Tractatus et Praxis De Canonizatione* (Lyons: Laurentii Durant, 1634), Caput XXIII, 277: "in compendio refert summo Pontifici."

34. Contelori, *Tractatus*, Cap. XXIII, 278: "qua relatione audita, si placet eidem Pontifici sine alia publica solemnitate, de Cardinalium consilio indulget, ut N. possit Beatus vocari."

35. Ditchfield, "Tridentine Worship," 209–210; Vauchez, *Sainthood*, 85–103; Gotor, *I Beati*.

36. Contelori, *Tractatus*, Caput. II, 16–17: "Beatificationem appellamus †, quae in effectu nihil est aliud, quam particularis quaedam canonizatio, ut dixit Dominus Franciscus Penia, olim Rotae Decanus, *in quaest de culut, & vener Sanct* . . . Summus Pontifex in beatificatione indulget, & concedit, ut aliquis cultus, & honor in aliqua Religione, Provincia, vel civitate beatificato deferatur, ut patet ex formula beatificationis."

37. Stanislaus Kostka was, for example, beatified in 1605 but only canonized in 1726. Filippo Neri enjoyed one of the shortest gaps between beatification and canonization, enjoying the former in 1615 and canonization in 1622. Many others were beatified but never canonized.

38. Gotor, *Chiesa*, 17–18. For the authoritative guide that details the transition from beatification to canonization and the ceremonies that should accompany such an event see Prospero Lambertini (the Pope Benedict XIV), *De servorum dei beatificatione et beatorum canonizatione*, vol. 1 (Bologna: Excusoris Archiepiscopalis, 1734), 201–213, 267–335.

39. See, for example, the massive festival in Milan and in Rome for the canonization of Carlo Borromeo, *Relatione della Festa Fatta in Milano per la canonizatione di S.to Carlo Card. Di S. Prassede, & Arcivescovo di detta Città nell'Anno 1610* (Milan: Appreso l'herede Di Pacifico Pontio, e Gio Battista Piccaglia, Stampatori della Corte Archiepiscopale, 1610). See also Noyes, "On the Fringes of the Center," for a discussion of the promoters of sanctity's production of images before and after a canonization.

40. BAV, Urbinati Latini (Urb. Lat) 1063, 362r: "passato ad altra vita il P[ad]re Filippo della chiesa nova . . . et uno de' fondatori de P[ad]ri della Valicella et p[e]r 25 [anni] era in op[inio]ne di santo [e] è stato grandissimo il co[nc]orso del Popolo a baciarli la mano, havendo anco p[re]detta hora della morte sua."

41. Giacomo Bacci, *The Life of Saint Philip Neri, vol. 2*, ed. Frederick Ignatius Antrobus (London: Kegan Paul, Trench, Trubner & Co., 1902), 114.

42. See discussion in the next chapter as well as the recounting of the dissection in Neri's first posthumous vita: Antonio Gallonio, *Vita Beati P. Philippi Nerii florentini Congregationis Oratorii fundatoris* (Rome: Apud Aloysium Zannetum, 1600), 227–229.

43. BAV, Barb. Lat. 2810, 307.

44. Gotor, *I Beati del Papa*, 43.

45. Alessio da Sezze, "Testimony," unnamed interviewer (Rome, August 18–20, 1621), in *Processus Sixtinus Fratris Felicis a Cantalice*, ed. M. D'Alatri (Rome: Institutum Historicum O.F.M.Cap., 1964), 344: "il padre generale commandò per santa obedienza al portinano che non mettesse gente dentro, perché era tanto grande la calca, et era il caldo grande."

46. Mariano D'Alatri, ed., *Processus Sixtinus Fratris Felicis a Cantalice* (Rome: Institutum Historicum O.F.M.Cap., 1964), 344: "Et il signor cardinale disse: 'Padre, bisogna trovare qui qualche remedio, perché le genti si affogano: o seppellire il corpo o veramente mandare a pigliare la guardia delli sguizzeri.'"

47. On Salviati's life and role in the Curia see Pierre Hurtubise, ed., introduction to *Correspondance du Nonce en France Antonio Maria Salviati (1572–1578)*, vol. 1 (Rome: Écloe Française du Rome, 1975), 1–124; Pietro de Angelis, *Il Cardinale Antonio Maria Salviati (1536–1602): benefattore insigne degli opsedali di San Giacomo in Augusta e di San Rocco delle Patorienti, nel 350 anno della sua morte* (Rome: Ferri, 1952).

48. ACDF, St. St. B-4-F, fasc. 1, 1r: "Illius conventus occasione sepeliendi Fratrem mortuu[m] inventu[m] fuisse cadaver alterius Fratris, qui obiit duodecim ab hinc annis integru[m], et flexis genibus, Praed[ictu]m Cadaver transportatu[m] fuisse in Sacrario, et repositum in Capsa; Praed[ictu]m Corpus a Guardiano [*sic*] pluribus Feminis ostentsum fuisse, quae ipsum venerati sunt."

49. On this issue of promoting sanctity through a variety of media see Ruth S. Noyes, "On the Fringes of the Center"; idem, "*Aut Numquid post annos Mille Quingentos Docenda est Ecclesia Catholica Quomdo Sacrae Imagines Pingantur?* Post-Tridentine Image Reform and the Myth of Gabriele Paleotti," *Catholic Historical Review* 99, no. 2 (April 2013): 239–261. For a clear argument for seeing canonization as an active campaign, or perhaps lobby, carried out by enthusiastic promoters see Simon Ditchfield, "'Coping with the Beati Moderni': Canonization Procedure in the Aftermath of the Council of Trent," in *Ite Inflammate Omnia. Selected Historical Papers from Conferences Held at Loyola and Rome in 2006*, ed. Thomas M. McCoog, S.J. (Rome: Institutum Historicum Societatis Iesu, 2010), 413–439.

50. ACDF, St. St. B-4-F, fasc. 10.

51. ACDF, St. St. B-4-P, fasc. 3, 3r: "Che mostravano le ossa . . . lodavano la sua vita, e molti per divotione le baciavano, che hanno distribuite di d[ett] a ossa per reliquie."

52. Ibid.: "Che dopo quest'ulti[m]a esumatione si sono fatti più ritrati di d[ett]a Caterina che non se n'era prima, essendo cresciuta l'opinione della sua santità [subject shifts to the friar doing the denouncing of the cult] l'ha vista dipinta senza raggi, e laurole, ma con la corona in mano."

53. Ibid., fasc. 11: "Simulacrum Scoti expositum publicae venerationi super Altare maius cum inscriptione Venerabilis."

54. Smoller, *The Saint and the Chopped-Up Baby*, 52–54. Smoller notes that even in an earlier period this was fairly common. Promoters of the sanctity of Vincent Ferrer engaged in a number of activities so as to increase devotion to him. These things included erecting an altar at his tomb, ringing

of bells to signal new miracles he worked, and the composition of a pilgrim book recording his miracles.

55. Ditchfield, "'Coping with the Beati Moderni,'" 433–435; Gotor, *I beati del Papa*, 57–65.

56. Gotor, *I beati del Papa*, 231–242.

57. ACDF, St. St., B-4-F, fasc. 16, 3v: "Nel presente anno 1655 quindici giorni in circa avanti la prima fiera, si divulgo', che ad una certa Donna Francesca di Cornelio Giulio da Montimag[gio]re Castello quivi viccino [*sic*], era di notte tempo l'apparso il detto santo, ricludendoli ripportarsi il di lui corpo sotto una pietra lunga, e larga per una statura di huomo."

58. Ibid., 2v: "ch'il suo corpo stava sotto sud[ett]a pietra, che non voleva star più tumulto."

59. Ibid.: "Di questo avvisato Mons[ignor] Vesc[ov]o col conseglio di m[ol]ti Religiosi vuolse chiarirsi della verità, mandò il Vicario con altri a far cavar sotto il sasso, e non si trovò niente."

60. Ibid.: "Q[uest]a diligenza non fece frutta alcuna, anzi alcuni dicevano, ch'il corpo era stato portato furtivam[en]te a Fano, altrui, che non essendo stato cercato, come si doveva con Oratione, il santo non haveva voluto lasciar di trovare."

61. Ibid.: "e cosi crebbero notabilm[en]te il Concorso, e l'elemosine, portandosi via alcuni pezzi di quella Pietra, come reliquia."

62. Ibid., 4r: "Cosi' mi portai [the inquisitor] quivi, ove feci murare ambidue le porte."

63. Urban VIII, *Decreta Servanda in Canonizatione, & Beatificatione Sanctorum* (Rome: Rev. Camera Apostolica, 1642), 27: "Sanctitas Sua expresse prohibuit . . . Congregationi, ne deinceps procedat in Causis Servorum Dei ad effectum Canonizationis seu Beatificationis, aut declarationis Martyrii, nisi lapsis quinquaginta annis ab obitu illius, quinimo etiam lapsis quinquaginta annis de similibus Processibus tam factis." See also Gotor, *Chiesa*, 88.

64. See, for example, the lengthy *non-cultu* process which preceded the canonization inquest for Gregorio Barbarigo Archivio Segreto Vaticano (ASV), *Congr. Riti, Processus* (hereafter RP) 3458. In this document witnesses are asked a number of questions to determine whether or not a cult had existed for Barbarigo prior to the opening of the canonization. On *non-cultu* processes in general see Philippe Boutry, "Le procès super non cultu, source de l'histoire des pèlerinages: Germaine Cousin et le sanctuaire de Pirbrac au lendemain de la Révolution française," *Bibliothèque de l'école des chartes* 154, no. 2 (1996): 565–590. I thank Simon Ditchfield for providing this helpful reference.

65. ACDF, St. ST., C-1-A, 1v–2r.

66. Maria Antonietta Visceglia, *Roma papale e Spagna: Diplomatici, nobili e religiosi tra due corti* (Rome: Bulzoni, 2010), 242–252.

67. Gotor, *I beati*, 224–225; Papa, *Le cause di canonizzazione*, 155.

68. See, for example, ACDF, St. St. B-4-F, fasc. 24, in which an inquisitorial proceeding against a prospective saint was opened due to a single denunciation.

69. Gotor, *Chiesa*, 42.

70. BAV, Stamp. Barb.LL.III.7, *Relatio Facta in Consitorio Secreto Coram S.D.N. Gregorio Papa XV A Francisco Maria Episcopo Portuensi S.R.E. Card A Monte Die [blank] Ianuarii MDCXXII Super Vita, Sanctitate, actis Canonizationis, & miraculis Beati Francisi Xavier e Societate Iesu*, 31.

71. ASV, RP 3156, 12–13.

72. ASV, RP 2443, 2v–3r.

73. The Rota considered cases ranging from disputes over benefices to marriage dispensation appeals, as well as cases related to the saints. For a good sampling of the various issues that they considered see Francisco Peña, *Recollectae Decisiones* (Lyons: Philip Borde, Larurent Arnaud, & Claude Rigaud, 1650).

74. Gotor, *Chiesa*, 42.

75. BAV, De Luca IV.6607, *Relatio Facta in Consistorio Secreto Coram S.D.N. Paulo Papa V. A Dominico Episcopo Hostiensi S.R.E. Cardinale Pinello Die Augusti MDCX. Super vita Sanctitate actis Canonizationis, & miraculis piae mem. Caroli Cardinalis Borromaei tit. Sanctae Praxedis Archiepiscopi Mediolanensis cum privilegio*, 19.

76. Gotor, *Chiesa*, 46.

77. Simon Ditchfield, "How Not to Be a Counter-Reformation Saint," 379–422.

78. BAV, Vat. Lat. 12294, 284v: "Et praedictus d[ominus] Orator a Palatio Campi Floris suae residentiae equester decedens associatus a multis curialibus, atque Nobilibus viris, et Baronibus Romanis, et ab aliquibus Praelatis venit ad Palatium ap[osto]licum, in quo de equo descendit, et ascendit supinus ad Cameras Ill[ustrissi]mi D[omini] Car[dina]lis Rusticucis Vicarii." On the cult of Saint Hyacinth and the negotiations that went into his canonization see Ronald Finucane, "Saint-Making at the End of the Sixteenth Century: How and Why Jacek of Poland (d. 1257) Became St. Hyacinth in 1594," *Hagiographica* 9 (2002): 207–258.

79. ASV 1681, 242r. Lists "Summa expensarum in Urbe actarum Pro canonizatione S. Caroli" with the number "26,300" appearing on the next page. I have assumed ducats given that most of the money was paid by Milan although no denomination is listed. Niels Rasmussen, "Liturgy and Iconography at the Canonization of Carlo Borromeo, 1 November 1610," in *San Carlo Borromeo*, ed. John Headley and John Tomaro (London: Associated University Presses, 1988), 276. Ramussen gives the price of the canonization as 31,143 gold scudi. A roman scudo was worth slightly more than a ducat.

80. J. R. Hale, *Renaissance War Studies*, History Series 11 (London: Hambledon Press, 1983), 309–311. Hale puts the price of keeping the largest Venetian Great Galley Flagship in the field for a year with a full crew, nearly 300 oarsmen, and over 100 soldiers at 31,929 ducats. I thank Brian Brege for his kindness in providing this reference.

81. L. Pelissier, "Le spese d'una canonizazione a Roma nel MDCVIII," in *Archivio della R. Società di Storia Patria* 16 (Rome: 1893): 239: "per la certa et alter cose fatte e spese per questa canonizazione, le quali tutte insieme

ascendono alla somma di scudi dieci nove milia in circa." For a recent study on the expenses and artistic effort expended during the final stages of canonization or beatification proceedings during this period, see Vittorio Casale, *L'Arte per le canonizzazioni: L'attività artistica intorno alle canonizzazioni e alle beatificazioni del Seicento* (Turin: Umberto Allemandi & C., 2011).

82. Ibid., 237.

83. Ibid., 238.

84. Tessa Storey, *Carnal Commerce in Counter-Reformation Rome* (New York: Cambridge University Press, 2008), xv.

85. Pelissier, "Le spese d'una canonizzazione a Roma nel MDCVIII," 239: "Per Nostro Signore: Piviale papale; stola per il piviale; cordone di seta amitto e camisola di zenzile; pianetta; stola per la messa' manipolo' soccintorio con un altro manipolo; tunicella e dalmatica di taffetano; sandali e calze; gremiale; borsa; coperta del faldistorio." I have been unable to find reliable translations for all the items listed in this summary.

86. Ibid.: "Al signor Prospero Farinacci, fiscale, una veste simile di saietta pavonazza col suo cappuccio come usano li advocati consistoriali."

87. Ibid., 238–239: "Alli sei camerieri secreti partecipanti della Camera di Nostro signore ed a ciascheduno di loro una veste col suo cappucchio di saietta di Milano rossa come usano nelle cappelle e pubblici concistori"; "Al medico di Nostro Signore una veste simile col suo capuccio."

88. On Benedict's changes to canonization procedure see Giuseppe Dalla Torre, "Santità ed economia processuale. L'esperienza giuridica da Urbano VIII a Benedetto XIV," in *Finzione e santità tra medioevo ed età moderna*, ed. Gabriella Zarri (Turin: Rosemberg & Sellier, 1991), 231–263; Maria Teresa Fattori, ed., *Storia, medicina e diritto nei trattati di Prospero Lambertini Benedetto XIV* (Rome: Edizioni di storia e letteratura, 2013).

89. ASV, RP 6866, 332r: "A quelli, che studiano, o votano sopra a queste Cause, non possano i Postulatori, e Procuratori di esse, sotto pena di privazione dell'Uffizio, ed altre più rigorose ad arbitrio della Sacra Congregazione de' Riti, dar verun Regalo, ancorché sia di soli Comestibili."

90. Ibid., 270r: "Per il Decreto della Canonizatione Scudi Mille d'oro stampe, si paga alla Sagristia della Basilica Vaticana o sia S. Pietro . . . Per la Bolla della Canonizatione——650."

91. Ibid.: "Per la funzione in S[an] P[iet]ro del gran soglio Pontificio, pitture di Medaglioni, Paratura Solenne della Basilica e gran Portico, cera puole Macchiae e solenne Processione state rappresentanti le virtù ed altro circa——20400."

92. Simon Ditchfield, *Liturgy, Sanctity, and History in Tridentine Italy* (New York: Cambridge University Press, 1995), 10.

93. Ditchfield, "Tridentine Worship," 208–209; Papa, *Le cause di canonizzazione*, 162. Simon Ditchfield has emphasized that the real separation of the apostolic from the ordinary phase of canonization was an innovation of the post-Tridentine period.

94. Each apostolic process opens with a remissorial letter deputing the local judges in charge of administering the process. For an example by an easy-to-read hand, see ASV, RP 2445 (Francisco Borgia Apostolic Process),

2v–3r. For a discussion of these letters from the period see Contelori, *Tractatus*, cap. 24; see also Ditchfield, "Tridentine Worship," 208.

95. On the role of notaries in this period in making evidence in all sorts of legal proceedings, see Laurie Nussdorfer, *Brokers of Public Trust: Notaries in Early Modern Rome* (Baltimore: Johns Hopkins University Press, 2009).

96. Although there is some variation based on the details of an individual's life, the set of questions for Borgia appears very similar to those asked for other saints. See, for example, the questions asked for Carlo Borromeo in 1604 (ASV, RP 1681, 57r–58r) or those for Maria Maddelena dei Pazzi in 1624 (ASV, RP 769 5r–5v).

97. ASV, RP 2445, 277r.

98. Ibid., 277v.

99. Ibid., 277v–278r.

100. Ibid., 278r.

101. ASV, RP 2445, 278r–283r.

102. For another example, see the apostolic phase of the canonization process for Rose of Lima, which includes almost exactly the same set of questions ASV, RP 1575, 12r–12v.

103. Laura A. Smoller, "Defining Boundaries of the Natural in Fifteenth-Century Brittany: The Inquest into the Miracles of Saint Vincent Ferrer (d. 1419)," *Viator* 28 (1997): 341. In this article, Smoller discusses the Church's concern to make sure that witnesses were reliable and could understand, at least at a rudimentary level, the difference between natural and non-natural explanations of why things happened. Certainly, there were many testators who could not do this and so either did not have their testimony count as evidence or had the information they gave reinterpreted by an expert. See below for examples of such reinterpretation.

104. ASV, RP 769, 5v.

105. Ibid., 6r: "It[em] ponunt quod maximam habuit charitatem erga proximum salutem proximos desiderando, et procurando infirmis monialibus, et aliis inserviendo novitias, et alias moniales instruendo, et alia opera pietatis circa moniales, et alios ex mon[aste]rio exercendo, et hoc est verum."

106. Ibid., 6v: "Item ponunt et ex corpore emanare liquorem, quemdm oleo similem, et odore sepulchrum eius, et odore suavissimo fragrante, et hoc fuit, et est verum."

107. Ibid.

108. Smoller, "Defining Boundaries of the Natural," 342–343; Massimo Vallerani, "I fatti nella logica del processo medievale. Note introduttive," *Quaderni storici*, 108, 36, no. 3 (December 2001): 665–694.

109. Ditchfield, "Tridentine Worship," 208–209. For a printed example, see the list appearing for each miracle in the canonization of Turibio of Mongrevjo: Congregatione Sacrorum Rituum, *Beatificationis & canonizationis Ven[erabile] Servi Dei Turibii Alphonsi Mogrobesii Archiepiscopi Limani. Positio Super Dubio* (Rome: Ex Typographia Rev. Camerae Apostolicae, 1675).

110. ACDF, St. St. B-4-P, fasc. 5, 7v: "Io per assicurarmi della verità ho esaminato Luca Boncinelli Intagliatore il quale ha messo assieme il so[pra]

detto Corpo, e depone che le mani, le calcagni de piedi diec'otto, o venti costole, tre noccioli della spina, un pezzo d'osso sacro, e molti pezzetti in varie parti, sono di legno, coperto di parta fatta con le ceneri d'alcuni fragmetti d'ossa abbruggiate a quest'effetto."

111. Congregatione Sacrorum Rituum, *Beatificationis & canonizationis Ven[erabile] Servi Dei Turibii Alphonsi Mogrobesii Archiepiscopi Limani,* 59–60.

112. Pamela O. Long, *Artisan/Practitioners and the Rise of the New Sciences, 1400–1600* (Corvallis: Oregon State University Press, 2011); Pamela Smith, *The Body of the Artisan: Art and Experience in the Scientific Revolution* (Chicago: University of Chicago Press, 2004), 59–94; Jim Bennett, "The Mechanical Arts," in *The Cambridge History of Science, Vol. 3: Early Modern Science,* ed. Katharine Park and Lorraine Daston (New York: Cambridge University Press, 2006), 673–695.

113. ASV, RP 3638, 117v.

114. Ibid., 117v–120v.

115. Ibid., 120v."Primo una Archa quatuor palmorum cum dimidio longitudinis et amplitudinis duorum palmores et aliorum duorm palmorum profunditatis cooperta velati purpurei suffulta trenis aureis et clavata claviculis deauratis sine recte clausa seu clausa cum clavibus quam p[raesen]ti DD[icti] Judices Remiss[oria]les mandarunt disclaudi, et aperui sicuti disclausa, et aperta fuit in presentia p[raesen]torum D.D. Juidcum Remiss[oria]lium . . . et mei p[raesen]ti et infra[scrip]t[i] Notarii per Simonem de Azevedo fabrum lignorum, qua Archa disclausa, et aperta fuit . . . reperta fuerunt ossa Infrascripta Corporis p[raesen]ti Servi Dei fr[atr]is Don Thomae de Villaneuva sine Carne involuta in gausippo." The bones are then identified and listed over the course of the next page. The small size of this box likely means that Thomas was moved into this box after his body had largely decayed into just bones. A palm in Valencia at the time was about nine modern inches in length.

116. Ibid., 121r.

117. ASV, RP 3523, 567r–569v.

118. On the new ways of writing about the natural world see Gianna Pomata and Nancy Siraisi, eds., *Historia: Empiricism and Erudition in Early Modern Europe* (Cambridge, MA: MIT Press, 2005); Gianna Pomata, "Observation Rising: Birth of an Epistemic Genre, 1500–1650," in *Histories of Scientific Observation,* ed. Lorraine Daston and Elizabeth Lunbeck (Chicago: University of Chicago Press, 2011),

119. Alison Sandman, "Mirroring the World: Sea Charts, Navigation, and Territorial Claims in Sixteenth-Century Spain," in *Merchants and Marvels: Commerce, Science, and Art in Early Modern Europe,* ed. Paula Findlen and Pamela Smith (New York: Routledge, 2002), 83–108. The Spanish Empire was actually involved at the same time in a number of other empirical enterprises in the New World that emphasized firsthand experience. See Antonio Barrera-Osorio, "Knowledge and Empiricism in the Sixteenth-Century Spanish Atlantic World," in *Science in the Spanish and Portuguese Empires, 1500–1800,* ed. Daniela Bleichmar et al. (Stanford, CA: Stanford University Press, 2009), 219–232.

120. Peter Dear, "*Totius in verba:* Rhetoric and Authority in the Early Royal Society," in *The Scientific Enterprise in Early Modern Europe: Readings from Isis,* ed. Peter Dear (Chicago: University of Chicago Press, 1997), 263–265; idem, *Discipline and Experience,* 21–26; Steven Shapin, "Pump and Circumstance: Robert Boyle's Literary Technology," *Social Studies of Science* 14, no. 4 (November 1984): 481–520.

121. ASV, RP 762, 149r: "Tale igitur Corpus ego Angelus Bonellus Florentin[us] videns, tangens, atque odorans annorum [ink smudged in original text] mortuis ducentum triginta tres, ultra naturae terminos ita eorum servatum suspicio atque admiror." On the cult of Andrea Corsini in general see Giovanni Ciappelli, *Un santo alla battaglia di Anghiari. La "Vita" e il culto di Andrea Corsini nella Firenze del Rinascimento* (Florence: Sismel—Edizioni del Galluzzo, 2007). I thank Simon Ditchfield for pointing me to this reference.

122. On the category of the supernatural see Lorraine Daston and Katharine Park, *Wonders and the Order of Nature, 1150–1750* (New York: Zone Books, 1998), 120–128. See also the discussion in Chapter 3 of this book.

123. ASV, RP 762, 149r.

124. Ibid.: "Tale igitur Corpus ego Angelus Bonellus Florentin[us] videns, tangens, atque odorans."

125. ASV, RP 762, 149r–150v.

126. ASV, RP 3523, 1134v: "fui processato già sedeci anni in circa criminalmente per imputatione di haver ammazzato un Comito Greco della Gallia." ASV, RP 3523, 1138v: "et cosi sano per severo doi anni senza mal nissuno ma in capo di doi anni gli venne poi la febre, et mori di febre, ma non pati mai piu di mal caduco."

127. For more information about Zacchia and his role in the development of a variety of aspects of early modern medicine see Alessandro Pastore and Giovanni Rossi, eds., *Paolo Zacchia alle origini della medicina legale 1584–1659* (Milan: Franco Angeli, 2008).

128. Zacchia makes it clear that the Rota specifically asked him to reevaluate this case due to the dubious nature of the evidence. Paolo Zacchia, *Quaestionum Medico-Legalium Tomus Posterior Quo Continentur Liber Nonus et Decimus, Necnon Decisiones Sacrae Rotae Romanae* (Lyons: Ioan, Ant. Huguetan, 1661), 123: "Agebatur coram Illustrissimis & Reverendissimis DD. Rotae Auditoribus de canonizatione Beati Laurentii Iustiniani, ad cuius sanctitatem magis magisque probandam multa proponebantur opera miraculosa, eius meritis, & invocatione successa circa quorum tamen nonnulla dubitare contigit, an vere miraculosa dici deberent, necne? Et nos ad instantias Religiosorum qui huiusmodi canonizationem promovebant, super nonnullis pro veritate scripsimus."

129. Zacchia, *Quaestionum Medico-Legalium Tomus Posterior Quo Continentur Liber Nonus et Decimus,* 123–127.

130. Gotor, *Chiesa.,* 79–80.

131. Maria Pia Donato, "Manfredi, Paolo," in *Dizionario Biografico degli Italiani,* vol. 68 (Rome: Istituto della Enciclopedia Italiana, 2007), http://www. treccani.it/enciclopedia/paolo-manfredi_%28Dizionario-Biografico%29/ .

132. Congregatione Sacrorum Rituum, *Beatificationis & canonizationis Ven[erabile] Servi Dei Turibii Alphonsi Mogrobesii Archiepiscopi Limani*. This work is divided into sections with the first being the summary of miracles and testimony, then the promotor fidei's objections, followed by Caccia and then Manfredi's responses.

133. See, for example, Manfredi's consideration of whether or not a woman liberated from a difficult pregnancy had been the subject of a miraculous cure. It includes both reliance on classical authority and clinical experience with the normal appearance of human fetuses. Such specific knowledge was far beyond the competency of most believers in the period. Ibid., sec. 4, entitled *Responsio Medicophysica Pauli Manfredi Medici Colleg[i] & publici Lectoris ad Animadversiones Rev.mi Promotoris Fidei . . .* , 13–15.

134. See, for example, the miracle in which the Archbishop used Toribio's cross to enact a miraculous cure; ibid., 54.

135. On the idea that artisanal techniques of knowledge making were appropriated and their origins excised, see Smith, *Body of the Artisan*, 182–236.

CHAPTER 2

1. Several scholars have commented on the importance of the canonizations of 1622 for the reassertion of Catholic identity. See, in particular, Marina Caffiero, "Istituzioni, forme e usi del sacro," *Roma moderna* (2002): 143–180; Miguel Gotor, *Chiesa e santità nell'Italia moderna* (Rome: Laterza, 2004), 53–55.

2. See appendix.

3. On the importance of the saint's body and his remains for the elaboration of his or her cult see Peter Brown, *The Cult of the Saints: Its Rise and Function in Latin Christianity* (Chicago: University of Chicago Press, 1981); Patrick J. Geary, *Furta sacra: Thefts of Relics in the Central Middle Ages* (Princeton, NJ: Princeton University Press, 1978); André Vauchez, *Sainthood in the Later Middle Ages*, trans. Jean Birrell (New York: Cambridge University Press, 1997), 427–443.

4. See, for example, the concerns voiced by Clement VIII over the veneration of noncanonized individuals recorded by his master of ceremonies Biblioteca Apostolica Vaticana (BAV), Barberini Latini (Barb. Lat.) 2810, 315; Miguel Gotor, *Chiesa e santità*; idem, *I beati del Papa: Santità, inquisizione e obbedienza in età moderna* (Florence: Leo S. Olschki, 2002), 127–134 .This is also discussed at greater length in Chapter 1 of the present volume.

5. On the growth of specific anatomical case studies in this period see Gianna Pomata, *"Praxis Historialis*: The Uses of *Historia* in Early Modern Medicine," in *Historia: Empiricism and Erudition in Early Modern Europe,* ed. Gianna Pomata and Nancy Siraisi (Cambridge, MA: MIT Press, 2005), 105–146; Anthony Grafton and Nancy Siraisi, *Natural Particulars: Nature and the Disciplines in Renaissance Europe* (Cambridge, MA: MIT Press, 1999), 1–21; Nancy Siraisi, "'Remarkable' Diseases, 'Remarkable' Cures, and Personal Experience in Renaissance Medical Texts," in *Medicine and*

the Italian Universities, 1250–1600 (Boston: Brill, 2001), 226–252; idem, *History, Medicine, and the Traditions of Renaissance Learning* (Ann Arbor: University of Michigan Press, 2007), 68–71. The first real collection of case studies of unusual phenomena in this period was Antonio Benivieni, *De abditis nonnullis ac mirandis morborum et sanationum causis* Florence: Philippi Giuntae, 1507).

6. Gianna Pomata, "Observation Rising: Birth of an Epistemic Genre, 1500–1650," in *Histories of Scientific Observation,* ed. Lorraine Daston and Elizabeth Lunbeck (Chicago: University of Chicago Press, 2011), 45–80.

7. Nancy G. Siraisi, "Signs and Evidence: Autopsy and Sanctity in Late Sixteenth-Century Italy," in *Medicine and the Italian Universities, 1250–1600* (Boston: Brill, 2001), 356–380.

8. L.J. Andrew Vilalon, "San Diego de Alcalá and the Politics of Saint-Making in Counter-Reformation Europe," *Catholic Historical Review* 83 (1997): 708–711.

9. L.J. Andrew Villalon, "Putting Don Carlos Together Again: Treatment of a Head Injury in Sixteenth-Century Spain," *Sixteenth Century Journal,* no. 2 (Summer 1995): 350–355. The group of medical practitioners attending Don Carlos consisted mostly of physicians, but also included at least one surgeon and one Moorish physician named Pintarete.

10. Villalon, "San Diego de Alcalá," 702. On the concept of the "odor of sanctity" see Jean-Pierre Albert, *Odeurs de sainteté: la mythologie chrétienne des aromates* (Paris: Editions de l' École des hautes études en sciences sociales, 1990); Martin Roch, *L'intelligence d'un sens: odeurs miraculeuses et odorat dans l'Occident du haut Moyen Âge* (Turnhout: Brepols, 2009). I thank Maria Pia Donato for pointing me to these helpful references.

11. Villalon, *San Diego de Alcalá,* 714.

12. "Relación de la enfermedad del Principe D. Carlos en Alcalá por el Doctor Olivares médico de su cámara," ed. Martin Fernandez de Navarrete, *Colección de documentos inéditos para la historia de España,* vol. 15. (Madrid: Academia de la Historia, 1849), 570: "á mi juicio no lo fué, porque el Principe se curó con los remedios naturales y ordinarios, con los cuales se suelen curar otros de la misma enfermedad estando tanto y mas peligrosos."

13. Ibid., 570–571: "Mas como está dicho fué por la orden natural, pues con los remedios que se le hicieron el Principe mejoró, y los milagros propriamente se llaman aquellos que exceden todas las fuerzas naturales, porque los que se remedian con los medios experimentados de los medicos, como se puede á ellos atribuir la salud no se dice que sanan por milagro, aunque todo se hace con la voluntad de Dios y con su favor y ayuda." This passage is also cited in Villalon, "San Diego de Alcalá," 703. On natural philosophical and theological ideas concerning the boundaries of nature in this period see the discussion in the next chapter.

14. Lucio Maria Núñez, "Documentos sobre la curación del príncipe D. Carlos y la canonización de San Diego de Alcalá," *Archivio ibero-americano* 1 (1914): 434: "Y este testigo tuvo el dicho suceso, por lo que tiene dicho, que *fué milagro.* . . . Puesto que a dos o tres de los dichos medicos oyó dezir que no lo tenjan por mjlagro, porque la salud de Su Alteza avia venjdo poco

a poco, y que, al parecer deste testigo, lo que dezian los dichos medicos no derogara la substancia y opinjon del mjlagro, ansi porque la dicha salud pudo venir poco a poco, aunque fuesse por milagro y special auxilio de Dios, como tiene dicho, como porque, al parecer deste testigo, los dichos medicos dezian lo suso dicho *por hazer mas sus partes que las del mjlagro*"(emphasis in the original). De Vega is also discussed in Villalon, "San Diego de Alcalá," 702.

15. Núñez, "Documentos sobre la curación," 433; "Relación de la enfermedad del Principe D. Carlos," 568.

16. Núñez, "Documentos sobre la curación," 442.

17. Pietro Galesini, *La vita, i miracoli e la canonizatione di San Diego d'Alcala d'Henares divisa in tre parti et tradotta nella lingua italiana dal Signor Francesco Avanzi, Venetiano* (Rome: Domenico Basa, 1589), 141.

18. Francesco Bracciolini, *Compendio della vita, morte, et miracoli di San Diego* (Milan: Gratiadio Ferioli, 1598), 31r–31v.

19. On the importance of incorruption as a sign of sanctity see Piero Camporesi, *The Incorruptible Flesh: Bodily Mutation and Mortification in Religion and Folklore*, trans. Tania Croft-Murray (New York: Cambridge University Press, 1988); John Gager, "Body Symbols and Social Reality: Resurrection, Incarnation and Asceticism in Early Christianity," in *Religion* 12, no. 4 (1982): 345–364; Vauchez, *Sainthood in the Later Middle Ages*, 24. See also Chapter 3 in the present book.

20. See Chapter 1 in this volume for a further discussion of the Rota.

21. Peter Godman, *The Saint as Censor Robert Bellarmine Between Inquisition and Index* (Boston: Brill, 2000), 90, 404–405. Godman argues that Peña's central goal in all his reforms was to increase papal power and authority.

22. Edward Peters, "Editing Inquisitors' Manuals in the Sixteenth Century: Francisco Peña and the Directorium inquisitorium of Nicholas Eymeric," *Library Chronicle* 40, no. 1 (1974): 97–98. On Peña see also Vincenzo Lavenia, "Peña, Francisco," in *Dizionario Storico dell'Inquisizione*, 4 vols., ed. Adriano Prosperi with Vincenzo Lavenia and John Tedeschi (Pisa: Edizioni della Normale, 2010), 1186–1189.

23. On the increasing papal dominance of inquisitional activities see Thomas F. Mayer, *The Roman Inquisition: A Papal Bureaucracy and Its Laws in the Age of Galileo* (Philadelphia: University of Pennsylvania Press, 2013). For a discussion of the role of the papacy in centralizing canonization see Chapter 1 of this volume and Gotor, *Chiesa e santità*.

24. Francisco Peña, *Relatione sommaria della vita, santità, miracoli, & atti della canonizatione di S. Carlo Borromeo Cardinale del titolo di Santa Prassede Arcivescovo di Milano canonizzato dalla Santità di N.S. Papa Paolo V* (Rome: Stamperia della Camera Apostolica, 1611), 56.

25. Gotor, *Chiesa e santità*, 40.

26. Francisco Peña, *De Vita, miraculis et actis canonizationis Sancti Didaci libri tres* (Rome: apud Georgium Ferrarium, 1589), 35–43.

27. Ibid.

28. Francisco Peña, *Relatione summaria della vita, de' miracoli, & delli atti della canonizatione di S. Raimondo di Penafort* (Rome: Niccolò Mutii,

1600), 26–27: "la fragrantia, e soave odore, che esce da i corpi morti, è segno che in quelli dimora l'Autor della vita, e soavità, poiché repugna alla natura, che de i corpi de' morti, de' quali suole uscir fetore, esca fragrantia, et odor soave, et perciò autori gravi, e santi hanno affermato, che così fatti odori soavi, che escono de i corpi, e sepolchri de' morti, sono miracolosi."

29. Francisco Peña, *Relatione summaria della vita, santità, miracoli et atti della canonizatione di Santa Francesca Romana,*(Rome: Bartolomeo Zannetti, 1608), 29: "Non si raccontaranno tutti li miracoli fatti ad intercessione della Santa, dopo la sua morte, perché farebbe cosa molto longa, e pero se ne referiranno alcuni più segnalati, fra quali è quello del suavissimo odore, che usciva dal suo corpo, co'l quale la Divina Misericordia illustrò molto la santità della serva sua."

30. Ibid.: "e quello, che fu di gran maraviglia, che non si guastò, né si corruppe, anzi come se fosse vivo, si rendeva morbido, flessibile, e trattabile."

31. Francisco Peña, *Directorium Inquisitorum F. Nicolai Eymerici Ordinis Praed. cum Commentariis Francisci Peñae Sacra Theologia ac Juris utriusque Doctoris* (Rome: apud Georgium Ferrarium, 1587), 439, 629.

32 Each apostolic process opens with a remissorial letter deputing the local judges in charge of administering the process. For an example by an easy-to-read hand, see Archivio Segreto Vaticano (ASV), *Congr. Riti, Processus* (hereafter: RP) 2445 (Francisco Borgia Apostolic Process), 2v–3r. For a discussion of these letters from the period see Felice Contelori, *Tractatus et Praxis De Canonizatione* (Lyons: Laurentii Durant, 1634), cap. 24; see also Simon Ditchfield, "Tridentine Worship and the Cult of the Saints," in *The Cambridge History of Christianity, vol. 6,* ed. R. Po-Chia Hsia (New York: Cambridge University Press, 2007), 208.

33. See, for example, the processes for Isidore the Laborer, ASV, RP 3192, 648r; Andrea Corsini, ASV, RP 762, 147r–147v; and Elizabeth of Portugal, ASV, RP 501, 40v–41r.

34. ASV, RP 11, 36r: "mandent nominari unum sive duos medicos et unum chirurgum sive facultatis peritos ad faciend[um] Visitatione corporis, ossium, et reliquiarum servi dei Fratris petri de Alcantara." I have translated *medicos* as "physicians" even though it normally might mean "medical practitioner" more broadly because (1) the letter specifies that other sorts of medical professionals, including surgeons, could be called in addition to the *medicos* and (2) physicians were in fact called in this case and normally in canonization proceedings. Please see also the discussion below regarding canonization officials preference for university-trained physicians in testimony before the Church.

35. Joseph Ziegler, "Practitioners and Saints: Medical Men in Canonization Processes in the Thirteenth to Fifteenth Centuries," *Social History of Medicine* 12, no. 2 (1999): 210.

36. Ibid., 220.

37. Ibid., 219–223.

38. David Gentilcore, *Healers and Healing in Early Modern Italy* (New York: Manchester University Press, 1998), 187–198; Fernando Vidal, "Miracles, Science, and Testimony in Post-Tridentine Saint-Making," *Science in*

Context 20, no. 3 (2007): 481–508. See also Jacalyn Duffin, *Medical Miracles: Doctors, Saints, and Healing in the Modern World* (New York: Oxford University Press, 2009), whose recent book is a thorough survey of doctors' involvement in healing miracles through the twentieth century.

39. Katharine Park, *The Criminal and the Saintly Body: Autopsy and Dissection in Renaissance Italy*, in *Renaissance Quarterly* 47 (1994): 1–33; idem, *Secrets of Women: Gender, Generation, and the Origins of Human Dissection* (New York: Zone Books, 2006); Nancy Siraisi, "Signs and Evidence: Autopsy and Sanctity in Late Sixteenth-Century Italy," in *Medicine and the Italian Universities, 1250–1600* (Boston: Brill, 2001), 356–380; Elisa Andretta, *Anatomie du Vénérable dans la Rome de la Contre-réforme. Les autopsies d'Ignace de Loyola et de Philippe Neri*, in *Conflicting Duties: Science, Medicine and Religion in Rome, 1550–1750* (London: Warburg Institute, 2009), ed. Maria Pia Donato and Jill Kraye, 255–280.

40. Andretta, "Anatomie du Vénérable," 258. Andretta makes the same point, that autopsy to discern holiness and medical verification of healing miracles require different sets of expertise.

41. Katharine Park, "The Criminal and the Saintly Body," 3–4, and Siraisi, "Signs and Evidence," have both observed that there were at least four reasons why bodies were dissected in the medieval period: (1) as funeral preparation for elites; (2) to determine the cause of death; (3) to check physical signs of a saint's holiness; and (4) to investigate murders. However, as the examples of already cited illustrate and as Park has observed in her *Secrets of Women*, 50, it was the exception rather than the rule to have holy bodies examined by a medical practitioner. Female mystics were generally the ones who were subject to the increased scrutiny.

42. Nancy Siraisi, *Medieval and Early Renaissance Medicine: An Introduction to Knowledge and Practice* (Chicago: University of Chicago Press, 1990), 81–86; Andrea Carlino, *Anatomical Ritual and Renaissance Learning*, trans. John Tedeschi and Anne C. Tedeschi (Chicago: University of Chicago Press, 1999), 2; Mondino dei Liuzzi, *Anatomies de Mondino dei Luzzi et de Guido de Vigevano* (Paris: E. Droz, 1926).

43. Siraisi, *Medieval and Early Renaissance Medicine*, 88; Carlino. 2.

44. Park, *Secrets of Women*, 39–60.

45. Ibid., 48–50.

46. Andrew Cunningham, *The Anatomical Renaissance: The Resurrection of the Anatomical Project of the Ancients* (Brookfield, VT: Ashgate, 1997); Mary Lindemann, *Medicine and Society in Early Modern Europe* (New York: Cambridge University Press, 2010), 91–97; Nancy Siraisi, *Medieval and Early Renaissance Medicine: A Guide to Knowledge and Practice* (Chicago: University of Chicago Press, 1990), 190–193. A few others have also pointed out that as early as the fifteenth century some physicians had begun to use firsthand observations and particular evidence to add to their overall knowledge of the human body. See Danielle Jacquart, "Theory, Everyday Practice, and Three Fifteenth-Century Physicians," *Osiris*, 2nd ser., vol. 6 (1990): 140–160; Katharine Park, "Natural Particulars: Medical Epistemology, Practice, and the Literature of Healing Springs," in *Natural Particulars*, 347–368.

47. Vivian Nutton, "The Rise of Medical Humanism: Ferrara, 1464–1555," *Renaissance Studies* 11 (1997): 2–19; Owsei Temkin, *Galenism: Rise and Decline of a Medical Philosophy* (Ithaca, NY: Cornell University Press, 1973), 125.

48. Pomata, "Observation Rising."

49. Carlino, *Books of the Body*, 2; Roger French, *Dissection and Vivisection in the European Renaissance* (Brookfield, VT: Ashgate, 1999), 96.

50. Numerous authors have written about the importance of Vesalius and debated to what extent 1543 counts as a turning point. See Carlino, *Books of the Body*, 1, 44; French, *Dissection and Vivisection*, 163–179; Lindemann, *Medicine and Society*, 92–95; Charles O'Malley, *Andreas Vesalius of Brussels, 1514–1564* (Berkeley: University of California Press, 1964).

51. Pamela O. Long, *Artisan/Practitioners and the Rise of the New Sciences, 1400–1600* (Corvallis: Oregon State University Press, 2011), 56–58.

52. Realdo Columbo, *De re anatomica libri XV* (Venice, 1559); Charles Estienne, *De dissectione partium corporis humani libri III* (Paris, 1545).

53. Roy Porter, "Medical Science," in *The Cambridge History of Medicine*, ed. Roy Porter (New York: Cambridge University Press, 2006), 136–175, here 138. On the increasingly important role of anatomy in medical education see Cynthia Klestinec, "Practical Experience in Anatomy," in *The Body as Object and Instrument of Knowledge: Embodied Empiricism in Early Modern Science*, ed. C. T. Wolfe and O. Gal (New York: Springer, 2010), 33–57.

54. French, *Dissection and Vivisection in the European Renaissance*, 177–189; Cynthia Klestinec, *Theaters of Anatomy: Students, Teachers, and Traditions of Dissection in Renaissance Venice* (Baltimore: Johns Hopkins University Press, 2011); Nancy Siraisi, "Giovanni Argenterio: Medical Innovation, Princely Patronage and Academic Controversy," in *Medicine and the Italian Universities*, 328–355.

55. I am referring here to the publications of of Fabricius of Acquapendente, who described the valves present in human veins in 1603; Gasparo Aselli of Padua (d. 1626) and Franciscus Sylvius of Leiden (d. 1672), who uncovered the workings of digestion; Gabriele Falloppio (d. 1562), who made significant contributions to both the anatomy of the ear and of female genitalia; and ultimately William Harvey who in 1628 demonstrated the circulation of blood in the human body.

56. Katharine Park, "The Criminal and the Saintly Body: Autopsy and Dissection in Renaissance Italy," *Renaissance Quarterly* 47 (1994): 1–33; idem, *Secrets of Women: Gender, Generation, and the Origins of Human Dissection* (New York: Zone Books, 2006), 47–52, 169–180. Previously, the body of a prospective saint had only rarely been a subject of medical inquiry and, in those few cases in which it was scrutinized, the evidence seems not to have been brought forth in the canonization attempt.

57. Giovanni di Polanco, "Epistola de Obitu S. Ignatii," in *Fontes Narrativi de S. Ignatio de Loyola et de Societatis Iesu Initiis*, vol. 1, ed. Dionysius Fernandez Zapic and Candidus de Dalmases (Rome: Monumenta Historica Soc. Iesu, 1943), 768: "pasado deste mundo el Padre nuestro, por conservar el

cuerpo, parecio conveniente sacar lo interior del, y embalsamarle en alguna manera"; Giovanni Baptista Carcano Leone, *Exenterationis Cadaveris Illustrissimi Cardinalis Borrhomaei Mediolani Archiepiscopi* (Milan: Ex Typographia Michaelis Tini, Ad instantiam Petri Tini, 1584), 3: "quo Cadaver Ill[ustrissim]is Cardinalis exenterare, eaque ratione ipsum tractarem, ut a corruptione, quantum fieri possit praeservarem."

58. Agostino Paravicini-Bagliani, *The Pope's Body*, trans. David S. Peterson (Chicago: University of Chicago Press, 2000), 134–143; Park, "The Criminal and the Saintly Body," 3–4; Siraisi, "Signs and Evidence," 356–380.

59. Pomata, "Observation Rising."

60. Loyola's autopsy has also been discussed in Andretta, "Anatomie du Vénérable," 255–280.

61. Polanco, "Epistola de Obitu S. Ignatii," 768.

62. Ibid., 765: "Y asi el miercoles me llamo, y me dijo que dijese al doctor Torres que tuviese tambien cargo del, como de los otros enfermos: porque no se teniendo por nada su mal, acudiase mas a otros que a el: y asi lo hizo."

63. Robert J. Moes and C. D. O'Malley, "Realdo Colombo: 'On Those Things Rarely Found in Anatomy,' An Annotated Translation from the 'De Re Anatomica' (1559)," *Bulletin of the History of Medicine* 34 (1960): 508–510. Moes and O'Malley note that Colombo had been a student of Vesalius, but later fell out with him when he began criticizing Vesalius's work. Pomata, "Observation Rising," 59. Pomata notes that a focus on case studies also was a way in which medical professionals sought to establish their knowledge and authority.

64. By dissection here I mean in the university theater or some other educational setting. Autopsy, instead, implies those more private instances in which Colombo explored the interior of the human body. On the different sorts of autopsy practices in the early modern period and the sort of knowledge they were thought to convey see Maria Pia Donato, "Il Normale, Il Patologico e La Sezione Cadaverica in Età Moderna," *Quaderni Storici* 136, 46, no. 1 (April 2011): 75–97; Klestinec, "Practical Experience in Anatomy."

65. Realdo Colombo, *De re anatomica libri XV* (Venice: Ex Typographia Nicolai Bevilacquae, 1559), book 15, p. 262: "De iis quae raro in anatome reperiuntur."

66. Ibid., 262: "Ego vero licet ab ineunte aetate innumera corpora dissecuerim, et ab hinc quindecim annos et amplius complura cadavera Patavii, Pisis, Romaeque in corona frequentis Academiae, tamen haec duntaxat."

67. Ibid.: "nullum genus hominu[m] mihi dissecandum defuisse, nisi mutum hominem ab ortu, quamvis quandoq[ue] anno uno quatuordecim cadavera mihi dissecare co[n]tigerit."

68. Moes and O'Malley, "Realdo Colombo," 512.

69. Klestinec, "Practical Experience in Anatomy," 33–57; idem, *Theaters of Anatomy*.

70. Colombo, *De Re Anatomica*, 266–267: "Lapides autem innumerabiles pene hisce manibus extraxi inventos in renibus colore vario, in pulmonibus, in iecore, in vena portae, ut tuis oculis vidisti Iacobe Bone in Venerabili Egnatio Generali congregationis Iesu vidi etiam lapillos in ureteris in vesica,

in intestino colo, in venis haemorrhoidalibus, atque in umbilico. In bilis quoque vesicula, quod tamen exciderat, varii coloris, variaeque figurae lapillos et in nonnullis complures inveni, vidi abscessum."

71. Ibid.: "Lapides autem innumerabiles pene hisce manibus extraxi . . . vidi abscessum. De abscessibus autem quid attinet dicere?" The last phrase implies that there is little utility in talking about abscesses because they are so common.

72. Dionysius Fernandez Zapic and Candidus de Dalmases, eds., *Fontes Narrativi de S. Ignatio de Loyola*, 761–762.

73. Polanco, "Epistola de Obitu S. Ignatii," 768: "Y aun en esto hubo gran edificación y admiración: que le hallaron el estómago y todas las tripas sin cosa ninguna dentro, y estrechas; de done los peritos desta arte seglares inferian las grandes abstinencias del tiempo pasado, y la grande constancia y fortaleza suya; que en tanta flaquesa tanto trabajaba, y con tan alegre y igual vulto." Curiously, Polanco names several physicians in his account, but Colombo is not among them.

74. Ibid.: "Vióse también el higado que tenia tres piedras; que refieren a la mesma abstinencia; por la qual el higado se endurecio."

75. Pietro Ribadenera, *Vita del P. Ignatio Loiola Fondatore della Religione della Compagnia del Giesu'*, trans. Giovanni Giolito de'Ferrara (Venice: I Gioliti, 1587), 430: "Tale era lo stato della Compagnia, quando Ignatio gia' carico d'anni, intorniato, & oppresso dalle infirmità, afflitto per i tempi travagliosi, e per le nuove calamità della Chiesa, & accesso di desiderio di vedersi con CHRISTO" (capitalization in original).

76. Ignatius of Loyola to Theotonius Braganza, Rome, January 1, 1554, in *Letters of St. Ignatius of Loyola*, ed. and trans. William J. Young (Chicago: Loyola University Press, 1959), 431.

77. Ribadenera, *Vita del P. Ignatio Loiola*, 431: "Erano all'hora in essa [Rome] molti infermi, visitati da' Medici, i quali non facevano caso della infirmità d'Ignatio, per parer loro, che fusse la sua ordinaria, e senza pericolo."

78. Polanco, "Epistola de Obitu S. Ignatii," 769: "que nuestro Padre vivia por milagro mucho tiempo habia; que con tal higado naturalmente no se como se podia vivir, sino que Dios nuestro Señor, por ser entonces necessario para la Compañia, supliendo la falta de los organos corporales, le conservó la vida."

79. Theodore Gerardi, "Fragmentum ex Ephermeridibus Romanis Theodorici Gerardi de Sancti Ignatii Obitu 1556," in *Fontes Narrativi de S. Ignatio de Loyola*, 772–776.

80. Ribadenera, *Vita del P. Ignatio Loiola*, 430–431. These pages discuss Loyola's death but make no mention of his autopsy. Furthermore, the summary of Loyola's deeds produced in the secret consistory for his canonization makes no mention of his body. See Francisco Maria Cardinal de Monte, *Relatio facta in Consistorio Segreto Coram S.D.N. Gregorio Papa XV: A Francisco Maria Episcopo Portuensi S.R.E. Card. A Monte Die xix Ianuarii MDCXXII Super Vita, Sanctitate, actis Canonizationis, & miraculis Beati Ignatii Fundatoris Societatis Iesu* (Lille: Ex Officina Petri de Rache, 1622).

81. The literature on Borromeo is enormous. For some basic biographic information see Michel de Certau, "Carlo Borromeo Santo," in *Dizionario Biografico degli Italiani*, vol. 20 (Rome: Istituto della Enciclopedia Italiana, 1977); R. Po-Chia Hsia, *The World of Catholic Renewal, 1540–1770* (New York: Cambridge University Press, 2005), 111–116; Diarmaid MacCulloch, *The Reformation* (New York: Penguin, 2003), 410–417.

82. Giovanni Baptista Carcano Leone, *Exenterationis Cadaveris Illustrissimi Cardinalis Borrhomaei Mediolani Archiepiscopi* (Milan: Ex Typographia Michaelis Tini, Ad instantiam Petri Tini, 1584), 3: "quo Cadaver Ill[ustrissimis] Cardinalis exenterare, eaque ratione ipsum tractarem, ut a corruptione, quantum fieri possit praeservarem."

83. Nancy Siraisi discusses Leone's treatment of Borromeo's body at length in "Signs and Evidence."

84. Giovanni Botero, *De morte Ill[ustrissi]mi ac Rev[erendissi]mi D. Cardinalis S. Praxedis Epistola ad Illustrissimum, ac Reverndissimum D. Andream Cardinalem Barthorium* (Milan: Michaelis Tini, 1584). The version I consulted can be found at Biblioteca Apostolica Vaticana (BAV), De Luca IV 6607.

85. Botero, 2v of an unpaginated treatise: "cum vero exenteratur, lien, & iecur corrupta & tabida inventa sunt, cor vero praegrande, & integrum; itemque pulmones, adeps autem nullus."

86. John Martin, "Inventing Sincerity, Refashioning Prudence: The Discovery of the Individual in Renaissance Europe," *American Historical Review* 102, no. 5 (December 1997): 1326–1333; Catrien Santig, "*De Affectibus Cordis et Palpitatione:* Secrets of the Heart in Counter-Reformation Italy," in *Cultural Approaches to the History of Medicine,* ed. Willem de Blécourt and Cornelie Usborne (New York: Palgrave Macmillan, 2004), 11–35; Scott Manning Stevens, "Sacred Heart and Secular Brain," in *The Body in Parts: Fantasies of Corporeality in Early Modern Europe,* ed. David Hillman and Carla Mazzio (New York: Routledge, 1997), 263–285; Heather Webb, *The Medieval Heart* (New Haven, CT: Yale University Press, 2010).

87. Luigi Firpo, "Botero, Giovanni," *Dizionario Biografico degli Italiani*, vol. 13 (Rome: Istituto della Enciclopedia Italiana, 1971).

88. Leone, *Exenterationis Cadaveris Illustrissimi Cardinalis Borrhomaei*, 6: "Neque n[on] cor praegrande erat, sicuti quidam in suo epistolo falso esse dixit, qui neque sectioni astitit, neque ab aliis relata recte fortassis intellexit, sed hoc potius animo suo confinxit." Leone clearly explains in this passage that he was motivated to write by the inaccurate letter which was circulating. Although he does not name Botero, it is likely that this was whom he intended, especially since Leone appears to be referencing Botero's phrase of "cor praegrande" to describe Borromeo's heart.

89. Leone, *Exenterationis Cadaveris Illustrissimi*, 6–7: "Cor itaque mediocris fuit magnitudinis et hoc optima ratione, quando sicuti mediocritatem in omnibus servavit (incredible fortassis videbitur) ita et cor mediocre iure esse debuit."

90. Aristotle, *De Partibus Animalium*, trans. William Ogle in *The Works of Aristotle*, vol. 5, ed. J. A. Smith and W. D. Ross (Oxford: Clarendon Press,

1912), 667a, III.4: "When the heart is of large size the animal is timorous, while it is more courageous if the organ be smaller and of moderate bulk . . . for the bulk of the heart is out of all proportion to the animal's heat, which being small is reduced to insignficance in the large space, and thus the blood is made colder than it would otherwise be." Carcano Leone cited Aristotle when discussing the heat of a heart on page 8: "Cum philosophus [Aristotle] in loco praeallegato magnarum adeo operationum causam efficientem reducere videatur in magnum calorem, cum dicat in magno corde calorem exolescere, in exiguo magis contineri."

91. Ibid., 3: "Secanti mihi abdomen a graecis epigastrium dictum nulla mihi sese obtulit pinguedinis nota; quod mirum mihi valde visum est: quando in caeteris, quae secui corporibus qua[m]vis emaciatis semper vestigium aliquod pinguedinis mihi sese obtulerit."

92. Ibid., 3: "ut quatuor manus digitorum invicem appositorum magnitudinem latitudinemve equare conspexerim."

93. On the boundary between the natural and supernatural in this period see my discussion in Chapter 3 as well as Lorraine Daston and Katharine Park, *Wonders and the Order of Nature, 1150–1750* (New York: Zone Books, 2001), 120–128; Lorraine Daston, "Marvelous Facts and Miraculous Evidence in Early Modern Europe," *Critical Inquiry* 18, no. 1 (Autumn 1991): 93–124.

94. Leone, *Exenterationis Cadaveris Illustrissimi*, 4. For a discussion of how contemporaries understood anatomical variation in the human body see Siraisi, "Vesalius and Human Diversity," 287–327. Instead of thinking of anatomy as being normal or abnormal, early modern anatomists thought of a broad spectrum of human diversity as falling under the category of the "natural."

95. Siraisi, "Signs," 363.

96. Ibid., 376; ASV, RP 1681. Although the full process of canonization for Borromeo is in the Biblioteca Ambrosiana, ASV RP 1681 contains a list of the testators in the case and Carcano Leone's name is not among them.

97. ASV, RP, 1681, 59v; Francesco Penia, *Relatio Sommaria della Vita Santita, Miracoli,& Atti della Canonizatione di S. Carlo Borromeo Cardinale del Titolo di Santa Prasede Arcivescovo di Milano Canonizato dalla Santità di N.S. Papa Paolo V* (Rome: Nella Stamperia della Cam[era] Apostolica, 1611), 28–29. This work includes many details of the saint's asceticism; pages 32–34 discuss Borromeo's death and burial, but do not mention Leone or the embalming process.

98. A sign that officials in Rome paid some attention to printed hagiography comes from the numerous cases brought before the Roman Inquisition in which unapproved vitae were denounced. See, for example, Archivio della Congregazione per la Dottrina della Fede (ACDF), Stanza Storica (St. St.) B-4-F, fasc. 6, 8, 10, 12, 20, 23, 24, 25 (each fascicle represents a separate case). These cases taken together with the popularity of Botero and Leone's accounts makes it likely that Peña and other canonization officials in Rome would have known of both accounts.

99. Angelo Turchini, *La fabbrica di un santo: Il processo di canonizzazione di Carlo Borromeo e la Controriforma* (Casale Monferrato: Casa Editrice Marietti, 1984).

100. On the growth of empiricisms around the year 1600 and their acceptance as knowledge-making techniques see Klestinec, "Practical Experience in Anatomy"; Long, *Artisan/Practitioners and the Rise of the New Sciences*, 128–131; Gianna Pomata and Nancy Siraisi, "Introduction," in *Historia: Empiricism and Erudition in Early Modern Europe*, 1–38; Alisha Rankin, *Panaceia's Daughters: Noblewomen as Healers in Early Modern Germany* (Chicago: University of Chicago Press, 2013), 25–60.

101. Romeo de Maio, *Riforme e miti nella Chiesa del Cinquecento* (Naples: Guida Editori, s.r.l., 1973), 257–264; Erin Rowe, "St. Teresa and Olivares: Patron Sainthood, Royal Favorites, and the Politics of Plurality in Seventeenth-Century Spain," *Sixteenth Century Journal* 37, no. 3 (Fall 2006): 721–737. On the conflict between the Spanish monarchy, local authorities, and the papacy surrounding the cult of Teresa, see also Gillian Ahlgren, *Teresa of Avila and the Politics of Sanctity* (Ithaca, NY: Cornell University Press, 1996); Erin K. Rowe, *Saint and Nation: Santiago, Teresa of Avila, and Plural Identities in Early Modern Spain* (University Park: Pennsylvania State University Press, 2011).

102. De Maio, *Riforme e miti nella Chiesa del Cinquecento*, 257.

103. On the importance of the miracle of incorruption to contemporaries, see Chapter 3 below as well as Camporesi, *The Incorruptible Flesh;* John Gager, "Body Symbols and Social Reality," 345–364; Vauchez, *Sainthood in the Later Middle Ages*, 24; Gianna Pomata, "Malpighi and the Holy Body: Medical Experts and Miraculous Evidence in Seventeenth-Century Italy," *Renaissance Studies* 21, no. 4 (2007): 568–586.

104. ASV, RP 3156, unfoliated, estimated ff. 268–269: "reperitque capsam in anteriori parte abruptam, et fere putrefactam [. . .] iacebat corpus incorruptum mira quadam integritate ita flexibile, tactuique suave, ac si vivum esset integrum una cum intestinis eodem modo, quod humatum fuit oleique copiam magnam effundens, ac odorem suavissimum emittens quod a peritissimis medicis aliisque personis spectatis auctoritatis visum tanquam miraculum reputatum et approbatum fuit."

105. Ibid.

106. ASV, RP 3156, unfoliated, estimated f. 712: "Ludovicus Vasquez medicus Civitatis Abulem . . . qui de praedictis testatur, et q[uod] d[ictu]m corpus non fuerat apertum nec unctum balsamo, quia tetigit eius ventrem plenum cum suis intestinis, et cum tanta carne in illis partibus, prout in vita extare poterat et declarat super incorruptione, odore, et liquore, et quia naturali, nisi miraculosa, illud esse non poterat."

107. Ibid.: "et q[uod] pro maiori confirmatione praedictorum diversis vicibus, et horis sine praeventione monialium ingressus fuit monast[eriu]m pro visitandis infirmis, et petiit, et obtinuit sibi ostendi dictum corpus, et praecipue quando maximus calor vigebat, et semper illud vidit eodem modo quo a principio, et erat valde leve, et indicavit illud pondus carnis sanctificatae."

108. Ibid., f. 713:. "de mand[at]o S[anctissi]mi fuit [a]p[er]tum corpus istius servae Dei restitutum Conventui de Alba et ex post facto diversis viribus et t[em]poribus idem corpus fuit visum, et repertum cum eade[m] incorruptione, odore, et liquore et [al]lis qualitatibus superius relatis, et . . . p[raese]nte ep[iscop]o Salamantino cum Medicis, et Notario in eode[m] Conventu Albae fuit discoopertum corpus, et visum, et repertum incorruptum cum o[mn]ibus qualitatibus praedictis, prout deponunt de visu."

109. Ibid., f. 715: "Doctor Christophorus de Medrano Medicus, et Cathedraticus in Civitate Salamantina 23. Testis deponens . . . et diligentia vidit, et tentavit d[ictu]m corpus integrum molle, et tractabile habere uterum, et ventrem, ubera, et mammas pectoris (partes qua citius corrupuntur, et consumuntur in corporibus mortuis) tam integra et plena, ac si Serva Dei viva esset, quod iudicavit pro evidenti miraculo, prout et pro tali habuit levitatem, et paruum pondus ipsius corporis, quod ipse se vidit, et manibus palpavit."

110. Padre Silverio de Santa Teresa, ed., *Procesos de Beatificatión y Canonización de Santa Teresa de Jesus*, vol. 3 (Burgos: Tipografia Burgalesa, 1935), 47–49. In Medrano's original Spanish testimony in these pages, curiously the mention of the womb or uterus is absent: "Y para los dichos efectos con particular cuidado vió y tentó el cuerpo de la dicha Santa, y le hallo entero y tan maravilloso y milagroso, cual nunca vió otro cuerpo; porque demas de estar entero, blando y tratable, tenia su vientre y las ubres de los pechos, que son las partes que mas presto se consumen y corrompen en los cuerpos muertos, tan enteros y llenos, como si fuera viva. Lo cual juzgo este testigo por evidente y claro milagro que Nuestro Señor obraba en aquel cuerpo de aquella su sierva."

111. Peña's name appears as part of the remissorial letters recorded in the Registry of Acts for her canonization, ASV, RP 3156, f. 110.

112. Padre Silverio de Santa Teresa, ed., *Procesos de Beatificatión y Canonización de Santa Teresa de Jesus*, vol. 3, lxix; anonymous, *Relatione della vita, miracoli, et canonizatione della gloriosa Vergine S. Teresa di Giesù fondatrice de' Carmelitani Scalzi* (Rome: l'Herede di Bartolomeo Zannetti, 1622), 37–38, 45–48.

113. Giacomo Bacci, *The Life of Saint Philip Neri, vol. 2,* ed. Frederick Ignatius Antrobus (London: Kegan Paul, Trench, Trubner & Co, 1902), 112–114. Bacci, who was one of Neri's early hagiographers, recounts in detail the incredible enthusiasm shown to the saint. Furthermore, the *avvisi*, or early newspapers, for the city of Rome record the enthusiasm of the people of Rome for Neri after his death. BAV, Urbinati Latini 1063, 362r: "passato ad altra vita il P[ad]re Filippo della chiesa nova . . . et uno de' fondatori de P[ad] ri della Valicella et p[e]r 25 [anni] era in op[inio]ne di santo è stato grandissimo il co[nc]orso del Popolo a baciarli la mano, havendo anco p[re]detta hora della morte sua." See also Chapter 1 for a discussion of devotion to the saints in general and Neri in particular.

114. On the importance of Cesalpino to the development of cardiac anatomy see Frederick A. Willius and Thomas Dry, *A History of the Heart and Circulation* (Philadelphia: Saunders, 1948), 292; Augusto de Ferrari,

"Cesalpino (Caesalpinus), Andrea," in *Dizionario Biografico degli Italiani*, vol. 24 (Rome: Istituto della Enciclopedia Italiana, 1980), 122–125.

115. Andrea Cesalpino, "Testimony for Filippo Neri" (Rome, October 3, 1595), in *Il primo processo per san Filippo Neri, vol. 1*, ed. Nello Vian and Giovanni Incisa della Rocchetta (Vatican City: Biblioteca Apostolica Vaticana, 1957), 235: "esamindando donde venisse questa palpitatione, scoprendoli il petto, lo ritrovai molto esenuato, con un tumore a piè delle costole, nel lato sinistro, vicino al cuore; et al tatto si cognosceva essere le costole innalzate in quel luogo, et, nel tempo della palpitatione, si alzava et abbassava a uso di mantaci."

116. Given Neri's fame and the prestige of the medical practitioners who dissected him, Neri's autopsy has been the subject of a number of article-length studies. See Andretta, "Anatomie du Vénérable," 255–280; Enzo Fagiolo, "La medicina a Roma nel secolo XVI. Malattie e medici di S. Filippo Neri," *Medicina nei secoli arte e scienza* 15, no. 3 (2003): 535–549; Catrien Santig, "De Affectibus Cordis et Palpitatione," 11–35; Siraisi, "Signs and Evidence."

117. Andrea Cesalpino, "Testimony for Filippo Neri" (Rome, October 3, 1595), in *Il primo processo per san Filippo Neri, vol. 1*, 235. Cesalpino testifies here that the autopsy on Neri helped to clarify the unusual palpitations and other physical issues the holy man was having during life.

118. There have been a number of recent studies that have argued that Rome was an important medical center in early modern Italy. See Maria Pia Donato, "La Medicina a Roma Tra Sei e Settecento Una Proposta di Interpretazione," *Roma moderna e contemporanea rivista interdisciplinare di storia* 13 (2005): 99–114; Daniela Mugnai Carrara and Maria Conforti, "L'insegnamento della medicina dall'istituzione delle università al 1550," in *Il Rinascimento Italiano e l'Europa*, vol. 5: *Le Scienze*, ed. Antonio Clericuzio, Germana Ernst, and Maria Conforti (Treviso: Fondazione Cassamarca, Angelo Colla Editore, 2008): 455–478; Silvia de Renzi, "'A Fountain for the Thirsty' and a Bank for the Pope: Charity, Conflicts, and Medical Careers at the Hospital of the Santo Spirito in Seventeenth-Century Rome," in *Health Care and Poor Relief in Counter-Reformation Europe*, ed. Ole Peter Grell, Andrew Cunningham, and Jon Arrizabalaga (New York: Routledge, 1999): 99–130; idem, "Medical Competence, Anatomy and the Polity in Seventeenth-Century Rome," *Renaissance Studies* 21, no. 4 (September 2007): 551–567.

119. Vittori was the principal physician to Pope Gregory XIII and a doctor of the Congregation from 1585. He testifies four times for Neri, in 1595, 1599, 1600, and 1610. In 1613 he published a treatise on Neri's autopsy, *De palpitatione cordis et admirabili fractura costarum beati Philippi Nerii, florentini, Congregationis Oratorii Romae fundatoris*, which is contained in a briefer edition in Vittori's testimonies of 1600 and 1610.

120. Cesalpino was the principal physician of Clement VIII. He produced a treatise on the circulation of the heart and testified three times during Neri's process, in 1595, 1597, and 1599.

121. Porto was the principal physician of Sixtus V. He testified three times for Neri, in 1595, 1597, and 1599. He was also the first doctor to produce a Latin medical treatise in which he discusses Neri's miraculous injuries. This document was dedicated to Federico Borromeo and the original is in the Biblioteca Ambrosiana. A printed version can be found in Luigi Belloni, ed., "L'aneurisma di S. Filippo Neri nella relazione di Antonio Porto," *Rendiconti del Istituto Lombardo di Scienze e lettere*, vol. 53 (1950): 665–690.

122. Silvestri was another principal physician for Gregory XIII. He testified twice for Neri, in 1595 and 1599.

123. Antonio Gallonio, *The Life of Saint Philip Neri*, trans. Jerome Bertram (San Francisco: Ignatius Press, 2005), 210–212. These details also appear in testimony in the canonization process, but Gallonio nicely summarizes the findings.

124. Vian, ed., *Il primo processo per san Filippo Neri, vol.* 2, 219: "Et, nello aprire, si trovò tutti li interiori netti, senza magagna alcuna, et si guardò minutamente al fegato, al polmone, al core et tutti li altri interiori, senza magagna alcuna."

125. Describing the interior of a corpse as "clean" or *netti* during an autopsy seems to have been standard terminology for indicating that the deceased had not been poisoned. See, for example, the forensic inquiry into poisoning which Giovanni Faber describes in a letter to Galileo: "Trovassimo tutti l'interiori netti, senza sospetto alcuno di veleno," in Giovanni Faber, Rome to Galileo, Florence, September 14, 1624, in *Le Opere di Galileo Galilei*, vol. 13, ed. Giuseppe Saragat (Florence: G Barbèra Editore, 1968), 207. The same phrase—"nettissimo"—was used in the case of Urban VII's death (1590), whose reign of only a few short weeks led many to believe that he had been poisoned. See BAV, Urb. Lat. 1058, fol. 500r: "Interiori netti" or "nettissimo" would seem to imply that one had not been poisoned in each of these accounts. This is exactly the phrase that del Bello uses when Neri's body is first opened. On contemporary ideas about the signs of poison in the human body, which largely included damage to the internal organs, see Alessandro Pastore, *Veleno: Credenze, crimini, saperi nell'Italia moderna* (Bologna: Il Mulino, 2010), 161–189; idem, "Casi di venefici tra Cinque e Seicento: teoria medico-legale e pratica penale," in *Paolo Zacchia alle origini della medicina legale 1584–1659*, ed. Alessandro Pastore and Giovanni Rossi (Milan: Franco Angeli, 2008), 249–265.

126. Vian, *Il primo processo per san Filippo Neri, vol.* 2, 219.

127. On the medical doctrine of "signs" and physicians' ability to read them in the early modern period, see Ian Maclean, *Logic, Signs, and Nature in the Renaissance: The Case of Learned Medicine* (New York: Cambridge University Press, 2002); Nancy Siraisi, "Disease and Symptom as Problematic Concepts in Renaissance Medicine," in *Res et Verba in der Renaissance*, ed. Eckhard Kessler and Ian Maclean (Wiesbaden: Harrassowitz Verlag, 2002), 217–240; Claudia Stein, "The Meaning of Signs: Diagnosing the French Pox in Early Modern Augsburg," *Bulletin of the History of Medicine* 80 (2006): 617–648.

128. Gallonio, *Vita Beati P. Philippi Nerii* (1600): 227–229: "Aperta anteriore parte thoracis inventae fuere, mirantibus qui aderant, sinistri lateris costae duae mendosae, ut vocant, fractae: erant hae quarta, & quinta. fractura in anteriore parte pectoris apparebat, ubi costae in cartilaginem desinunt: costae adeo elevate erant . . . quo palpitans cor non lederetur . . . aperto Thorace nullum in praecordiis vitium apparuit. Cor cum inspiceretur, magnum apparuit, & musculosius ultra quam esse soleat: a calore [e]n[im] ob ferventium spirituum vim superfluente ita effectum esse Andreas Caesalpinus, atque Antonius Portus iurati publico testimonio confirmarunt. Vena deinde arteriosa (ut à medicis, aliisque ex astantibus accepi) cuius actio sanguinem ad pulmones ferre, quo ibi attenuatus, cum aere ad sinistrum cordis ventriculum eius nutriendi, refrigerandique causa transferri possit, duplo maior reperta est, quam natura soleat . . . Corde dein, cuius incisa cutis fuit, inspecto, in pericardio, quod veluti capsula illud involuit, Angelo Victorio & Iosepho Zerla testibus, aque nihil repertum fuit."

129. Siraisi, "Signs and Evidence," 374–375; Willius and Dry, *A History of the Heart and Circulation*, 292. As Nancy Siraisi has demonstrated, Angelo Vittori changed his opinion about the existence of pulmonary transit based on the information he found in this case, as it better explained Neri's anatomy. In many ways, Neri was the first famous proof of the circulation of the blood.

130. Gotor, *I Beati*, 225.

131. Luigi Belloni, ed., "L'aneurisma di S. Filippo Neri nella relazione di Antonio Porto." The description here of Neri's body is an expansion of what Porto wrote in a letter to Federico Borromeo in 1595 and is now contained in the Biblioteca Ambrosiana in Milan. Angelo Vittori, *Medica disputatio. De palpitatione cordis: fracturs costarum aliisque affectionibus B. Philippi Neri* (Rome: Ex Typographia Camera Apostolica, 1613).

132. Vittori, *Medicae Consultatioes*, 415–443.

133. That it was included in Neri's canonization process, both in the ordinary and apostolic phase, is evidenced by the numerous medical witnesses, who testify to Neri's miraculous anatomy.

134. *Relatio facta in Consistorio Secreto coram S.D.N. Gregorio Papa XV . . . die XIX Ianuarii MDCXXII super vita, sanctitate, actis canonizationis, & miraculis Beati Francisci Xavier e Societate Iesu* (Rome: apud Haeredes Bartholomaei Zannetti, 1622), 48.

135. Ibid., 48–49.

136. Ibid., 49: "Et quoniam rei miraculum excedebat fidem: de mandato Proregis ab insigni medico corpus inspectum, pertentatumque fuit, & compertum incorruptum, succosum, & molle, integris, ac solidis intestinis."

137. Charlton T. Lewis and Charles Short, "Pertento," in *A New Latin Dictionary*, ed. E. A. Andrews (New York: Harper and Brothers Publishers, 1891), 1358. The best contemporary dictionary, Charles Du Cange's *Glossarium Mediae et Infimae Latinati*, vol. 5 (Paris: Firmin, 1845), does not have a citation for *pertento* or its various conjugations. I thank the anonymous reader of my manuscript for signaling the importance of this word to me.

138. On the meaning *experimentum* in the sixteenth century see Michael McVaugh, "The Experimenta of Arnald of Villanova," *Journal of Medieval and Renaissance Studies* 1 (1971): 107–118; idem, "Two Montpellier Recipe Collections," *Manuscripta* 20, no. 3 (1976): 175–178; Rankin, *Panaceia's Daughters*, 38–40.

139. *Relatio facta in Consistorio Secreto coram S.D.N. Gregorio Papa XV*, 49: "Et quoniam rei miraculum excedebat fidem: de mandato Proregis ab insigni medico corpus inspectum, pertentatumque fuit, & compertum incorruptum, succosum, & molle, integris, ac solidis intestinis."

140. Vittori, *Medicae consultationes*, A3. In this address to the reader, Vittori explains that his judgments on saints found in this volume were produced when consulting for the Rota: "Hic habes, nec omnibus obvia exempla, praecipue, quae Auctor ipse respondit consultus coram sacra Rota Romana de quorundam sanctorum gestis, cum de illorum canonizatione, stricte, ut moris est, ageretur."

141. Vittori, *Medicae consultationes*, 381–445.

142. See also Paolo Zacchia, *Quaestionum medico-legalium tomus posterior quo continentur . . . decisiones Sacrae Rotae Romanae ad praedictas materias spectantes* (Lyons: Ioan. Ant. Hugeutan, 1661). In this volume Zacchia, commonly considered the father of forensic medicine, published forty of the cases which he presented before the Rota, several of which involved canonization proceedings.

143. De Renzi "Witnesses of the Body," 219–242.

144. Vittori, *Medicae Consultationes*, 410: "Statuendum igitur est ex supradictis omnino mirabile, et supra naturae modum excedens, ut ad simplex vulnus dentibus inflictum in eodem cadavere sanguis effluxerit liquidus prout in hominibus vivis vulneratis accidere solet."

145. For a discussion of the boundaries of nature in the early modern world see Chapter 3 as well as Daston and Park, *Wonders and the Order of Nature*, 120–128; Daston, "Marvelous Facts and Miraculous Evidence in Early Modern Europe," 93–124.

146. F. M. Episcopo Portuensis S.R.E Card. A Monte, *Relatio Facta in Consistorio Secreto*, 48–51. Postmortem miracles number 1–4 focus on Xavier's miraculous corpse.

147. ASV, RP 3192, 655r: "ad ecclesia parrochem S[anc]ti Andrea huius d[ict]i oppidi Madriti ubi existit corpus p[raedic]ti Servi Dei Isidori ad ef[fect]um illud visitandi ut in his Remiss[oriali]b[us] huius causa mandatur."

148. ASV, RP 3192, 655r–655v.

149. Ibid., f. 657r: "et pectus et ventrem plenum inapertum [*sic*] et non extractis intestinis, neque inbalsatum quia non est insutum in aliqua parte."

150. Ibid., f. 657r–657v: "corpus quod sic repertum fuit pro ut dictu[m] est, vid[ru]nt, et visita[ve]runt p[raedic]ti Medici et Chyrurgus, illudq[ue] inspexer[un]t et considerarunt magna cu[m] attentione et dilig[enti]a, et mediante juram[en]to quod praestiterunt ad S[anc]tas scripturas et evangelia ac in forma iuris declararunt quod pr[aes]ens corpus quoad structura[m] et compositionem tam partium solidam q[uo]d carnosaru[m] eiusque integritate est miraculosum et super naturam ac extra ordine a natura observatum

erga caetera corpora quae per aliquot annos sine spiritu extiterunt, maxime cum elapsi fuerint pro ut est pubb[licu]m et notorium ac traditio antiqua plusque quadragenti anni."

151. BAV, Stamp. Barb.LL.III.7, *Relatio facta in consistorio Secreto Coram S.D. N. Gregorio Papa XV A Francisco Maria Episcopo Portuensi S.R.E Card. A Monte Die Ianuarii MDC XXII Super Vita, Sanctitate, actis Canonizationis, & miraculis Beati Isidori Agricolae de Matrito*, 15. No printer information appears on this version of the *Relatio facta*, so I have included the location in which I found it at the Vatican Library. Another printed version also records his miraculous incorruption as a miracle: *Relatio facta in consistorio Secreto Coram S.D. N. Gregorio Papa XV A Francisco Maria Episcopo Portuensi S.R.E Card. A Monte Die Ianuarii MDC XXII Super Vita, Sanctitate, actis Canonizationis, & miraculis Beati Isidori Agricolae de Matrito* (Milan: Apud haer. Pacifici Pontii, & Joan. Baptistam Piccaleum, Impressores Archiepiscopales, 1622), 8–9.

152. Pomata, "Observation Rising."

153. The wondrous corpses of these saints appeared in a number of hagiographies produced at the time of their canonizations. See, for example, Anonymous, *Relatione della vita, miracoli, et canonizatione della gloriosa Vergine S. Teresa di Giesù fondatrice de' Carmelitani Scalzi* (Rome: l'Herede di Bartolomeo Zannetti, 1622), 37–38, 45–48; Melchior Ramirez, *Relatione sommaria della vita, santità, miracoli et atti della canonizatione di S. Isidoro Agricola Patrone, e Protettore della villa di Madrid Corte della Maestà Cattolica* (Rome: Alessandro Zannetti, 1622), 25; Mutio Vitelleschi, *Compendio della vita del S.P. Francesco Xaverio della Compagnia di Giesù canonizzato con S. Ignatio fondatore dell'istessa religione dalla Santità di N.S. Gregorio XV* (Rome: l'herede di Bartolomeo Zannetti, 1622), 134–135; Antonio Gallonio, *Vita Beati P. Philippi Nerii florentini Congregationis Oratorii fundatoris* (Rome: Apud Aloysium Zannetum, 1600), 227–229.

CHAPTER 3

This chapter revises and greatly expands the argument presented in my article "Negotiated Sanctity: Incorruption, Community, and Medical Expertise," *Catholic Historical Review* 102, no. 1 (2016): 1–25.

1. Archivio Segreto Vaticano (ASV), Congregazione dei Riti Processus (RP) 2155, fol. 22r: "Item ponit & quod corpus ipsius Beati Gregorii Decimi post lapsem 346 [*sic*] annorum ab eius obitu integrum et incorruptem inspicitur, et suis pontificiis vestibus ornatum in marmoreo eminenti sepulchro suavem emittens odorem, quod in die testificatis eiusdem omnibus fidelibus patet, quod fuit, et est verum publicum et notorium palam." For a discussion of the phases of Gregory's trial and its context see Simon Ditchfield, "How Not to Be a Counter-Reformation Saint: The Attempted Canonization of Pope Gregory X, 1622–45," *Papers of the British School at Rome*, 60 (1992): 379–422.

2. André Vauchez, *Sainthood in the Later Middle Ages*, trans. Jean Birrell (New York: Cambridge University Press, 1997), 427–433. Vauchez observes

that a good-smelling, incorrupt body was a key element of sanctity in the Middle Ages. For a broader work on bodily incorruption in popular culture see Piero Camporesi, *The Incorruptible Flesh: Bodily Mutation and Mortification in Religion and Folklore*, trans. Tania Croft-Murray (New York: Cambridge University Press, 1988).

3. ASV, RP 2155, 43v, 55r, 88r. Canonization officials summoned three medical practitioners who discussed the state of Gregory's body. They defined themselves respectively as "medico fisico," "Dottore di Filosofiae Medicina," and "Dottor' di Filosofia e medicina." Thus, all three were physicians. This would match with canonization judges' preference for physicians in canonization trials, as observed in the last chapter. This preference seems especially pronounced in cases like this one, when the testators needed only to interpret observed evidence and not actually handle the remains.

4. On the divisions of nature see Lorraine Daston and Katharine Park, *Wonders and the Order of Nature, 1150–1750* (New York: Zone Books, 1998), 120–128; Lorraine Daston, "Marvelous Facts and Miraculous Evidence in Early Modern Europe," *Critical Inquiry* 18, no. 1 (Autumn 1991): 93–124. See also the discussion of this topic later in this chapter.

5. ASV, RP 2155, 90v: "Io ho veduto più volte quando ero giovanetto il corpo di questo Beato Pontefice integro e incorrotto con li suoi habiti Pontificii entro il sepolchro marmoreo che sopra ho deposto il quale da poco tempo in qua non mi par cosi integro come ho memoria d'haverlo veduto prima."

6. ASV, RP 2155, 59r: "Io l'ho visto molte volte da cinquant'anni in dietro nel qual tempo detto corpo era molto più intiero, che non è di p[rese]nte o che ciò sia nato per essersi per corto del tempo corrosa la cassa di legno e tavola dove sia posato d[etto] corpo, o perché sia stato toccato con corone, et altro da fedeli come sopra ho deposto, o che il caldo de[i] lumi de quali si sono tenuti le persone che hanno voluto vedere detto corpo o della lampada, che dentro si soleva tenervi accesa, o per altro accidente non per più di presente cosi intiero e solido come prima."

7. Ditchfield, "How Not to Be a Counter-Reformation Saint," 419–422.

8. Ibid., 394–395.

9. See discussion below and in the previous chapter.

10. Aviad M. Kleinberg, *Prophets in Their Own Country* (Chicago: University of Chicago Press, 1992), 4.

11. John Gager, "Body Symbols and Social Reality: Resurrection, Incarnation and Asceticism in Early Christianity," *Religion* 12, no. 4 (1982): 345–364; Vauchez, *Sainthood in the Later Middle Ages*, 427–428. Vauchez notes on these pages that "public opinion was very exacting on this point, and if the corpse of a servant of God did not emit 'the odour of sanctity', the veneration might stop as quickly as it had begun." Romeo de Maio has observed that there was even biblical precedent for incorruption being an important sign of holiness, and both medieval and early modern authors pointed to Psalms 15:10 and Acts 2:27, in the Latin Vulgate, as places where incorruption was indicated as a sign of holiness. See Romeo de Maio, *Riforme e miti nella Chiesa del Cinquecento* (Naples: Guida Editori, s.r.l., 1973), 273.

12. Carlos M.N. Eire, *War Against the Idols* (New York: Cambridge University Press, 1986), 1–2, 312.

13. See discussion of this miracle in the previous chapter.

14. Gianna Pomata, "Malpighi and the Holy Body: Medical Experts and Miraculous Evidence in Seventeenth-Century Italy," *Renaissance Studies* 21, no. 4 (2007): 568–571.

15. Theophilis Raynaudus, *De incorruptione cadaverum, occasione de mortui foeminei corporis post aliquot secula incorrupti, nuper refossi Carpentoracti* (Avignon: ex typographia Iacobi Bramereau, 1665). For more information on Raynaudus see Jean-Pascal Gay, "Théophile Raynaud et le choix de la théologie comme rhétorique en soi," *Histoire, Monde, et Cultures Religieuses* 3, no. 35 (2015): 35–52. I thank Maria Pia Donato for this helpful reference. For a brief biography of Raynaud, see Andrew Steinmetz, *History of the Jesuits*, vol. 3 (London: Richard Bentley, 1848), 565–566.

16. Raynaudus, *De incorruptione cadaverum*, a2v: "multorum sanctorum in pace sepulta corpora, tabe & carie superiora repraesento, in quibus immortalitatis prolusio intra mortis fines ac regnum adeo conspicua micat."

17. Francesco Zuccarone, *Prediche Quaresimali del Padre Francesco Zuccarone della Compagnia di Giesu*, 3rd ed. (Venice: Paolo Baglioni, 1671), 324–325: "sapendo bene ch'i cadaveri de' Giusti, gli son dati in tutela, acciò li vada benificando, negotiando, accrescendo, e che nel giorno poi destinato a rendere I conti, dovrà restituire per un cadavero un corpo vivo, per la putredine le doti gloriose, per un mucchio di polvere, e d'ossa un'animato di perpetua durata."

18. Raynaudus, *De incorruptione cadaverum*, 193: "Sed & Lutheri cadaver quantumvis summa cura conditum, etiam priusquam sepulchro inferretur foetorem emisisse qui ferri non poterat."

19. Jonathan Seitz, "Natural or Supernatural? Witchcraft, Inquisition and Views of Nature at the Dawn of the Scientific Revolution" (Ph.D. diss., University of Wisconsin, Madison, 2006), 82.

20. Vincent Puccini, *The Life of St. Mary Magdalene of Pazzi, A Carmelite Nunn*, trans. anonymous (London: Randal Taylor near Stationers Hall, 1687), 27–28.

21. For a brief overview of the religious tensions in England at this moment see Mark Kishlansky, *A Monarchy Transformed: Britain, 1603–1714* (New York: Penguin Books, 1996), 263–286.

22. Charles H. Parker, "Diseased Bodies, Defiled Souls: Corporality and Religious Difference in the Reformation," *Renaissance Quarterly* 67, no. 4 (Winter 2014): 1265–1266.

23. On Contelori, see Giovanni Camillo Peresio, *Vita di Monsig. Felice Contelori* (Rome, 1684).

24. Felice Contelori, *Tractatus et Praxis De Canonizatione* (Lyons, 1634), 144–145.

25. Ibid., 209.

26. Contelori, *Tractatus*, 145: "& haec putrefactio, & corruptio provenit homini ultra infirmitatem naturae in poenam peccati primi Parentis."

27. Fernando Vidal, "Brains, Bodies, Selves, and Science: Anthropologies of Identity and the Resurrection of the Body," *Critical Inquiry* 28, no. 4 (Summer 2002): 939–940.

28. Caroline Bynum, "Material Continuity, Personal Survival and the Resurrection of the Body: A Scholastic Discussion of Its Medieval and Modern Contexts," *History of Religions* 30, no. 1, The Body (August 1990): 52; idem, *The Resurrection of the Body in Western Christianity, 200–1336* (New York: Columbia University Press, 1995), 154–155; idem, *Christian Materiality: An Essay on Religion in Late Medieval Europe* (New York: Zone Books, 2011), 187–192.

29. Bynum, *The Resurrection*, 200.

30. Ibid., 210.

31. Ibid., 110.

32. Pomata, "Malpighi and the Holy Body," 578–582.

33. Paolo Zacchia, *Quaestionum Medico-Legalium Tomi Tres Edito Nova, a Variis Mendis Purgata, Passimque Interpolata, et Novis Recentiorum Authorum Inventis ac Observationis aucta*, 4.1.1 (Frankfurt: Sumptibus Joannis Baptistae Schonwetteri 1666), 282: "In nonullis ergo miraculis examinandis sacra Rota Romana, ut plenam, & indubitatam veritatem assequatur Medicos interdum accersi iubet, eorumque sententiam exposcit . . . Nos enim, qui Naturae operibus indesinenter insistimus, facile ea, quae ab eius operibus desciscunt, eiusque operandi potentiam exuperant, cognoscere possimus."

34. On Zacchia see below as well as Silvia De Renzi, "Per una biografia di Paolo Zacchia: nuovi documenti e ipotesi di ricerca," in *Paolo Zacchia Alle origini della medicina legale, 1584–1659*, ed. Alessandro Pastore and Giovanni Rossi (Milan: Franco Angeli, 2008), 50–73. Zacchia served as protomedico for the Papal States, was a personal physician to Pope Innocent X, and was a regular expert witness before various Roman tribunals.

35. The most relevant recent literature on the early modern boundaries of nature includes Daston, "Marvelous Facts and Miraculous Evidence in Early Modern Europe"; Daston and Park, *Wonders and the Order of Nature*; Peter Dear, "Miracles, Experiments, and the Ordinary Course of Nature," *Isis* 81, no. 4 (December 1990): 663–683; Peter Harrison, "Miracles, Early Modern Science, and Rational Religion," *Church History* 75, no. 3 (September 2006): 493–510; Andrew Keitt, *Inventing the Sacred: Imposture, Inquisition and the Boundaries of the Supernatural in Golden Age Spain* (Boston: Brill, 2005); Jonathan Seitz, *Witchcraft and the Inquisition in Early Modern Venice* (New York: Cambridge University Press, 2011); Laura A. Smoller, "Defining Boundaries of the Natural in Fifteenth-Century Brittany: The Inquest into the Miracles of Saint Vincent Ferrer (d. 1419)," *Viator* 28 (1997): 333–359; Fernando Vidal, "Miracles, Science, and Testimony in Post-Tridentine Saint-Making," *Science in Context* 20, no. 3 (2007): 481–508. For a discussion of these boundaries by early modern authors that is especially relevant for this essay, see Zacchia, *Quaestionum Medico-Legalium*, 4.1.2, 283–284; Contelori, *Tractatus*, 166–177. Both Zacchia and Contelori put forward the same tripartite

division recognized by modern scholars, but also add further subdivisions to the category of supernatural.

36. Gentilcore, *Healers and Healing in Early Modern Italy*, 188–189.

37. Keitt, *Inventing the Sacred*, 179.

38. On the issue of affected or false sanctity as a preternatural phenomenon, see Valerio Marchetti, "La simulazione di santità nella riflessione medico-legale del sec XVII," in *Finzione e santità tra medioevo ed età moderna,* ed. Gabriella Zarri (Turin: Rosenberg and Sellier, 1991), 202–227; Anne Jacobson Schutte *Aspiring Saints: Pretense of Holiness, Inquisition and Gender in the Republic of Venice, 1618–1750* (Baltimore: Johns Hopkins University Press, 2001), 132–153; Moshe Sluhovsky, *Believe Not Every Spirit: Possession, Mysticism & Discernment in Early Modern Catholicism* (Chicago: University of Chicago Press, 2007).

39. Daston and Park, *Wonders and the Order of Nature*, 120–128.

40. According to the definition by papal physician Paolo Zacchia, who is discussed below. Paolo Zacchia, *Quaestionum Medico-Legalium Tomi*, 4.1.10 (Frankfurt, 1666), cit., 321: "At vera cadaveris incorruptibilitas est inter miracula magnae considerationis, ac Dei omnimodam virtutem requirens."

41. Raynaudus, *De incorruptione cadaverum*, cap. 6, 124–178.

42. Ibid., cap. 7, 195–203.

43. See discussion in the last chapter on the increase in practical knowledge of anatomy and the application of empirical techniques in the understanding of the human body.

44. ASV, RP 2009 (Giacomo della Marca), fol. 446r: "Thoracem sine visceribus invenimus albo mundoque go[s]sipio . . . repletum, gos[s]ipium extricavimus, totumque Thoracem manibus satis iudicavimus, sed praeter illud nihil in ipso invenimus." ASV, RP 762 (Andrea Corsini), fol. 149r.

45. ASV, RP 501, fol. 596r: "et non solum vidi, sed etiam illud manu tetigi ab humero dextro per totum brachium usque ad manum."

46. ASV, RP 3156, unfoliated, estimated fol. 712: "Ludovicus Vasquez medicus Civitatis Abulem . . . qui de praedictis testatur, et q[uod]d[ictu]m corpus non fuerat apertum nec unctum balsamo, quia tetigit eius ventrem plenum cum suis intestinis, et cum tanta carne in illis partibus, prout in vita extare poterat et declarat super incorruptione, odore, et liquore, et quia naturali, nisi miraculosa, illud esse non poterat, et q[uod] pro maiori confirmatione praedictorum diversis vicibus, et horis sine praeventione monialium ingressus fuit monast[eriu]m pro visitandis infirmis, et petiit, et obtinuit sibi ostendi dictum corpus, et praecipue quando maximus calor vigebat, et semper illud vidit eodem modo quo a principio, et erat valde leve, et indicavit illud pondus carnis sanctificatae."

47. ASV, RP 3361, fols. 1516r–1516v: "inspexerunt corpus praefati Beati Ludovici, conspicientes super ab omni parte, et saepius tangentes, viderunt quod totus corpus erat integru[m], et articulatu[m], et quod solum ei deficiebant tres digiti manu sinistri."

48. Charles du Cange, et al., "Inspicio," *Glossarium mediae et infimae latinitatis,* éd. augm. (Niort: L. Favre, 1883–1887), t. 4, col. 381c, http://ducange.enc.sorbonne.fr/INSPICIO.

49. Ibid., fols. 1517r–1517v: "et quod corpus praefati Beati Ludovico manet, et continuo servatum fuit Integrum absque aliqua putrefactione, et absque aliquo signo praecedentis corruptionis no[n] solum in partibus internis et extremis, sed etia[m] in capite, pectore, abdomine."

50. See Chapter 2 for a discussion of sixteenth- and seventeenth-century innovations in medicine.

51. Ian Maclean, *Logic, Signs, and Nature in the Renaissance: The Case of Learned Medicine* (New York: Cambridge University Press, 2002); Nancy Siraisi, "Disease and Symptom as Problematic Concepts in Renaissance Medicine," in *Res et Verba in der Renaissance,* ed. Eckhard Kessler and Ian Maclean (Wiesbaden: Harrassowitz Verlag, 2002), 217–240; Claudia Stein, "The Meaning of Signs: Diagnosing the French Pox in Early Modern Augsburg," *Bulletin of the History of Medicine* 80 (2006): 617–648.

52. Maclean, *Logic, Signs, and Nature,* 126–128; Siraisi, "Disease and Symptom," 224.

53. Anita Guerrini, "Experiments, Causation, and the Uses of Vivisection in the First Half of the Seventeenth Century," *Journal of the History of Biology,* no. 46 (2013): 228; Maria Pia Donato, "Il Normale, Il Patologico e La Sezione Cadaverica in Età Moderna," *Quaderni Storici* 136, 46, no. 1 (April 2011): 75–97.

54. Maclean, *Logic, Signs, and Nature,* 8.

55. Craig Martin, "Interpretation and Utility: The Renaissance Commentary Tradition on Aristotle's Meteorologica IV" (PhD diss., Harvard University, 2002), 148. Martin argues that from the late sixteenth to the early eighteenth centuries book 4 of the *Meteorology* came to be considered a central medical text and the key work on how bodies decay.

56. Paolo Zacchia, *Quaestionum Medico-Legalium Tomus Posterior Quo Continentur Liber Nonus et Decimus Necnon Decisiones Sacrae Rotae Romanae ad Praedictas Materias Spectantes, A D. Lanfranco Zacchia Collectae* (Lyons: Sumptibus Ioan. Ant. Huguetan & Marci-Ant, 1661).

57. On Zacchia see Silvia De Renzi, "Per una biografia di Paolo Zacchia."

58. Zacchia, *Quaestionum Medico-Legalium,* 4.1.10, 318.

59. Ibid., 319.

60. Ibid., 320–321.

61. Ibid., 321: "Cum vero, ut notum est, naturaliter omnia cadavera corrumpantur & putrefiant, sciendum est ad majorem miraculi evidentiam, ut superius dixi, cadaver ex miraculo incorruptum servatum, debere non solum secundum solidiores & sicciores partes tale conservari, etiam secundum moliores & humidiores, & secundum eas, quae magis sunt putrefactioni obnoxiae: & hae quidem ab omni genere putrefactionis immunes sint, oportet."

62. Ibid., 320: "Habitus ipsius cadaveris in causa, est facilioris, aut difficilioris putrefactionis; pinguia, & humiditate multa referta, citissimè corrumpuntur."

63. Ibid., 321: "Observantur igitur aliquando cadavera sese movere, vel secundum partes, vel secundum totum; sanguinem effundere, rubore perfundi maculari & rubris stigmatibus conspergi, calida per longum tempus ab

obitu permanere, et aliquam etiam per se stare. In quibusdam etiam ungues visuntur crescere, seu potius convulsi quidam membrorum motus; quibusdam etiam Penis erigitur, ad multum tempus ita perdurant,quod pluries in his suspenduntur, animadvertitur."

64. Ibid., 322: "Eadem ex causa omnes commaculationes, rubores, livores, stigmata, & his similia, quae in cadaveribus fieri observantur eveniunt . . . sic etiam & sanguinis emissio aliqua ex parte, ut ex ulcere, ex ore, ex naribus, ex vulneribus, cum enim omnis iam naturalis calor evanuerit, & extinctus sit, & cum eo virtutes conciderint, praecipue autem retentiva, iam turgentes humores, luxuriansque putredinem sanguis impetu facto quo quolibet erumpunt. Notandum autem, quod cum haec ex Naturae praescripto fiunt, non longe ab obitu accidere consueverunt, & postridie, aut tertio ad summum die ab obitu comparent, aliter enim si multos post dies evenirent, multo miraculi suspicionem facerent; & idcirco notoriam miraculi evidentia accidit."

65. Ibid., 322–323. Nam foetor semper consequitur putredinem, odor vero contra laudabilem humorum & corporis constitutionem. Imo neque naturalis est odor qualiscunque, qui gratus quoquo modo esse possit, non modo morturoum cadaveribus, sed neque viventibus corporibus quantumcumque perfecta sanitate, & eucrasia fruantur . . . corpora Sanctorum cum caetera foetebat, bene olere ob id creditum est, vi Divinitatis adversus Naturae decreta pugnante. Nec tamen secundum Naturae decreta pugnante. Nec tamen secundum naturam impossibile est, humanum cadaver recens non male olere; at bene olere, inquam ergo, est impossible; quia bonus odore ex calore naturali in cadavere emanare non potest."

66. On the importance of Zacchia's work and its wide circulation in the seventeenth century see Maria Gigliola and Renzo Villata, "Paolo Zacchia, la medicina come sapere globale e la 'sfida' al diritto," in *Paolo Zacchia alle origini della medicina legale 1584–1659, 9–49.*

67. For only some of the most important examples, in which Zacchia was used as the main authority in dealing with a controversy, see ASV, RP 2659, fasc. 7 (debate over miracles for Stanislaus Kostcha); ASV, RP 2574, 967v (Giovanni Maria Lancisi's judgment on Pope Innocent XI's corpse); Benedict XIV, *De Servorum Dei Beatificatione et Beatorum Canonizatione*, Lib. IV (Padua: Typis Seminarii, 1743), Lib. IV, cap. 31 (Pope Benedict XIV's reevaluation of the miracle of incorruption); ASV, RP 3478, 626v–627v (Giovan Battista Morgagni's concerns about Gregorio Barbarigo's body).

68. Zacchia, *Quaestionum Medico-Legalium*, 4.1.10, 320.

69. Vatican City, Archivio della Congregazione per la Dottrina della Fede (ACDF), Stanza Storica (St. St.), C-1-D, b. 1, 20r.

70. Maria Antonietta Visceglia, *Roma papale e Spagna: Diplomatici, nobili e religiosi tra due corti* (Rome: Bulzoni Editore, 2010), 243–244. Visceglia discusses Simon's case as an example of how Spanish interested played out in the Roman Curia.

71. Ibid., 242.

72. Ibid.

73. ACDF, St. ST., C-1-A, fols. 1v–2r.

74. ACDF, St. St., C-1-C, 1118r–1118v, 1122r: "nel medesimo giorno di San Marco, in cui morì il Servo di Dio Don Simo, incominciò la Divina Bontà a manifestare la di lui nascosta santità"; "l'odore della di lui santità [*sic*]."

75. Ibid., fol. 1471 r; ASV, RP 4235, fol. 908r. The experts were Paulo Josephus Leonart and Miguel Tudela, both listed as "Medicinae Doctor." Leonart is also described as being a professor at the University of Valencia (St. St., C-1-A, fol. 40r). It therefore seems likely that both practitioners were physicians.

76. ACDF, St. St. C-1-D, b. 10, 16r: "Pietro Cabesas Spagnuolo . . . venne in Roma a contradire la Causa della Canonizatione del P[adr]e Don Francesco Geronimo Simon."

77. ACDF, St. St. C-1-C, fols. 493r–493v: "havevano portato alla Chiesa, lavatolo con acque di molti odori, colocassero il cadavero dirimpetto ad una finestra, nella quale vi erano le vetrate, con tal disposizione che il Sole riverberasse nella di lui faccia, talche pareva, che gli uscissero li splendori, quandoche non erano altro, che il riflesso del sole."

78. Ibid., fol. 5r.

79. Visceglia, *Roma papale e Spagna*, 242–252.

80. ACDF, St. St. C-1-D, busta 10, 9v: "che il D[otto]r Tudela gli disse, che in salute, et in infirmità haveva visitato il P[adre] Simone, ma già mai haveva trovato in lui segni di santo, prova la falsità di questo Testim[oni]o, perche interrogato il D[otto]r Tudela avanti il vescovo dice il Contrario."

81. ACDF, St. St. C-1-B, 233r: "che uno delli maggiori banditori della di lui santità è stato il d[ett]o Dottor Tudela per compiacere il Popolo."

82. Visceglia, *Roma papale e Spagna*, 242.

83. ACDF, St. St., B-4-C, fasc. 12, 1: "Denuntio facta sub die 6 Julii 1629 in S[ancto] Uf[fici]o Romae a P Generali Cong[regatio]nis Theatinorum, in qua exponit, se recepisse a pluribus Patribus eius Cong[regatio]ni Collegis S. Pauli Neapoli epistolae, in quibus enunciant Funeralia, expositione cadaverii in eminenti feretro, gratiae, et miracula fictitia propalata praecipue a P[ad]re. D. Eustatio de St. Sisto."

84. ACDF, St. St., B-4-C, fasc. 12, fols. 32r–32v.

85. ASV, RP 3638, fol. 123v: "quae reperta fuerunt erant integra, et non corrupta absque ullo genere mali odoris."

86. Ibid.

87. Ibid., fol. 120v. The record describes the bones as "involuta in gausippo." Wrapping it in cotton was likely an attempt to prevent too much moisture from reaching the body and thereby to slow its decay.

88. Ibid., fol. 116v: "ut secreto fiat d[emu]m actum visitandi ne tumulus concitetur et ut concursus populi evitetur."

89. ASV, RP 2574, 899r: "ancor Io, che vi assistei, come Medico presi un pezzo di costa, et in oltre bagnai il fazzoletto nel suo sangue, et hora mi [re] pento di non haverne presa piu perché la Principesse, e le Dame, e Personaggi anche stranieri con lettera havendomi fatto piu volte Instanza d'havere qualche reliquia di questo servo di Dio, non ho potuto consolar tutti, per non restar Io totalm[ent]e privo."

90. ASV, RP 220, 157r.

91. ASV, RP 811, 247r: "Io ho devotione a questa Beata particolarmente doppo haver veduto operare a sua intercessione un miracolo nella Persona del sudetto Fra Tomaso consistente nella sua miracolosa sanatione da detta sua infermità desidero la sua canonizatione ma io non faccio parti da Procuratore."

92. ASV, RP 3528, 106v: "Questo corpo . . . è un scheletro molto consumato."

93. Ibid., 107r: "Tutto questo Corpo scheletro è stato messo insieme et alligato parte con filo d'argento, et parte con tela et colla, ma con puoco [sic] giudizio dell'arte; Dal ch' ne nasce una deformità dello scheletro assai grande."

94. Gio. Battista Maffei, *Vita di S. Lorenzo Giustiniano Primo Patriarca di Venetia* (Rome, 1690), 57.

95. Ibid., 58.

96. See, for example, Tiepolo's efforts surrounding the incorruption of Giustiniani's corpse: ASV., RP 3528., fols. 105r–107v.

97. Ibid., fol. 105v.

98. Benedict XIV, *De servorum Dei beatificatione et beatorum canonizatione liber tertius* (Bologna, 1737), 426, 588. Silvia de Renzi has noted that the physician Giulio Mancini only received 9 scudi for three months salary at one point in his career. However, a physician at the Santo Spirito Hospital in Rome would enjoy a salary of 100 scudi per year in the seventeenth century. Silvia de Renzi, "Medical Competence, Anatomy and the Polity in Seventeenth-century Rome," *Renaissance Studies* 21, no. 4 (September 2007): 551–567, here 558; idem, "'A Fountain for the Thirsty' and a Bank for the Pope: Charity, Conflicts, and Medical Careers at the Hospital of Santo Spirito in Seventeenth-Century Rome," in *Health Care and Poor Relief in Counter-Reformation Europe*, ed. Ole Peter Grell and Andrew Cunningham (New York: Routledge , 1999), 99–130, here 110.

99. Pomata, *Contracting a Cure*, 140–171.

100. Pompeo Molmenti, *Venice: Its Individual Growth from the Earliest Beginnings to the Fall of the Republic*, vol. 6, trans. Horatio F. Brown (Chicago: A. C. Mclurg, 1908), 155.

101. ASV, RP 1575, 493r–493v.

102. Ibid., 493v: "In Civitate Limana die 27. Mensis marti 1632. D[ict]i Domini judices Apostolici dixerunt quod cum Doctor Melchior de Amusgo Protomedicus qui erat nominatus ad . . . visitationi facendae hodie d[ict]o die . . . egrotat et sic impeditus vacare non potest ad hunc effectum nominabant et nominarunt Doctorem Joannem de Tesseda Medicum qui vice illius intersit huiusmodi visitationi cum suius Dominationibus et subscripserunt "

103. Ibid., 497r: "venerunt ad Conventum S[anct]i Dominici in prosecutionem visitationis facendae corporis et ossarum ac sepoltam d[ict]a serva dei et in praesentiam Patris Magistri fratris Sabricilis de Zarate provincialis d[ict]i Ordinis ac Doctorum Joannis de Tesseda ac Joannis de Vega Medicorum necnon Segretariorum [sic] Joannis de Valenzuela et Bartolomei de diurico ac Alosii de Molina Cirurghi quia non fuit repertus Petrus di Villa Real nominata."

182   Notes to Chapter 3

104. In Amusco's case this is particularly plausible since he died the following year. Perhaps he was already suffering from the ailment which would eventually kill him? On the dates of Amusco's tenure as protomedico see Abraham Zavala Batlle, "El Protomedicato en el Perú," *Acta médica peruana* 27, no. 2 (2010): 153.

105. According to the Ordinary Process for her canonization, Rose of Lima's body was thought to wondrously resist rot from the time of her death onward. See ASV, RP 1571, fol. 11r–11v.

106 ASV, RP 1575, fol. 499v: "dixit che questo testimonio si trovo nella detta visita con li detti sig[no]ri giudici per esser stato nominato a questo effetto hieri 27 di questo mese e vidde tutti li ossi principali e la testa della benedetta Rosa li quali erano separati e divisi l'uno dal altro et in alcuni la carne secca e consumata da i quali e dalla cassa dove stavano esalava et usciva un odore suave simile a quello delle Rose secche molto diverso di quello che sogliono havere i cadaveri in simile stato."

107. ASV, RP 1575, fol. 499r: "dixit che questo Testimonio fu nominato per trovarsi presente nella visita degli ossi della detta serva di Dio nella quale si trovo hieri 27 di questo mese e ch' quel che vidde et intese e che tutti li ossi principali e la testa de Corpo della detta benedetta Rosa ch'erano divisi e s[e]parati l'uno dall'altro et alcuni con la carne seca e consumata dalli quali e dalla cassa di legname nella quale si trov[a]rono usciva un odore soave simile alle Rosse secche e molto diverso di quello che sogliono havere i corpi defunti in simile stato." Such similarity in testimony is unusual as I have not found this level of agreement in any other medical examination of a holy individual in this period.

108. Mar Rey Bueno, "*Concordias Medicinales de Entramos Mundos: El Proyecto Sobre Materia Médica Peruana de Matías d Porres (Fl. 1621),*" *Revista de Indias* 66, no. 237 (2006): 351–352; John Tate Lanning, *The Royal Protomedicato: The Regulation of the Medical Professionals in the Spanish Empire,* ed. John Jay TePaske (Durham, NC: Duke University Press, 1985), 48–49.

109. Lanning, *The Royal Protomedicato,* 49.

110. Batlle, "El Protomedicato en el Perú," 153.

111. For a longer consideration of this case please see Bradford Bouley, "Contested Cases: Medical Evidence, Popular Opinion, and the Miraculous Body," in *Médecine et religion: Collaborations, compétitions, conflits (XIIe-XXe siècles),* ed. Maria Pia Donato et al. (Rome, 2013), 139–162.

112. On Vallisneri see Dario Generali, ed., *Antonio Vallisneri: La figura, il contesto, le immagini storiografiche* (Florence, 2008); idem, *Antonio Vallisneri: Gli anni della formazione e le prime ricerche* (Florence, 2007); Ivano Lombardi, *Un nume del Settecento: Antonio Vallisneri* (Lucca, 1998).

113. On Morgagni, see Valentina Gazzaniga and Elio de Angelis., eds., *Giovan Battista Morgagni, Perizie medico-legali* (Rome, 2000).

114. ASV, RP 3478, fols. 619r–629r.

115. ASV, RP 3478, fols. 619v–620r.

116. Ibid., 620r: "Et statim DD[icti] Judices quemlibet ex dictis Peritis separatim monuerunt, ut infra triduum, nempe die sabbati, quae erit 20 me[n]

s[is] Decembris curren[tis] facta per eos magis matura reflexione, et ponderatione referant, et unusquisque eorum referat in scriptis quid sibi videatur de statu dicti ven[erabi]lis Corporis, et in specie an dici possit incorruptum, et in statu miraculoso. Qui Periti se promptos, ac paratos exhibaerunt satisfaciendum infra tempus praedictum omne sibi imposito, et referendum suam opinionem in scriptis."

117. Vallisneri to Muratori, Padova, December 19, 1727, in *Carteggi con Ubaldini . . . . Vannoni, Nazionale del Carteggio di L. A. Muratori, vol. 44*, ed. Michela L. Nichetti Spanio (Florence, 1978), Letter 225, p. 311: "A me toccò dare il duro giudizio, perché erano preoccupati dal miracolo, ma per dire il vero non lo trovammo in troppo buono stato, onde mi riserbai di porre il mio parere in iscritto, in cui anderò cautissimo e fedele, perché mi fecero giurare colle mani sopra l'Evangelo di dire la verità, altrimenti, come spergiuro sarei scomunicato, non potendomi assolvere se non il Pontefice, o un penitenziere in articulo mortis, onde immaginate se voglio dir menzonge adulatrici. Non è mica menzogna, né sarà mai s'io dico che sono." I thank Paula Findlen for bringing this collection of letters to my attention.

118. Muratori to Vallisneri, Modena, January 2, 1728, in ibid., Letter 226, p. 312: "Brutto cimento che è quello a cui vi veggo esposto (e n'ho dispiacere) per la ricognizione del cadavere del fu venerabile card. Barbarigo; perché dire la verità è necessario' e pure gli avvisi di Mantova già stampati mettono voi, e il sig. Morgagni come autentici testimoni della sopranaturale incorruttibilità, e il dire diversamente sarà odioso costì. A me è noto che la spezieria aiutò. In sì fatto labirinto starò a vedere come saprete condurvi." Although Muratori is writing back to Vallisneri after Vallisneri had already submitted his report, it seems likely that the *avvisi* were circulating before Vallisneri gave his final verdict on Barbarigo. After all, Vallisneri initially wrote to Muratori on December 19 and Muratori wrote back on January 2. In the period between many printers would have closed for various Christmas holidays. Also, Muratori was not in Mantua and so would have only seen the *avvisi* after they had been in circulation for at least a few days. I figure, therefore, that for Muratori to have seen the *avvisi* and write about them by January 2, they must have been printed at about the same time or before Vallisneri visited Barbarigo's tomb.

119. ASV, RP 3478, fols. 624v–625v.

120. Ibid., fol. 625v: "Haec omnia mihi diligenter, ac singillatim perpendenti admiranda sane visa sunt. Utrum tamen ad haec prestanda miraculum supra naturae ordinem intercesserit, nec ingenii, nec facultatis meae est definire."

121. Vallisneri to Muratori, Padova, January 17, 1728, in *Carteggi con Ubaldini*, letter 227, p. 313: "Sono stato al certo in pensiero molto, ma finalmente parmi d'essermi riuscito di liberarmi dagli imbrogli con destrezza. Sua Eminenza è restato sodisfatto, e tanto a me basto."

122. Ibid.: "Né io, né il sig. Morgagni abbiamo mai detto della sopranaturale incorruttibilità, ma solo dicemmo che vi era del *mirabile*, ch'è ne'confini del miracolo, ma non è miracolo, a chi ben intende."

123. Antonio Vallisneri to Ludovico Antonio Muratori, Padova, May 6, 1726, in *Carteggi*, Letter 200, 289–290: "Una cosa sola mi dispiace, che può far dire gli eretici de'quali ne sono continuamente in Padova, ed è che tutti, o quasi tutti, per farlo veder santo, alludono all'incorruttibilità del corpo . . . quando nella spezieria dello Scarella mostrano la ricetta de'balsami co'quali fu imbalsamato, e vi è gente ancor viva che era presente quando l'imbalsamarono, e tutta Padova il confessa, e lo dice. Questo è pure un manifestamente imporre, e dar campo agli eretici che si burlino, e si faccian beffe delle vite, e de'miracoli de' nostri Santi."

124. Rome, Biblioteca Lancisiana, Fondo Lancisi, MS. 262, p. 632: "mando a V[ostro] S[ignore] Ill[ustrissi]mo il mio Libricciuolo . . . vi troverà da per tutto seminato un libero, e filosofico ardimento particolarmento contro i Franzesi [*sic*], che si poco stimano noi altri Italiani."

125. Ibid.: "Oh se sentise quante favole ha detto il volgo! Che gli avevo fatto cavar sangue, e che saltò fuora dalle vene, come se fosse stato vivo, altri che gli aveo tagliato un braccio e che corse il sangue vivo, altri ch'era incorrotto e pareva che dormisse, quando era tutto nero e faceva quasi paura."

126. ASV, RP 3478, 624 r.: "Observatum leviter dexterum brachium flexile cedensque, mortui recetnis ad instar apparvuit."

127. Zacchia, *Quaestionum Medico-Legalium*, 6.3.1, p. 496.: "dicamus cum Aristotele, honorem esse exhibitionem reverentiae in virtutis testimonium: vel dicamus quod honor est significatio quaedam excellentiae virtutis per actus civiles."

128. Steven J. Harris, "Confession-Building, Long-Distance Networks, and the Organization of Jesuit Science," *Early Science and Medicine* 1, no. 3 (October 1996): 287–318, here 288.

129. Steven Shapin, *A Social History of Truth: Civility and Science in Seventeenth-Century England* (Chicago: University of Chicago Press, 1985), 42–63.

130. Pomata, "Malpighi and the Holy Body," 585. Pomata makes a similar observation to what I have concluded here, stating that the physicians in the case she examined must have had a sort of "double vision" in which they saw the body in both a spiritual and a medical light.

CHAPTER 4

1. Agostino Paravicini-Bagliani, *The Pope's Body*, trans. David S. Peterson (Chicago: University of Chicago Press, 2000), 134–143; Maria Antonietta Visceglia, *Morte e elezione del papa: norme, riti e conflitti, L'Età moderna* (Rome: Viella, 2013), 40–47. Although the practice began in the late Middle Ages, Visceglia notes that opening papal bodies only became routine in the sixteenth century, starting with Julius II (d. 1513). Prior to that such procedures had been more ad hoc.

2. Io Francisco Marenco Albensi, "De Pii V. Pont. Max. morbo, quo obiit," in *Degli Archiatri Pontifici,* ed. Gaetano Marini (Rome: Stamperia Pagliarini, 1784), 319: "et inter mingendum in pectine et toto pene dolebat vehementer, praesertimque in eius summo, nec solum dum mingeret ita torquebatur, sed etiam post mictionem."

3. Ibid., 321.

4. Ibid.

5. Ibid.: "Cum autem diem suum obierit tunc exenteratus fuit, ac dissecta vesica inventi sunt tres lapides pari magnitudine, colore, duritie, ac figura, siquidem erant circulari, planaque figura, magnitudine quantum pollice, ac indice digitus complecti posset, colore subnigro, ac levi superficie, qualis est in b[e]zoar lapide vocato, duritie marmoris."

6. Elisa Andretta, "Medici e pubblico al capezzale dei papi. Gian Francesco Marengo, "Michele Mercati e la narrazione della morte del pontefice," in *Pubblico e pubblici di antico regime,* ed. Benedetta Borello (Pisa: Pacini, 2009): 73–100; idem, *Roma medica: Anatomie d'un système medical au XVIe siècle* (Rome: École Française de Rome, 2011), 275–276; Richard Palmer, "Medicine at the Papal Court in the Sixteenth Century," in *Medicine in the Courts of Europe, 1500–1837,* ed. Vivian Nutton (New York: Routledge, 1990): 49–78. Palmer and Andretta have emphasized the insecurity of the office of papal *archiater,* but also the desirability and potential profitability of that office.

7. See discussion of the bodies of Carlo Borromeo and Ignatius of Loyola in Chapter 2.

8. Marengo, "Michele Mercati e la narrazione della morte del pontefice," 322: "nam cum esset annorum quinquaginta degeretque in Coenobiis Dominici Ordinis, calidus erat temperatura, et gracilissimus, et longa itinera pedibus obibat, famem ac sitim perferebat diutius, multis jejuniis, victuque tenui corpus exsiccabat, quaproper circiter ea tempora mihi probabile est genitos fuisse lapides."

9. André Vauchez, *Sainthood in the Later Middle Ages,* trans. Jean Birrell (New York: Cambridge University Press, 1997), 300–301.

10. Giuseppe Alberigo, "Carlo Borromeo come modello di vescovi nella chiesa post-tridentina," *Rivista storica italiana* 79 (1967): 1031–1052; Joseph Bergin, "The Counter-Reformation Church and its Bishops," *Past and Present* 165 (November 1999): 30–73; Mario Rosa, "L'immagine del vescovo nel seicento," *Ricerche di storia sociale e religiosa* 46 (1994): 49–59. Certainly scholars have uncovered that in a number of places the reforms required in the Decrees of the Council Trent were not uniformly applied and probably the majority of bishops did not act any more saintly or rigorous than their predecessors. Yet the idea that they should be better educated and more pious was emplaced and did seem to gain traction by the seventeenth century.

11. On the introduction of new empirical techniques to medicine and the rising prestige of anatomy in the sixteenth and seventeenth centuries, see Chapters 1 and 2 of the present volume.

12. Paolo Alessandro Maffei, *Vita di S. Pio Quinto Sommo Pontefice, dell'Ordine de' Predicatori* (Venice: Giacomo Tommasini, 1712), 272, 357.

13. Kerstin Aspegren, *The Male Woman: A Feminine Ideal in the Early Church,* ed. René Kieffer (Stockholm: Almqvist & Wiskell International, 1990), 14; Peter Brown, *The Body and Society: Men, Women, and Sexual Renunciation in Early Christianity* (New York: Columbia University Press, 1988), 223; Conrad Leyser, *Authority and Asceticism from Augustine to*

Gregory the Great (Oxford: Clarendon Press, 2000), 167; Teresa M. Shaw, *The Burden of the Flesh: Fasting and Sexuality in Early Christianity* (Minneapolis: Fortress Press, 1998), 9, 25, 174–181.

14. Leyser, *Authority and Asceticism from Augustine to Gregory the Great*, 33; Philip Rousseau, *Ascetics, Authority and the Church in the Age of Jerome and Cassian*, 2nd ed. (Notre Dame, IN: University of Notre Dame Press, 2010), 9–11.

15. Rousseau, *Ascetics, Authority and the Church*, 125–131.

16. Peter Brown, *Augustine of Hippo: A Biography, A New Edition with Epilogue* (Berkeley: University of California Press, 2000), 207–221, 340–353; Leyser, *Authority and Asceticism from Augustine to Gregory the Great*, 3–32. The literature on Augustine and late antique theology is vast. These two authors provide a brief overview and indicate other resources on the subject.

17. Leyser, *Authority and Asceticism from Augustine to Gregory the Great*, 131–188.

18. Donald Weinstein and Rudolph Bell, *Saints and Society: The Two Worlds of Western Christendom, 1000–1700* (Chicago: University of Chicago Press, 1982), 220.

19. Caroline Bynum, *Holy Feast and Holy Fast: The Religious Significance of Food to Medieval Women* (Berkeley: University of California Press, 1987), 94–112; Weinstein and Bell, *Saints and Society*, 233–235.

20. Although there have been now numerous studies on late medieval female sanctity, the two best known are Rudolph M. Bell, *Holy Anorexia* (Chicago: University of Chicago Press, 1987); Bynum, *Holy Feast, Holy Fast*. Several recent scholars have questioned to what extent this was an active choice on the part of women to portray their sanctity this way. Rather, they have pointed out that lives of medieval female saints were almost always written by male hagiographers and so the description may be more a male view of female sanctity than a representation of how the women actually wanted to portray themselves. On this see Catherine Mooney, *Gendered Voices: Medieval Saints and Their Interpreters* (Philadelphia: University of Pennsylvania Press, 1999); Amy Hollywood, *The Soul as Virgin Wife: Mechthild of Magdeburg, Marguerite Porete, and Meister Eckhart* (Notre Dame, IN: University of Notre Dame Press, 1995), 36–38.

21. Dyan Elliott, *Fallen Bodies: Pollution, Sexuality, and Demonology in the Middle Ages* (Philadelphia: University of Pennsylvania Press, 1999); idem, "The Physiology of Rapture and Female Spirituality," in *Medieval Theology and the Natural Body*, ed. Peter Biller and A. J. Minnis (York: York Medieval Press, 1997), 141–175; Ian Maclean, *The Renaissance Notion of Woman* (New York: Cambridge University Press, 1980), 6–46.

22. Nancy Caciola, *Discerning Spirits: Divine and Demonic Possession in the Middle Ages* (Ithaca, NY: Cornell University Press, 2003), 274–320; Dyan Elliott, *Proving Woman: Female Spirituality and Inquisitional Culture in the Later Middle Ages* (Princeton, NJ: Princeton University Press, 2004); 233–296; André Vauchez, "La nascita del sospetto," in *Finzione e*

santità tra medioevo ed età moderna, ed. Gabriella Zari (Rurin: Rosenberg and Sellier, 1991), 39–51.

23. Although there were not necessarily more women than men charged with false or affected sanctity, theologians seem to have expressed greater concern about the ability of women to deceive and their susceptibility to demonic deception. See Jean-Michel Sallmann, "Esiste una falsa santità maschile?" in *Finzione e santità tra medioevo ed età moderna,* ed. Gabriella Zarri (Turin: Rosenberg and Sellier, 1991), 119–128; Anne Jacobson Schutte, *Aspiring Saints: Pretense of Holiness, Inquisition and Gender in the Republic of Venice, 1618–1750* (Baltimore: Johns Hopkins University Press, 2001), 42–60.

24. Katharine Park, *Secrets of Women: Gender, Generation and the Origins of Human Dissection* (New York: Zone Books, 2006), 39–76.

25. Heiko A. Oberman, *Luther: Man Between God and the Devil,* trans. Eileen Walliser-Schwarzbart (New York: Image Books, 1992), 77–78, 125–129.

26. George Yule, "Luther and the Ascetic Life," in *Monks, Hermits, and the Ascetic Tradition,* ed. W. J. Sheils (Padstow: Blackwell, 1985), 229.

27. Angelo Rocca, *De Canonizatione Sanctorum* (Rome: Ex Typographia Rev. Cam. Aposrolica, 1610), cap. 8, 12–13. Rocca, who wrote one of the first comprehensive canonization manuals following the Reformation, presented in this section the requirements for canonization "Quaenam in eo, qui canonizandus est, requirantur." Among these requirements he included certain aspects of asceticism "castitatem, sobrietatem, & abstinentiam," but warned canonization officials about trusting appearances "Vitae sanctimonia potest esse simulata & ficta, cuiusmodi vita Hypocritatum est." On the importance of Rocca's work for the period, see Simon Ditchfield, "How Not to Be a Counter-Reformation Saint: The Attempted Canonization of Pope Gregory X, 1622–45," *Papers of the British School at Rome 60* (1992): 380–381.

28. There has been a wealth of recent literature on this topic, but see in particular Andrew Keitt, *Inventing the Sacred: Imposture, Inquisition and the Boundaries of the Supernatural in Golden Age Spain* (Boston: Brill, 2005); idem, "The Miraculous Body of Evidence: Visionary Experience, Medical Discourse, and the Inquisition in Seventeenth-Century Spain," *Sixteenth Century Journal 6/1* (2005): 77–96; Adriano Prosperi, *Tribunali della coscienza: inquistori, confessori missionari* (Turin: Einaudi, 1996), 431–464; Schutte *Aspiring Saints;* idem, "Pretense of Holiness in Italy: Investigations and Persecutions (1581–1876),"*Rivista di Storia e Letteratura Religiosa* 27, no. 2 (2001): 299–321; Moshe Sluhovsky, *Believe Not Every Spirit: Possession, Mysticism & Discernment in Early Modern Catholicism* (Chicago: University of Chicago Press, 2007); Zarri, ed., *Finzione e santità tra medioevo ed età moderna.*

29. Romeo de Maio, *Riforme e miti nella Chiesa del Cinquecento* (Naples: Guida, 1973), 257.

30. Ibid., 258–264.

31. Ibid., 266–271.

32. Schutte, *Aspiring Saints*, 138–143.

33. Prosperi, *Tribunali*, 431–440. I am thinking here not just of Luther, but also of Bernardino Ochino and Peter Martyr Vermigli's flights to Protestantism in 1542.

34. Felice Contelori, *Tractatus et Praxis De Canonizatione* (Lyons: Laurentii Durant, 1634), cap. 10, 105: "Quarto, quia Ecclesia utitur in canonizatione testimonio humano, per testes enim inquirit de vita, & miraculis canonizandi . . . quod testimonium est fallible."

35. Ibid., 106: "Quae vulgo affertur: *Multa corpora Sanctorum venerantur in teris, quorum animae cruciantur in tormentis*" (emphasis in the original).

36. Ibid., 114: "quod Summus Pontifex in canonizatione Sanctorum non innititur solum testimoniis hominum, sed divinae promissioni, qua Christus pro Petro rogavit."

37. The main canonization officials stressing the need for medical expertise in verifying saintliness were Francisco Peña (discussed in Chapter 2) and Felice Contelori (Chapter 3). In addition to these authors, several inquisition or exorcism manuals also advise seeking medical advice in determining whether an unusual illness might be supernatural. These include Giorgio Polacco, *Pratiche per discerner lo spirito buono dal maluagio, e per conoscer gl'indemoniati, e maleficiati* (Bologna: Carlo Zenero, 1638), 118–119, on the need to bring in doctors to discern spirits. Candido Brognolo, *Alexiacon Hoc Est Opus de Maleficiis ac Morbis Maleficis Duobus Tomis Distributum* (Venice: Typis Io: Baptistae Catanei, 1668), 2. In this work, Brognolo calls upon medical doctors and exorcists to work together; Eliseo Masini, *Sacro arsenale ovvero pratica dell'uffizio della santa inquisizione* (Rome: S. Michele a Ripa, 1730), 298. Masini recommends in these pages that inquisitors consult with physicians when they suspect bewitchment.

38. On the boundaries between natural, preternatural, and supernatural phenomena please see discussion in Chapter 3.

39. Gianna Pomata, "Observation Rising: Birth of an Epistemic Genre, 1500–1650," in *Histories of Scientific Observation*, ed. Lorraine Daston and Elizabeth Lunbeck (Chicago: University of Chicago Press, 2011), 45–80. On the growth of case histories in medicine in this period see Gianna Pomata, "*Praxis Historialis:* The Uses of *Historia* in Early Modern Medicine," in *Historia: Empiricism and Erudition in Early Modern Europe*, ed. Gianna Pomata and Nancy Siraisi (Cambridge, MA: MIT Press, 2005), 105–146; Nancy Siraisi, "'Remarkable' Diseases, 'Remarkable' Cures, and Personal Experience in Renaissance Medical Texts," in *Medicine and the Italian Universities 1250–1600* (Boston: Brill, 2001), 226–252. See also Chapter 2 of the present volume for a discussion of the medical and religious synthesis that *observationes* allowed in dealing with holy bodies.

40. Marcello Donato, *De Medica Historia Mirabili Libri Sex* (Mantua: Per Franciscum Osanam Donati, 1586); Paulus Lentulus, *Historia Admiranda, de Prodigiosa Apolloniae Schreierae, Virginis in Agro Bernensi, Inedia* (Bern: Ioannes Le Preux, 1604); Fortunio Liceti, *De his qui diu vivunt sine alimento libri quatuor* (Padua: Pietro Bertelli, 1612). Anne Schutte also

discusses at greater length some of the case histories and arguments found in these volumes; see Schutte, *Aspiring Saints*, 139–142.

41. Paolo Zacchia, *Quaestionum Medico-Legalium Tomi Tres Edito Nova, a Variis Mendis Purgata, Passimque Interpolata, et Novis Recentiorum Authorum Inventis ac Observationis* (Frankfurt: Sumptibus Joannis Baptistae Schonwetteri, 1666), Lib. II, Tit. I, Quaest. XVIII (on Lymphatics, Demoniacs, Ecstatics, etc.), Lib. IV, Tit. I, Quaest. VI (on fake ecstasies and raptures), Lib. IV, Tit. I, Quaest. VII (on unusually long fasts), Lib. VII, Tit. IV, Quaest. I (on stigmata), as well as other sections in book IV on miracles. See also Elena Brambilla, "Patologie miracolose e diaboliche nelle Quaestiones medico-legales di Paolo Zacchia," in *Paolo Zacchia alle Origini della medicina legale 1584–1659,* ed. Alessandro Pastore e Giovanni Rossi (Milan: Franco Angelli, 2008), 138–162.

42. Paulo Zacchia, *Quaestiones Medico-Legales* (Avignon: Ex Typographia Johannes Piot, Sancti Offici Typographi, 1657), Lib. IV, Tit. I, Quaest. VII: De longo Iejunio, 215: "Est ergo, ut ad rem veniamus, varius hic terminus tolerandi jejunium in homine, quam varietatem faciunt temperamenta, aetates, regiones, anni tempora, consuetudo, et alia nonnulla."

43. James J. Bono, *The Word of God and the Languages of Man* (Madison: University of Wisconsin Press, 1995), 98–102; Lois N. Magner, *A History of Medicine* (New York: Taylor and Francis, 2005), 125–127; Sidney Ochs, *A History of Nerve Functions: From Animal Spirits to Molecular Mechanisms* (New York: Cambridge University Press, 2004), 24–26. Nancy Siraisi, *Medieval and Early Renaissance Medicine: An Introduction to Knowledge and Practice* (Chicago: University of Chicago Press, 1990), 97–106.

44. Siraisi, *Medieval and Early Renaissance Medicine*, 9, 101–137.

45. On the endurance of this system even late into the seventeenth century, see Owsei Temkin, *Galenism: Rise and Decline of a Medical Philosophy* (Ithaca, NY: Cornell University Press, 1973), 152–161. For a good overview of Paracelsus and iatrochemistry in this period see Allen G. Debus, *The Chemical Philosophy: Paracelsian Science and Medicine in the Sixteenth and Seventeenth Centuries* (Mineola, NY: Dover, 2002).

46. On medical ideas about the range of natural variation in the human body see Maria Pia Donato, "Il Normale, Il Patologico e La Sezione Cadaverica in Età Moderna," *Quaderni Storici* 136, 46, no. 1 (April 2011): 75–97; Nancy Siraisi, "Vesalius and Human Diversity in *De humani corporis fabrica*," in *Medicine and the Italian Universities*, 287–327.

47. N.F.J. Eloy, *Dictionnaire historique de la médecine ancienne et moderne*, vol. 3 (Paris: Chez H. Hoyois, 1778), 158.

48. Marcello Donati, *De Medica Historia Mirabili*, 215v: "Sic enim senes facile ieiunium ferunt test Hip. Aff. 12.1 lib eo quod illis calor minor et languidor insit . . . is parum appetet et facile paucis vel nullis alimentis transiget."

49. Zacchia, *Quaestiones Medico-Legales* (1657), 221: "Primo enim calor nativus non acer, nec validus, sed debilis fit oportet saltem respectu copiae et qualitatis crudorum humorum, ut infra dicemus: ex caloris enim debilitate maior pituitae et crudorum humorum copia emerget, ex qua etiam maior erit ipsius appetentis facultatis satietas, et ab externo alimento cessato.

Hoc enim ita se habere satis commonstrat experientia, ea autem ex causa
multo plures foeminae, quam viri, visae sunt, quae naturaliter longum ser-
vaverint ieiunium."

50. Donati, *De Medica Historia Mirabili*, 214–218; Schutte, *Aspiring
Saints*, 140–142.

51. On women who survived for an extended period through eating only
the Eucharist see Bell, *Holy Anorexia*, 20, 26–29, 156–157; Bynum, *Holy
Feast, Holy Fast*, 73–93.

52. Ochs, *A History of Nerve Functions*, 25.

53. Zacchia, *Quaestiones Medico-Legales* (1657), 212: "universaliter
autem naturalis sequenti modo fieri solet: Facta vehementi imaginatione, ac
fixa circa rem aliquam, ut circa amatam mulierem, vel etiam circa coelestia,
circa Angelos, circa Sanctos (nam non ob id, quod Ecstasis fiat ex contempla-
tione supernaturalium rerum, idcirco supernaturalis smper et ipsa est) con-
fluunt in cerebrum animales omnes spiritus, externis sensibus, ac internis,
et motui quoque destinari, unde contingit . . . magis multo, quam in somno
ipsi exerni sensus obligati, et ipsum animal omni motu carere appareat; eo
enim spirituum animalium omnium confluxu a sensibus prorsus alienatur
homo, qui in ea imaginatione haerens non secus ac in somniantibus eveniat,
se praesens habere existimat, ac realiter videre, et audire, quacunque imagi-
natur, cum Angelis, et sanctis Dei colloqui, si circa illos imaginatio fuerit, vel
coelesti, ac Dei gloriam, aut inferna, et damnatorum poenas contemplari, vel
cum ipsissima amata confabulari."

54. Ibid., 213: "Ecstasim nimirum, quae naturaliter fit, esse morbum
quendam, sue affectum, vel symptoma praeternaturam."

55. On rapture and other mystical experiences as a key element of late
medieval female sanctity see Bynum, *Holy Feast, Holy Fast*, 26–28; Elliot,
Proving Woman, 180–230.

56. Zacchia, *Quaestionum Medico-Legalium* (1666), Lib. IV, Tit. I,
Quaest. VIII: "De Morte miraculosa, & de morbis divinis immissis."

57. Zacchia, *Quaestionum Medico-Legalium* (1666), Lib. III, Tit. II,
Quaest. VI: "De simulato morbo cum defectu Animi, & sensus amissione, ut
Syncope, Apoplexia, Epilepsia, Ecstatsi, & aliis."

58. Paolo Zacchia, *Quaestionum Medico-Legalium Tomi Tres* (Frankfurt:
Johannis Melchioris Bencard, 1688), Lib. IV, Tit. I, Quaest. VIII, 360: "Adhi-
bendae insuper & in hoc judicio conjecturae ex temperatura, ex aetate, ex
statu, & ex habitu aegrotantis, vel pereuntis: videndumque quantum morbus,
aut interitus ab aegroti, aut morientis temperatura, habitu, aetate, aliisque con-
ditionibus desciscat: quae enim secundum Naturae vires eveniunt, consenta-
neum est secundum easdem conditiones evenire, & in summa quandocunque
morbus occurrit difficilis, sive repentinus interitus, cuius causae sapientibus
sint ignotae, & ipse morbus, aut interitus naturalibus, apparentibusque causis non modo minime conformis, sed undequaque repugnans, & alia ex parte
urgeant praesumptiones, & conjecturae etiam extra artem Medicam quaesi-
tae, de miraculo suspicari licet, & ad eius cognitionem habendam, praedicta
exquisite examinanda" The versions of Zacchia that I have used vary based on
which version I had access to at various points during my research.

59. On the medical doctrine of signs in the early modern period see Ian Maclean, *Logic, Signs, and Nature in the Renaissance: The Case of Learned Medicine* (New York: Cambridge University Press, 2002), 126–128; Nancy Siraisi, "Disease and Symptom as Problematic Concepts in Renaissance Medicine," in *Res et Verba in der Renaissance*, ed. Eckhard Kessler and Ian Maclean (Wiesbaden: Harrassowitz Verlag, 2002), 217–240.

60. Zacchia, *Quaestionum Medico-Legalium* (1666), 254: "Vidi ego mulierem mihi satis notam, quae se, ubi frequens hominum coetus in templis, sacrisque locis convenisset, raptam in Ecstasim effingebat, & admiratione non parva dignum erat, quam apte simularet. Stabat extensis brachiis in Crucis modum, palpebris immobilibus, oculis fixis, & per horae spatium, ac ultra, eo in actu perseverabat. Interdum veluti ad coelum volatura, & in aerem se elevatura corpus attollebat, illud mirum in modum extendens; sed admirationem omnem superare mihi visum est, quod vultum in mille colores vel ictu oculi commutaret; nam modo rubescebat; & quasi ardore quodam incendi videbatur, modo adeo pallescebat, ut quasi emortua langueret, denuo, ac dicto citius, rubore perfundebatur ac denique veluti animo deficiens ad seipsam redire simulabat, ita ut circumstantes omnes eam divino raptu prehensam pro sancta venerarentur, & ad illius vestimenta devotionis ergo tangenda, mulierculae & homunciones aderant, acurrerent, non sine mei ipsius risu, & multo majori, ut credo, ipsiusmet foemina derisu, quam ego quidem intus & in cute agnoscebam; erat autem Sicula."

61. Paolo Zacchia, *Quaestionum Medico-Legalium Tomus Posterior Quo Continentur Liber Nonus et Decimus Necnon Decisiones Sacrae Rotae Romanae ad Praedictas Materias Spectantes, A D. Lanfranco Zacchia Collectae* (Lyons: Sumptibus Ioan. Ant. Huguetan & Marci-Ant, 1661). Book 10 of this edition contains a recounting of eighty-five cases in which Zacchia served as an expert medical witness before the Rota Tribunal. Not a single one treats the discernment of spirits or examination of living saints.

62. The printed collections of case studies penned by Donati, Lentuolo, and Liceti, which are mentioned above, deal with examples that might fall under the rubric of extreme asceticism. However, in each of the cases in which wondrous ascetic behavior appears, the medical practitioner was called by local and usually secular officials to investigate it.

63. On the destruction of many of the records of the Roman Inquisition in the early nineteenth century see John Tedeschi, *The Prosecution of Heresy: Collected Studies on the Inquisition in Early Modern Italy* (Binghamton, NY: Medieval and Renaissance Texts and Studies, 1991), 23–45.

64. Vatican City, Archivio della Congregazione per la Dottrina della Fede (ACDF), Stanza Storica (St. St.), C-1-F, tome 2, 267–268. In this case, Lucia Gambona was examined by a medical professional who checked a bleeding lance wound in her side. But the inquisitors trying the case did not ask the physician about its possible origin. See also Francesco Barbierato, "Il medico e l'inquisitore. Note su medici e perizie mediche nel tribunale del Sant'Uffizio veneziano fra Sei e Settecento," in *Paolo Zacchia alle Origini della medicina legale*, 266–285. Barbierato concluded that the Inquisition employed doctors largely to check the health of the incarcerated, to see if an accused was strong

enough to be put to torture, or to offer another opinion on a person's sanity. Jonathan Seitz, *Witchcraft and Inquisition in Early Modern Venice* (New York: Cambridge University Press, 2011), 73–95, has found that in cases in which witchcraft was thought responsible for an illness, inquisitors called on medical experts in an attempt to rule out natural causes.

65. Schutte, *Aspiring Saints*, 147.

66. See, for example, the case of Francisco Girolamo Simon, ACDF, C-1-A, B, C, D, or an anonymous body examined by surgeons in Ancona in ACDF, St. St., B-4-P, fasc. 13, 2nd document in set, fol. 3.

67. Niccolò del Re, *La Curia Romana: Lineamenti storico-giuridici* (Rome: Sussidi eruditi, 1970), 243–259.

68. Peter Godman, *The Saint as Censor: Robert Bellarmine Between Inquisition and Index* (Boston: Brill, 2000), 91–92. Godman has noted here that some inquisitors also worked for the Rota as well and were involved with saint-making.

69. On the beginning of an Inquisition investigation see Thomas F. Mayer, *The Roman Inquisition: A Papal Bureaucracy and Its Laws in the Age of Galileo* (Philadelphia: University of Pennsylvania Press, 2013), 166–171.

70. On the amount of publicity surrounding the treatment of the body of a prospective saint see Chapter 1 in this volume. In addition, the fact that Lentuolo and Liceti were able to publish accounts of wondrous fasts meant that such cases were high profile and of general interest.

71. Adriano Prosperi, "Il 'Budget' di un Inquisitore: Ferrara 1567–1572," in *L'Inquisizione romana: letture e ricerche* (Rome: Edizioni di storia e letteratura, 2003), 125–140. Prosperi has found that regional branches of the Inquisition operated on budgets as small as 82 lire per year. A medical consult could, therefore, be a substantial part of the budget given contemporary medical wages. Silvia de Renzi, "Medical Competence, Anatomy and the Polity in Seventeenth-century Rome," *Renaissance Studies* 21, no. 4 (September 2007): 558, notes that Giulio Mancini was paid a "meagre" 9 scudi every three months while serving as a chief physician for a Roman jail. In another article, idem, "'A Fountain for the Thirsty' and a Bank for the Pope: Charity, Conflicts, and Medical Careers at the Hospital of Santo Spirito in Seventeenth-Century Rome," in *Health Care and Poor Relief in Counter-Reformation Europe,* ed. Ole Peter Grell and Andrew Cunningham (New York: Routledge, 1999), 110, de Renzi notes that the doctors at the Santo Spirito Hospital in Rome received 100 scudi annually in 1595. The doctor on retainer for the Holy Office in Rome in 1653 was paid 25 scudi a year; see ACDF, *Oeconomica* 6, 8r. Although relative currency values fluctuated, a papal scudo was generally worth more than a lira in this period, so even if we assume a one-to-one ratio it would still have been prohibitively expensive for most branches of the Inquisition to solicit expert medical testimony.

72. Biblioteca Nazionale di Roma, ms. San Lorenzo in Lucina 60, 209 v. "Si vedevono spesse volte da suoi Confessori et altre Persone nelle di Lei mani, piedi, e lato sinistro le ciccatrici rossegianti di sangue come se fosse state le stimmate della ricevute passione."

73. Ibid., 210r: "procedesse d'alcune spine che p[ri]ma intorno alla d[ett] a piaga havevano cominciato ad uscire fuori con le punte, e toccate dal Confessore si sentivano inviscerate nella Carne."

74. Zacchia, *Quaestionum Medico-Legalium* (1666), Lib. VII, Tit. IV, Quaest. I: "Quid sunt Stigmata, de quibus hic, & historica eorum disquisitio." His section on stigmata deals with unusual physical signs, though not this exact abnormality.

75. Biblioteca Nazionale di Roma, ms San Lorenzo in Lucina 60, 210v: "considerava il Tribunale parere non smosso in Termini di Santa, che una femina di cosi poca età, senza la precedenza d'una lunga penitenze e continuato esercizio delle più eroiche virtue fosse si toste prevenuta a godere I privilegii delli gran Santi Franc[esc]o d'Assisi o Catarina da Siena, ancorche con maggior prerogativa di quelli a quali non si erano mai vedute ne spine, ne chiodi et altre esterne visibili apparenze come di q[ues]ta si è detto."

76. On Borromeo as a model for the early modern Catholic bishop see Alberigo, "Carlo Borromeo come modello di vescovi nella chiesa post-tridentina."

77. Giovanni Baptista Carcano Leone, *Exenterationis Cadaveris Illustrissimi Cardinalis Borrhomaei Mediolani Archiepiscopi* (Milan: Ex Typographia Michaelis Tini, Ad instantiam Petri Tini, 1584), 3: "Secanti mihi abdomen a graecis epigastrium dictum nulla mihi sese obtulit pinguedinis nota; quod mirum mihi valde visum est: quando in caeteris, quae secui corporibus qua[m]vis emaciatis semper vestigium aliquod pinguedinis mihi sese obtulerit." On Borromeo's dissection and the meaning of the fat found in his body see Chapter 1 in this volume and Nancy G. Siraisi, "Signs and Evidence: Autopsy and Sanctity in Late Sixteenth-Century Italy," in *Medicine and the Italian Universities, 1250–1600* (Boston: Brill, 2001), 356–380.

78. Realdo Colombo, *De re anatomica libri XV* (Venice: Ex Typographia Nicolai Bevilacquae, 1559), 266–267."Lapides autem innumerabiles pene hisce manibus extraxi inventos in renibus colore vario, in pulmonibus, in iecore, in vena portae, ut tuis oculis vidisti Iacobe Bone in Venerabili Egnatio Generali congregationis Iesu vidi etiam lapillos in ureteris in vesica, in intestino colo, in venis haemorrhoidalibus, atque in umbilico. In bilis quoque vesicula, quod tamen exciderat, varii coloris, variaeque figurae lapillos et in nonnullis complures inveni, vidi abscessum."

79. *Relatio Facta in Consistorio Secreto Coram S.D.N. Alexandro P. VII . . . Super Vita, Sanctitate, actis Canonizationis, & miraculis Beati Francisci de Sales Episcopi Genevensis* (Rome: Ex Typographia Rev. Cam. Apost., 1662), 14: "Secto corpore ne gutta quidem humoris in cistula fellis reperta est, sed parvi lapilli in ea erant varii coloris & figurae in modum coronae dispositi, & velut invicem cohaerentes."

80. Giuseppe Fozi, *Vita del Venerabile Servo di Dio Annibale d'Afflitto Arcivescovo di Reggio* (Rome: Per Nicolò Angelo Tianssi, 1681), 156–157: "nell'aprirlo, gli fu trovata nella vescica una pietra grossa più d'una Noce."

81. ASV, RP 797, 462r: "Hidropisia, inflatione di corpo grandissima, da febbre, e mal di pietra . . . le qual cos' l'havevano tenuta un'anno continuo in letto."

82. ASV, RP 797, 462r–462v: "gettò 30 o 32 pietri le quali i medici dissero, non con virtù o potenza naturale essere stato da lei gittato, ma per virtu, et potenza superiore, et divina, affirmando essi, che di tanta grandezza e numero, esse tal pietro naturalm[ent]e con la vita. D. d[ett]a S. Cattrina non potevano haver esito et in particolare con questa circonstantia, che v'erano che le gitte senza alcuno dolore, o passioni."

83. Mary Lindemann, *Medicine and Society in Early Modern Europe* (New York: Cambridge University Press, 2010), 39–40; Marsilio Cagnati, *Relatione dell'Infermità del Cardinale Salviati* (Rome: Appresso Luigi Zannetti, 1603), 15. Cagnati commented that there were only few and small stones in Salviati's body—implying perhaps that it was almost a healthy abnormality.

84. For two prominent early modern accounts of kidney function that are largely in agreement see Andreas Vesalius, *On the Fabric of the Human Body*, book 5, trans. William Frank Richardson (Novato, CA: Norman Publishing, 2007), chap. 10; Realdo Colombo, *De re anatomica libri XV* (Venice: Ex Typographia Nicolai Bevilacquae, 1559), book 11, cap. 11, 132–133.

85. Wallace B. Hamby, "Paré, Ambroise," *Complete Dictionary of Scientific Biography*, vol. 10, ed. Charles Gillispie (New York: Cengage Learning, 2008), 315–317.

86. Ambroise Paré, *Ten Books of Surgery with the Magazine of the Instruments Necessary for It*, trans. Robert White Linker and Nathan Womack (Athens: University of Georgia Press, 1969), 175.

87. Ibid., 181.

88. Levinus Lemnius, *Della complessione del corpo humano libri due* (Venice: Appresso Domenico Nicolino, 1564), 18v: "Iddio scrutatore del cuore, et delle reni, cioè ha comprese tutte le cose e penetra tutti I luoghi nascosi."

89. N.F.J. Eloy, *Dictionnaire Historique de la Médecine Ancienne et Moderne*, vol. 3 (Paris: Chez H.Hoyois, 1778), 50.

90. Lemnius, *Della complessione del corpo humano libri due*, 18v–19r.

91. S. V. Ramge, "Innocent XI, Pope, BL," in *The New Catholic Encyclopedia*, vol. 7 (Detroit: Thomson Gale, 2003), 480–481.

92. Maria Pia Donato, *Morti improvvise: Medicina e religione nel Settecento* (Rome: Carocci, 2010), 56–57. On anatomy at the Santo Spirito see Silvia de Renzi, "'A Fountain for the Thirsty' and a Bank for the Pope: Charity, Conflicts, and Medical Careers at the Hospital of Santo Spirito in Seventeenth-Century Rome," 104–105.

93 Carlo Castellani, "Lancisi, Giovanni Maria," *Complete Dictionary of Scientific Biography*, vol. 7 (New York: Charles Scribner's Sons, 2008), 613–614; *Gale Virtual Reference Library*, March 22, 2011, http://find.galegroup.com/grnr/infomark.do?&source=gale&idigest=a630090 61cb4723de8392cb6fdoea984&prodId=GRNR&userGroupName=psu cic&tabID=T001&docId=CX2830902444&type=retrieve&contentSet=-EBKS&version=1.0; Donato, *Morti improvvise*, 56–60.

94. Donato, *Morti improvise*, 57.

95. ASV, RP 2574, 899r.

96. ASV, RP 2574, 889r: "d'un infermità, che duro 58 giorni continui mista di febre, di resipole, di ascessi supporati alli piedi, e di Podagra, che con le piaghe, e con le fistole negl'articoli de piedi le facevano soffire un'Indicibile Martirio, alle quali gravissimie infermita' vi era aggiunto un male de Reni, che di 33 anni in dietro l'haveva contin[u]am[ent]e afflitto."

97. ASV, RP 2574, 890r–890v: "e pure questi male, che separatamente in ogn'altro haverebbero portato all'Infermo eterna Smania et Inquietitudini nel Santo Pontefice io non osservai gia mai minimo atto d'impatienza."

98. Biblioteca Lancisiana, Fondo Lancisi ms. 149, fols. 5–6; Donato, *Morti improvvise*, 58. Maria Pia Donato notes that this letter also contained clear religious and political advice for Clement XI, including an argument against nepotism and a call for Clement to maintain the independence of the papacy. Hence, Lancisi later used the dissection as a way to talk about politics in the papal capital and endorse a certain program of action.

99. ASV, RP 2574, 889r: "un male de Reni, che di 33 anni in dietro l'haveva contin[u]am[ent]e afflitto, e questo consisteva in due grossissime pietre che occupavano internamente Li Reni, li quali riconosciute doppo [*sic*] la morte d'una grandezza smisurata."

100. ASV, RP 2574, 889v: "ma crebbe in oltre in me la maraviglia nell'osservare, che dalle Pietre si era affatto consumata la sostanza de Reni, e solo vi era rimasta in ciascuno una grossa membrana, che come una borsa chiudeva, e stringeva la Pietra."

101. ASV, RP 2574, 889v: "e la credi come cosa sopra naturale."

102. See, for example, the short pamphlet that appears to have circulated in early modern Rome: *Relazione dell'Ultima Infermità e Morte di Nostro Signore PP. Innocenzo Undecimo Di Felicissima Memoria Pontefice Ottimo Massimo* (Rome: Gio Francesco Buagni, 1689), 6: "Dipoi si venne all'apertura del suo corpo per imbalsamarlo; e ne' reni li furono trovate due pietre di smisurata grandezza, una per ciascheduno."

103. ASV, RP 3356, 1829v, 2302r.

104. Vincenzio Puccini, *Vita della Madre Suor Maria Maddalena de'Pazzi Fiorentina* (Florence: Giunti, 1609), 13: "E Messer Iacopo Tronconi uno de quattro, che piu' seguito di visitarla replicò piu volte, che con tutto lo studio che vi havesse posto non mai haveva potuto ritrovare la cagione, ne la qualità di tal malattia, e che bisognava lasciar fare a Dio: perché da umano artifizio non si poteva sperare giovamento veruno."

105. Ibid., 186: "I medici non seppero mai trovare ragione, onde quel corpo potesse tanto tempo mantenersi in vita, e far retta a tante, e si atroci pene."

106. See above discussion of raptures in Zacchia's *Quaestiones*.

107. The 1687 publication date of this work in England was almost certainly connected to polemics against the Catholic James II and the fears that his attempts to expand Catholic rights in England aroused. For a brief overview of the religious tensions in England at this moment see Mark Kishlansky, *A Monarchy Transformed: Britain, 1603–1714* (New York: Penguin

Books, 1996), 263–286; Michael Mullett, *James II and English Politics, 1687–1688* (New York: Routledge, 1994).

108. Vincent Puccini, *The Life of St. Mary Magdalene of Pazzi, A Carmelite Nunn*, trans. Father Lezin de Sainte Scholastique (London: Randal Taylor, 1687), 15.

109. Ibid., 30.

110. Schutte, *Aspiring Saints*, 42–59.

111. ASV, RP 769, 39r–40v; RP 771, 183r–185r.

112. Teresa of Avila and Rose of Lima, for example, were famous for their feats of asceticism.

113. Both Teresa and Rose were examined posthumously by medical practitioners to check for incorruption. See the discussion of each saint's body in Chapters 2 and 3, respectively.

CHAPTER 5

1. Francesco Maria Maggio, *Compendioso Ragguaglio della Vita, Morte e Monisteri della Venerabil Madre D. Orsola Benincasa Napoletana* (Naples: Gio Francesco Paci, 1669), 104: "se le gonfiò il petto in maniera, che dava segno di bollimento alla parte del cuore. Il che fù con tanto empito e forza, che ruppe la legatura delle veste. Se le videro ancora tutte le vene del volto ingrossate e ripiene: e il viso lasciando il torbido e nero, divenne rubicondo: e incominciò dal naso a versar gocciole di sangue."

2. Ibid., 104–105: "Fè poi instanzia il signor D. Antonio Carmignano, che si sparasse, per veder la cagione di quell'arsura petto." On the Carmignano family and a brief reference to Antonio, see Giuseppe Fiengo, *L'Acquedotto di Carmignano e lo sviluppo di Napoli in età barocca* (Florence: Leo S. Olschki, 1990), 88–95.

3. Maggio, *Compendioso Ragguaglio*, 105: "Piacque ciò alle Vergini, e alla Duchessa; ma vollero I Padri, che si facesse con segretezza, per non essere oppressi dalle persone divote."

4. On the crowds that might attend the medical examination of a holy corpse, see Chapter 1 of this current volume. On the ways in which crowds in general could form with any activity related to investigations into the holiness of a saint, see Laura Smoller, *The Saint and the Chopped-Up Baby* (Ithaca, NY: Cornell University Press, 2014), 76–83.

5. Maggio, *Compendioso Ragguaglio*, 105: "Onde, senz'aspettar maestri periti, o ricercar gli strumenti, che in ciò si sogliono adoperare; con una fega di ferro, un puntaruolo, e cortelli [*sic*], fu il cadavero aperto."

6. Ibid., 105: "tutti con affetto, e divozione incredibile, sentivano somma consolazione e allegrezza: benchè pareva più opera di macello, che osservazione di Medici, e Anatomisti." Jean-Michel Sallmann, *Naples et ses saints a l'âge baroque (1540–1750)* (Paris: Presses Universitaires de France, 1994), 308–309. Drawing on information from the canonization process, Sallmann reports a slightly different version of events in which a surgeon was present, but he had merely forgotten his tools. He used a small knife and then a saw to open Benincasa.

7. Maggio, *Compendioso Ragguaglio*, 105: "tutti videro, che nel petto non era il cuore, ma tutto consumato dal fuoco: e così erano eziandio vuote, e arrostite le'nteriora."

8. Ibid., 105: "E con tutto ciò, fu di non minor maraviglia, la grassezza del suo corpo, pingue in tutte le parti benchè non tanto di cibo terreno si sia pasciuta, qua[n]to del Divinissimo Sacramento."

9. Giovanni Baptista Carcano Leone, *Exenterationis Cadaveris Illustrissimi Cardinalis Borrhomaei Mediolani Archiepiscopi* (Milan: Ex Typographia Michaelis Tini, Ad instantiam Petri Tini, 1584), 3. In his dissection of Carlo Borromeo, Leone makes clear the connection between a lack of fat and holiness. Similarly, the physician Levinus Lemnius associated fat with weakness and laziness. Levinus Lemnius, *Della complessione del corpo humano libri due* (Venice: Appresso Domenico Nicolino, 1564), 48r–48v.

10. Katharine Park, *Secrets of Women: Gender, Generation and the Origins of Human Dissection* (New York: Zone Books, 2006), 223–227; Heather Webb, *The Medieval Heart* (New Haven, CT: Yale University Press, 2010), 136–139. The meaning of a missing heart can be ambiguous. Park recounts a story of a miser's heart found to be missing on opening the body and then later discovered with his gold. Webb relates the experience of Catherine of Siena, whose heart was supposedly taken by Jesus and then replaced with his own.

11. Park, *Secrets of Women*, 39–51.

12. Joseph Bergin, "The Counter Reformation Church and Its Bishops," *Past and Present*, no. 165 (November 1999): 30–73; R. Po-Chia Hsia, *The World of Catholic Renewal, 1540–1770* (New York: Cambridge University Press, 2005), 111–126; Gabriella Zarri, "From Prophecy to Discipline, 1450–1650," in *Women and Faith: Catholic Religious Life in Italy from Late Antiquity to the Present*, trans. Keith Botsford, ed. Lucetta Scaraffa and Gabriella Zarri (Cambridge, MA: Harvard University Press, 1999), 83–112.

13. Tessa Storey, *Carnal Commerce in Counter-Reformation Rome* (New York: Cambridge University Press, 2008), 234; Merry E. Wiesner, *Women and Gender in Early Modern Europe* (New York: Cambridge University Press, 1993), 179–217, 255.

14. Park, *Secrets of Women*, 216–221; Monica H. Green, *Making Women's Medicine Masculine: The Rise of Male Authority in Pre-Modern Gynaecology* (New York: Oxford University Press, 2008), 316.

15. Lorraine Daston and Katharine Park, "The Hermaphrodite and the Orders of Nature: Sexual Ambiguity in Early Modern France," *GLQ: A Journal of Lesbian and Gay Studies* 1 (1995): 419–438; Dorinda Outram, "Gender," in *The Cambridge History of Science, Vol. 3: Early Modern Science,* ed. Katharine Park and Lorraine Daston (New York: Cambridge University Press, 2006), 797–817. For a survey of a slightly earlier period that is still very useful for thinking about early modern gender see Joan Cadden, *Meanings of Sex Difference in the Middle Ages: Medicine, Science, and Culture* (New York: Cambridge University Press, 1993), 198–202.

16. Daston and Park, "The Hermaphrodite and the Orders of Nature," 420–431.

17. Park, *Secrets of Women*, 26–27. For a consideration of the various ways in which sixteenth- and seventeenth-century Europeans conceived of differences between the sexes, see Ian Maclean, *The Renaissance Notion of Woman* (New York: Cambridge University Press, 1980), 28–46.

18. Park, *Secrets of Women*, 121–131.

19. Ibid., 129–131.

20. On the spiritual importance of the heart in the medieval and early modern periods see Nancy Caciola, *Discerning Spirits: Divine and Demonic Possession in the Middle Ages* (Ithaca, NY: Cornell Unviersity Press, 2003), 182–183; Catrien Santing, "*De Affectibus Cordis et Palpitatione:* Secrets of the Heart in Counter-Reformation Italy," in *Cultural Approaches to the History of Medicine,* ed. Willem de Blécourt and Cornelie Usbourne (New York: Palgrave Macmillan, 2004), 11–35; Scott Manning Stevens, "Sacred Heart and Secular Brain," in *The Body in Parts: Fantasies of Corporeality in Early Modern Europe,* ed. David Hillman and Carla Mazzio (New York: Routledge, 1997): 263–285; Webb, *The Medieval Heart.*

21. Park, *Secrets of Women*, 39–52; 70–71.

22. Dyan Elliott, *Proving Woman: Female Spirituality and Inquisitorial Culture in the Later Middle Ages* (Princeton, NJ: Princeton University Press, 2004), 144–145; Park, *Secrets of Women*, 35.

23. See discussion of female spirituality in Chapter 4. For a general discussion of the embodied elements of late medieval female sanctity see Caroline Bynum, *Holy Feast and Holy Fast: The Religious Significance of Food to Medieval Women* (Berkeley: University of California Press, 1987); André Vauchez, *Sainthood in the Later Middle Ages*, trans. Jean Birrell (New York: Cambridge University Press, 1997), 369–386.

24. On the continued importance of female saints through the early years of the sixteenth century and the concern which male churchmen expressed about them, see Gabriella Zarri, *Le sante vive: cultura e religosità femminile nella prima età moderna* (Torino: Rosenberg & Sellier, 1990).

25. Park, *Secrets of Women*, 170–171.

26. Ibid., 162–164; Gianna Pomata, "A Christian Utopia of the Renaissance: Elena Duglioli's Spiritual and Physical Motherhood (ca. 1510–1520)," in *Von der dargestellten Person zum erinnerten Ich: Europäische Selbstzeugnisse als historische Quellen (1500–1850),* ed. Kaspar von Greyerz, Hans Medick, and Patrice Veit (Cologne: Böhlau Verlag, 2001), 323–353.

27. Park, *Secrets of Women*, 164–165.

28. On the popularity of the genre of medical case studies in this period see Chapter 2 of this book. See also, Gianna Pomata, "*Praxis Historialis:* The Uses of *Historia* in Early Modern Medicine," in *Historia: Empiricism and Erudition in Early Modern Europe,* ed. Gianna Pomata and Nancy Siraisi (Cambridge, MA: MIT Press, 2005), 105–146; Anthony Grafton and Nancy Siraisi, *Natural Particulars: Nature and the Disciplines in Renaissance Europe* (Cambridge, MA: MIT Press, 1999), 1–21; Nancy Siraisi, "'Remarkable' Diseases, 'Remarkable' Cures, and Personal Experience in Renaissance Medical Texts," in *Medicine and the Italian Universities, 1250–1600* (Boston: Brill, 2001), 226–252. The first real collection of case studies

of unusual phenomena in this period was Antonio Benivieni, *De Abditis Nonnullis ac Mirandis Morborum et Sanationum Causis* (Florence: Philippi Giunate, 1507).

29. See discussion of this in Chapter 3.

30. Teodoro Valle, *Breve Compendio de gli piu illustri padri nella santità della vita, dignità, uffici, e lettere ch'ha prodotto la Prov. Del Regno di Nap. Dell'Ord de Predic* (Naples: Per Secondino Roncagliolo, 1651), 315.

31. Nancy G. Siraisi, "Signs and Evidence: Autopsy and Sanctity in Late Sixteenth-Century Italy," in *Medicien and the Italian Universities, 1250–1600* (Boston: Brill, 2001), 374–375.

32. Santig, *"De Affectibus Cordis et Palpitatione,"* 12.

33. ASV, RP 2812, 3r: "lo [del Pas] sparai, et lo trovai dentro bellissimo, et senza infettione alcuna, et quando cavai gl'interiori con il resto, cavai il Cuore appartato, dove ci trovai in detto Cuore un taglio a guise di una ferita, et mettendolo in un vaso detto al barillo di Terra, dove si mettono le confettioni, lo asciuttavo con fazzoletti, et altre pezze di lino, et di queste pezze e una delli sopradette che posti sopra il Braccio del patienti, come ho detto."

34. See, for example, the process of canonization for Gregory Barbarigo ASV, RP 3478, 620r: "Et statim DD[icti] Judices quemlibet ex dictis Peritis separatim monuerunt, ut infra triduum, nempe die sabbati, quae erit 20 me[nsi]s Dece[m]bris curren[tis] facta per eos magis matura reflexione, et ponderatione referant, et unusquisque eorum referat in scriptis quid sibi videatur de statu dicti ven[erabi]lis Corporis, et in specie an dici possit incorruptum, et in statu miraculoso."

35. Anton-Maria da Vicenza, *Vita del venerabile servo di Dio P. Angelo del Pas, vol. 2* (Rome: G. Aureli, 1867), 206–208. According to this well disposed hagiographer, the most eminent adherents to del Pas's cult in the years following his death were primarily the Duke of Acquasparta, his fellow Franciscans, the Roman populace, and some adherents in Barcelona. Compared with holy people who achieved canonization in the early modern period, this is fairly light political backing. See Chapter 1 for an extended discussion of this issue.

36. The literature on how the Reformation affected gender roles is vast and contentious. I cite here only some of the best-known surveys: Scott Hendrix, "Masculinity and Patriarchy in Reformation Germany," *Journal of the History of Ideas* 56, no. 2 (1995): 177–193; Hsia, *The World of Catholic Renewal*, 144–158; Steven Ozment, *When Fathers Ruled: Family Life in Reformation Europe* (Cambridge, MA: Harvard University Press, 1983); Lyndal Roper, *The Holy Household: Women and Morals in Reformation Germany* (New York: Oxford University Press, 1989); Wiesner, *Women and Gender in Early Modern Europe*, 179–217; Merry E. Wiesner-Hanks, *Christianity and Sexuality in the Early Modern World: Regulating Desire, Reforming Practice* (New York: Routledge, 2000).

37. Jean-Michel Sallmann, "La sainteté mystique féminine à Naples au tourant des XVIe et XVIIe siècles," in *Culto dei santi: istruzioni e classi sociali in età preindustriale,* ed. Sofia Boesch Gajano and Lucia Sebastiani (Rome: Japadre Editore, 1984), 701; Donald Weinstein and Rudolph Bell,

Saints and Society: The Two Worlds of Western Christendom, 1000–1700 (Chicago: University of Chicago Press, 1982), 225; Wiesner, *Women and Gender*, 198; Zarri, "From Prophecy to Discipline," 83–112.

38. Giacomo Bacci, *The Life of Saint Philip Neri, vol. 2*, ed. Frederick Ignatius Antrobus (London: Kegan Paul, Trench, Trubner & Co., 1902 [originally published 1622]), 56–57.

39. Giacomo Bacci, *The Life of Saint Philip Neri, vol. 1*, ed. Frederick Ignatius Antrobus (London: Kegan Paul, Trench, Trubner & Co., 1902 [originally published 1622]), 32.

40. Pietro Gisolfo, *Vita del P.D. Antonio de Colellis* (Naples: Per Giacinto Passaro, 1663), 208: "Fù nemico d'ascoltare le Confessioni delle Donne, e quando occorreva per qualche grave necessità confessarne alcuna, lo facea con gran cautela, & essortava del continuo i suoi à portarsi con molta circospettione nel praticare con quelle."

41. Wietse de Boer, "Sollecitazione in confessionale," in *Dizionario Storico dell'Inquisizione*, vol. 3, ed. Adriano Prosperi with Vincenzo Lavenia and John Tedeschi (Pisa: Edizioni della Normale, 2010), 1451–1455.

42. *Biblioteca mistica carmelitana*, vol. 18 (Burgos: Tipografia de El Monte Carmelo, 1913), 9, quoted in Gillian T.W. Ahlgren, "Negotiating Sanctity: Holy Women in Sixteenth-Century Spain," *Church History* 64, no. 3 (September 1995): 381; Alison Weber, *Teresa of Avila and the Rhetoric of Femininity* (Princeton, NJ: Princeton University Press, 1990), 17–18. Weber observes that throughout Teresa's canonization process she was routinely described as a "virile woman."

43. For a good summary of early modern medical ideas about the female body, see Maclean, *The Renaissance Notion of Woman*, 28–46.

44. Erin Rowe, "The Spanish Minerva: Imagining Teresa of Avila as Patron Saint Seventeenth-Century Spain," *Catholic Historical Review* 92, no. 4 (October 2006): 583.

45. Leonard Hansen, *Vita Mirabilis Mors pretiosa Sanctitas Thaumaturga, S. Rosae Peruanae* (Rome: Typis Nicolai Angeli Tinassii, 1680), 90–91.

46. Rowe, "The Spanish Minerva," 581.

47. Outram, "Gender," 797–817.

48. Michel de Montaigne, *The Complete Works of Montaigne*, trans. Donald M. Frame (Stanford, CA: Stanford University Press, 1967), 69.

49. Ambroise Paré, *On Monsters and Marvels*, trans. Janis L. Pallister (Chicago: University of Chicago Press, 1982), 31–33.

50. Paré, *On Monsters and Marvels*, 32.

51. Ibid., 33.

52. Daston and Park, "The Hermaphrodite and the Orders of Nature," 419–438.

53. Paré, *On Monsters and Marvels*, 85–97.

54. For a sampling of the literature on the role of the female body as the repository of family virtue and honor see Michael Rocke, "Gender and Sexual Culture in Renaissance Italy," in *The Italian Renaissance Essential Readings*, ed. Paula Findlen (Oxford: Blackwell, 2002), 192–211; Daniela

Hacke, *Women, Sex and Marriage in Early Modern Venice* (Aldershot: Ashgate, 2004), 13–18; Ulinka Rublack, *The Crimes of Women in Early Modern Germany* (Oxford: Clarendon Press, 1999), 134–162.

55. Laura Gowing, *Common Bodies: Women, Touch and Power in Seventeenth-Century England* (New Haven, CT: Yale University Press, 2003), 24–25; Storey, *Carnal Commerce in Counter-Reformation Rome*, 62.

56. For numbers of prospective saints subjected to a posthumous medical exam in the early modern period, see appendix.

57. Antonio Gallonio, *Vita Beati P. Philippi Neri Fiorentini* (Rome: Apud Aloysium Zanneti, 1600), 227: "Illud inter sectionem mirabile accidit, in quo maxime Deus illius confirmasse virginitatem mihi videtur. Convenerant iam eius corporis exenterandi gratia sectores aderant multi ex Patribus, cum defunti corpus quo disecari facilius posset, denudasset, exanduis illius corporis manus, & spiritu destituti (mirum dictu) supra naturae vires moveri, easque corporis partes, quas indecorum ostendi vivo fuisset, occultare coeperunt."

58. Biblioteca Apostolica Vaticana (BAV), De Luca IV 6607, Ioannis Boteri Benensis, *De morte Ill.mi ac Rev.mi D. Cardinalis S. Praxedis Epistola Ad Illustrissimum, ac Reverendissimum D. Andream Cardinalem Barthorium* (Milan: Ex Typographia Micahelis Tini, 1584), 2v: "Neque alia pene re constare videbatur, praeter quam ossibus, & cute admodum firmat."

59. Gisolfo, *Vita del P.D. Antonio de Colellis*, 209: "Doppo la sua morte, essendo veduto il suo Cadavero [sic caps] ignudo (coll'occasione di toglierne l'interiora) da' Medici, affermarono tutti, che stava così intiero, & acconcio nelle parti genitali, come se fosse stato d'un' bambino di tre, o quattro mesi nato."

60. Christoforo Giarda, *Compendio della Vita del Venerabil Servo di Dio Monsignor Francesco di Sales Vescovo di Geneva; e Fondatore dell'Ordine della Visitatione di Santa Maria Libri Quattro* (Rome: Appresso Filippo de' Rossi, 1648), 212: "I medesimi, e Medici, e Chirurgi dall'inspettione del medesimo corpo determinarono, che fosse Vergine, come un fanciulo poco avanti nato."

61. Jacqueline Murray, "'The Law of Sin That Is in My Members': The Problem of Male Embodiment," in *Gender and Holiness: Men, Women, and Saints in Late Medieval Europe*, ed. Samantha J.E. Riches and Sarah Salih (New York: Routledge, 2002), 18.

62. Peter Brown, *The Body and Society: Men, Women, and Sexual Renunciation in Early Christianity* (New York: Columbia University Press, 1988), 223; Conrad Leyser, *Authority and Asceticism from Augustine to Gregory the Great* (Oxford: Clarendon Press, 2000), 167; Teresa M. Shaw, *The Burden of the Flesh: Fasting and Sexuality in Early Christianity* (Minneapolis: Fortress Press, 1998), 9, 25, 174–181.

63. Leo Steinberg, *The Sexuality of Christ in Renaissance Art and in Modern Oblivion*, 2nd ed. (Chicago: University of Chicago Press, 1996), 244–247. Steinberg has observed that in some medieval paintings Christ appeared without genitalia to represent "an ideal of manhood without the blight of sex."

64. ASV, RP 3156, 715: "Doctor Christophorus de Medrano Medicus,
et Cathedraticus in Civitate Salamantina 23. Testis deponens [. . .] et diligentia vidit, et tentavit d[ictu]m corpus integrum molle, et tractabile habere
uterum, et ventrem, ubera, et mammas pectoris (partes qua citius corrupuntur, et consumuntur in corporibus mortuis) tam integra et plena, ac si Serva
Dei viva esset, quod iudicavit pro evidenti miraculo, prout et pro tali habuit
levitatem, et paruum pondus ipsius corporis, quod ipse se vidit, et manibus
palpavit." Pages are not numbered in this volume, so 715 represents my count
from the first page. See also Padre Silverio de Santa Teresa, ed., *Procesos
de Beatificatión y Canonización de Santa Teresa de Jesus*, vol. 3 (Burgos:
Tipografia Burgalesa, 1935), 47–49: "Y para los dichos efectos con particular cuidado vió y tentó el cuerpo de la dicha Santa, y le hallo entero y tan
maravilloso y milagroso, cual nunca vió otro cuerpo; porque demas de estar
entero, blando y tratable, tenia su vientre y las ubres de los pechos, que son
las partes que mas presto se consumen y corrompen en los cuerpos muertos,
tan enteros y llenos, como si fuera viva. Lo cual juzgo este testigo por evidente y claro milagro que Nuestro Señor obraba en aquel cuerpo de aquella
su sierva." In Medrano's original Spanish testimony in these pages, the mention of the womb or uterus is curiously absent. Perhaps the Latin phrase was
added to the apostolic process to give Medrano additional authority? See
below on the role that knowledge of the uterus had in constructing anatomical authority.

65. ASV, RP 769, 37r.

66. James A. Brundage, *Law, Sex, and Christian Society in Medieval
Europe* (Chicago: University of Chicago Press, 1987), 457.

67. Jean de Roye, *Journal de Jean de Roye, connu sous le nom de Chro-
nique scandaleuse, 1460–1483, vol. 1*, ed. Bernard de Mandrot (Paris:
Librairie Renouard, 1894), 27: "Et si y avoit encores trois bien belles filles,
faisans personnages de seraines toutes nues, et leur veoit on le beau tetin
droit, separé, rond et dur, qui estoit chose bien plaisant." On the sexuality
of the breast in late medieval culture, see also Steinberg, *The Sexuality of
Christ*, 382.

68. Kathryn Schwarz, "Missing the Breast: Desire, Disease, and the Singular Effect of Amazons," in *The Body in Parts*, 148–151; Pomata, "A Christian Utopia," 347–348.

69. ASV, RP 501, 43v–44r: "sequebantur pectora cum suis uberibus erectis simil[i]t[e]r admodu[m] alba et sicca et imposita manu remanebant solida
et firma."

70. Jacopo Berengario da Carpi, *Commentaria cum amplissimis addi-
tionibus super anatomia Mundini* (Bologna: Hieronymum de Benedictis,
1521), cccvi r: "Iuuant etiam mamillae in incitando coitum pertractando eas
tam in mare quam in femina licet magis in femina . . . & hoc est verissi-
mum si tangatur papilla mamillae statim ipsa papilla erigitur sicut virga &
ita propter comunitatem matricis & virgae cum mamillis fit aliqua comotio
in virta & in matricae maxime in dispositis & in paratis ad coitum." I have
relied on Gianna Pomata's translation of this passage in rendering the text
into English. See Pomata, "A Christian Utopia," 348–349.

71. Ibid., 596r: "totum hoc valde compositum, et non solum vidi, sed etiam illud manu tetigi ab humero dextro per totum brachium usque ad manum."

72. Ibid.: "Capilli in capite versus partem dexteram flavi tam pulchri, ac si denuo lavati fuissent."

73. Archivio Diocesano di Padova, no specific shelfmark, but on the spine of the volume was written "Documenti Vari di : 1. S. Gaetano Thiene 2. B. Elena Enselmini 3. B. Beatrice d'Este. 4. S. Rocco presunto vinacealo," 241v, 243r. The medical teams investigated the incorruption of Enselmini's corpse, including her genitalia, but do not seem to have opened the body.

74. Park, *Secrets of Women*, 27.

75. Bette Talvacchia, *Taking Positions: On the Erotic in Renaissance Culture* (Princeton, NJ: Princeton University Press, 1999), 161–187; Park, *Secrets of Women*, 200.

76. Green, *Making Women's Medicine Masculine*, 265.

77. Park, *Secrets of Women*, 27.

78. Maureen C. Miller, "Masculinity, Reform, and Clerical Culture: Narratives of Episcopal Holiness in the Gregorian Era," *Church History* 72, no. 1 (March 2003): 25–52.

79. Carolyn Merchant, *The Death of Nature: Women, Ecology, and the Scientific Revolution* (New York: Harper & Row, 1989).

80. Lyndal Roper, *The Holy Household: Women and Morals in Reformation Augsburg* (New York: Oxford University Press, 2001), 2.

CONCLUSION

1. Roy Porter, *Flesh in the Age of Reason* (New York: Allen Lane, 2003), 19. Porter also uses this example to talk about the evolution of the concept of the interconnectedness of body and spirit.

2. Gianna Pomata, "Observation Rising: Birth of an Epistemic Genre, 1500–1650," in *Histories of Scientific Observation,* ed. Lorraine Daston and Elizabeth Lunbeck (Chicago: University of Chicago Press, 2011), 45–80.

3. Gianna Pomata, "*Praxis Historialis*: The Uses of *Historia* in Early Modern Medicine," in *Historia: Empiricism and Erudition in Early Modern Europe,* ed. Gianna Pomata and Nancy Siraisi (Cambridge, MA: MIT Press, 2005), 105–146; Nancy Siraisi, "'Remarkable' Diseases, 'Remarkable' Cures, and Personal Experience in Renaissance Medical Texts," in *Medicine and the Italian Universities, 1250–1600* (Boston: Brill, 2001), 226–252; idem, *History, Medicine, and the Traditions of Renaissance Learning* (Ann Arbor: University of Michigan Press, 2007), 68–71.

4. Katharine Park, "The Criminal and the Saintly Body: Autopsy and Dissection in Renaissance Italy," *Renaissance Quarterly* 47 (1994): 1–33; idem, *Secrets of Women: Gender, Generation, and the Origins of Human Dissection* (New York: Zone Books, 2006); Nancy Siraisi, "Signs and Evidence: Autopsy and Sanctity in Late Sixteenth-Century Italy," in *Medicine and the Italian Universities, 1250–1600* (Boston: Brill, 2001), 356–380.

5. Siraisi, "Signs and Evidence," 358–361.

6. Pamela O. Long, *Artisan/Practitioners and the Rise of the New Sciences, 1400–1600* (Corvallis: Oregon State University Press, 2011), 1–9, 30–62; Gianna Pomata and Nancy Siraisi, "Introduction," in *Historia: Empiricism and Erudition in Early Modern Europe,* ed. Gianna Pomata and Nancy Siraisi (Cambridge, MA: MIT Press, 2005), 1–38; Alisha Rankin, *Panaceia's Daughters: Noblewomen as Healers in Early Modern Germany* (Chicago: University of Chicago Press, 2013), 25–60.

7. Park, *Secrets of Women,* 27.

8. Gerardo di Flumeri, ed., *Le stigmate di Padre Pio da Pietrelcina. testimonianze relazioni* (San Giovanni Rotondo: Edizioni Padre Pio da Pietrelcina, 1995), 151, quoted in Sergio Luzzatto, *Padre Pio: Miracles and Politics in a Secular Age,* trans. Frederika Randall (New York: Metropolitan Books, 2010), 37. I would like to thank David Kertzer for bringing this reference to my attention.

9. Luzzatto, *Padre Pio,* 37.

10. Gerardo di Flumeri, *Il beato padre Pio da Pietrelcina* (San Giovanni Rotondo: Edizioni Padre Pio da Pietrelcina, 2001), 472, quoted in Luzzatto, *Padre Pio,* 289.

11. "Esumato il corpo di Padre Pio 'È Conservato perfettamente,'" *La Repubblica,* March 3, 2008, http://www.repubblica.it/2008/01/sezioni/cronaca/padre-pio-riesumato/condizioni-corpo/condizioni-corpo.html, accessed September 9, 2015.

12. Lorraine Daston and Katharine Park, *Wonders and the Order of Nature, 1150–1750* (New York: Zone Books, 1998), 320–364.

13. For a recent evaluation of the various ways in which Benedict has been interpreted in the historiography, see Maria Teresa Fattori, ed., *Le Fatiche di Benedetto XIV: Origine ed evoluzione dei trattati di Prospero Lambertini (1675–1758)* (Rome: Edizioni di Storia e Letteratura, 2011), xiii–v.

14. On Benedict and the Catholic Enlightenment see Giuseppe Cenacchi, "Benedetto XIV e l'Illumismo," in *Benedetto XIV (Prospero Lambertini): convengo internazionale di studi storici,* vol. 2 (Ferrara: Cento, 1982), 1079–1102; Paula Findlen, "Science as a Career in Enlightenment Italy: The Strategies of Laura Bassi," *Isis* 84 (1993): 457–460; Maria Pia Paoli, "'Lavorare a tempo rubbato' Benedetto XIV e Muratori nella Repubblica delle Lettere," in *Storia, medicina, e diritto nei trattati di Prospero Lambertini Benedetto XIV,* ed. Maria Teresa Fattori (Rome: Edizioni di Storia e Letteratura, 2013), 77–94.

15. On the changes to canonization under Benedict see Pierluigi Giovannucci, "Dimostrare la santità per via giudiziaria," in Fattori, *Storia, medicina, e diritto nei trattati di Prospero Lambertinii,* 277–296; Mario Rosa, "Prospero Lambertini tra 'regolata devozione' e mistica visionaria," in *Finzione e santità tra medioevo ed età moderna,* ed. Gabriella Zarri (Turin: Rosenberg and Sellier, 1991), 521–550; Riccardo Saccenti, "La lunga genesi dell'opera sulle canonizzazioni," in *Le Fatiche di Benedetto XIV,* 3–37; Fernando Vidal, "Miracles, Science, and Testimony in Post-Tridentine Saint-Making," *Science in Context* 20, no. 3 (2007): 503–504.

16. Prospero Lambertini, *De Servorum Dei Beatificatione et Beatorum Canonizatione Liber Quartus, & Ultimus Pars Prima* (Bologna: Formis

Longhi Excusoris Archiepiscopalis, 1738), 263: "Lancisius *in Opere citato de Aneurysmate cap. 6. proposit.* 48. Demonstrat, aliquando molem totius cordis cum Aneurysmate auctam repertam fuisse: ex quibus proinde aliquis facile deducere posset, omnia juxta naturalem rerum cursum in S. Philippo Nerio contigisse."

17. On anatomy and medicine in Benedict's reevaluation of sanctity see Lucia Dacome, "Ai confini del mondo naturale: anatomia e santità nell'opera di Prospero Lambertini," in Fattori, *Storia, medicina, e diritto nei trattati di Prospero Lambertini Benedetto XIV*, 319–338.

18. Lambertini, *De Servorum Dei*, 4.33.19, 471: "Tantum vim, & efficaciam nonnulli phantasiae & imaginationi in proprium imaginantis corpus tribuerunt."

19. Ibid., 4.33.21, 473: "ex imaginatione plrues morbos ortum habuisse, & multos aegrotantes ab imaginatione sanitatem recepisse."

20. Benedict XIV, *De Servorum Dei Beatificatione et Beatorum Canonizatione*, Lib. IV (Padua: Typis Seminarii, 1743), 23, 288: "Uti consideranti patebit, facilius est, transacto termino naturali corruptioni constituto, distinctionem admittere miraculorum inter incorruptionem, & continuationem incorruptionis, quam effugere multplicationem miraculorum fere in infinitum. Si enim transacto primo termino naturali, intra quem sequi debuisset corruptio, extat miraculum incorruptionis, & continuatio habetur pro novo miraculo."

21. Jacalyn Duffin, *Medical Miracles: Doctors, Saints, and Healing in the Modern World* (New York: Oxford University Press, 2009), 114.

22. Archivio Segreto Vaticano (ASV), *Congr. Riti, Processus* (RP) 700, 273r–282r. On Domenica's life see Tamar Herzig, *Savonarola's Women: Visions and Reform in Renaissance Italy* (Chicago: University of Chicago Press, 2008), 6, 31–33. On eighteenth- and early nineteenth-century attitudes toward electricity in Italy see Giuliano Pancaldi, *Volta: Science and Culture in the Age of the Enlightenment* (Princeton, NJ: Princeton University Press, 2003).

23. Rudolph M. Bell and Cristina Mazzoni, *The Voices of Gemma Galgani: The Life and Afterlife of a Modern Saint* (Chicago: University of Chicago Press, 2003), 188–189. On the Church's views of animal magnetism see David Armando, "Spiriti e fluidi. Medicine e religione nei documenti del Sant'Uffizio sul magnetismo animale (1840–1856)," in *Médecine et religion: Compétitions, Collaborations, Conflits (XIIe-XXe Siècles)*, ed. Maria Pia Donato et al. (Rome: École Française de Rome, 2013), 195–225. On the enduring popularity of mesmerism and animal magnetism until the beginning of the twentieth century see Alison Winter, *Mesmerized: Powers of Mind in Victorian Britain* (Chicago: University of Chicago Press, 1998).

24. Leonardo Ancona, "S. Maria Maddalena de' Pazzi alla luce della psicologia," *Carmelus* 13, no. 1 (1966): 3–20; Armando Favazza, *Bodies Under Siege: Self-Mutilation, Nonsuicidal Self-Injury, and Body Modification in Culture and Psychiatry* (Baltimore: Johns Hopkins University Press, 2011), 37; Kathryn J. Zerbe, *The Body Betrayed: Women, Eating Disorders, and Treatment* (Washington, DC: American Psychiatric Press, 1993), 116.

25. E. J. Dingwall, *Very Peculiar People: Portrait Studies in the Queer, the Abnormal and the Uncanny* (New York: Rider and Company, 1950), 127.

26. Enzo Fagiolo, "La Medicina a Roma Nel Secolo XVI. Malattie E Medici di S. Filippo Neri," *Medicina Nei Secoli* 15, no. 3 (2003): 535–550.

ACKNOWLEDGMENTS

This project would not have been successful without the help of a great number of people and institutions who generously gave time, energy, and funding. I can only express a small measure of my gratitude here to all those who have helped me along the way. Any errors that still remain in the finished project are of course my own.

First, I would like to thank the several institutions that have housed and funded me during the tenure of this research, including the University of Washington, Stanford University, the University of Southern California, and the Pennsylvania State University. The friendships I made at these places encouraged me to further my academic pursuits, sustained me in times of despair, and inspired me to be enthusiastic about the field I love. In particular, I would like to thank Marcelo Aranda, Lydia Barnett, Daniel Beaver, Daniela Bleichmar, Matthew Boswell, Brian Brege, Jon Brockopp, Genevieve Carlton, Christopher Celenza, Elizabeth Coggeshall, Amy Greenburg, Jason Harris, R. Po-Chia Hsia, Matthew Kahle, Keir Lockridge, Peter Mancall, Hannah Marcus, Craig Martin, Noah Millstone, Jeffrey Miner, Gregg Roeber, David Rosoff, Jacob Soll, Andrew Stone, Suzanne Sutherland, Molly Taylor, and Corey Tazzara. I owe a large thank you to Jessica Batke and the Weinbergs, who are not only great friends but who also housed me during a month of research. Matthew Restall has been a friend and mentor throughout my time at Penn State and I have found inspiration and support through my friendship with him.

This project has benefitted from a number of research grants, without which it would not have been possible. In particular, I received funding from the Fulbright Commission, the American Academy in Rome, the University of Southern California Provost's Postdoctoral Fellowship, The Mellon Foundation's Vatican Film Library Grant, a

Lane Grant for the History of Science, a Weter Grant from Stanford University, and a Foreign Language Area Scholarship.

I received generous help from the staff at a number of libraries and archives during the course of my research. The staff at the Archivio di Stato in Rome was consistently friendly and kind to me, and I would especially like to thank Giuliana Adorni for helping me to locate specific files there. At the Archivio della Congregazione per la Dottrina della Fede, I enjoyed the friendship and expert help of Daniel Ponziani as well as the regular aid of the two Fabrizios. I spent a large amount of time at the Archivio Segreto as well as the Biblioteca Apostolica, and the staff at both institutions was continually friendly and helpful. The staff at the Archivio Diocesano di Padua, the Biblioteca Communale di Padua, the Archiginnasio in Bologna, the Biblioteca Nazionale, Biblioteca Casan-atense, Biblioteca Vallicelliana in Rome, the British Library, the Well-come Institute, the Huntington Library, the Vatican Film Library, and the National Library of Medicine all greatly aided my research. The archives would have been far less enjoyable without my coffee crew, so I also must thank Benedetta Albani, Miguel Dionisio, Igor Salmic, and Johannes Schwaiger. The librarians at my home institutions of Stanford, the University of Washington, and the University of Southern Califor-nia were unfailingly helpful with my work. I would like to single out Penn State's Pattee and Paterno Libraries and its research librarian, Eric Novotny, for special recognition. Eric and the entire staff have gone out of their way to fulfill numerous and difficult requests, and I have been pleasantly surprised at their ability to occasionally obtain photocopies of rare documents from the seventeenth century for me.

A large body of scholars in both Italy and the United States have read drafts, pointed me to documents, and otherwise helped improve this project. Maria Pia Donato, Craig Martin, and Paula Findlen have generously read through entire drafts of the manuscript, which has been inestimably improved through their advice. I also would like to thank the three anonymous readers of the manuscript who read the work for the University of Pennsylvania Press. Their critical eye undoubtedly made this a much better piece of scholarship. Philippe Buc, Jessica Riskin, Gregg Roeber, Laura Stokes, Simon Ditchfield, Laura Smoller, and Nancy Siraisi all offered critical advice on early versions of this work and I am grateful to them for pointing me in the right direction.

While abroad I received schoarly advice, friendship, and hospital-ity from Renata Ago, Elisa Andretta, Francesco Barcellona, Patrizia

Cavazzini, Maria Conforti, James Nelson Novoa, and Fabiola Zurlini. In particular, I must again thank Maria Pia Donato and her partner, Luc Berlivet, who have been wonderful friends in Italy and have gone out of their way to encourage my research and make me feel welcome in Rome and in their home.

I would like to thank Jerry Singerman and the entire staff at the University of Pennsylvania Press for helping me turn this manuscript into an actual book. When I first sent Jerry chapter drafts and a proposal, the book was admittedly in a poorly formed state. I am grateful to him for staying with it and helping me create a much better final product than that which I started with. I would also like to thank the *Rivista di storia del cristianesimo* and the *Catholic Historical Review* for the permission to reprint sections of Chapters 2 and 3, respectively, which previously appeared in these journals.

I owe an especially large thanks to Paula Findlen, who is a model of academic excellence to be emulated. At every stage in my career she has been supportive and kind. Despite an incredibly busy life, she never seems rushed, always gives careful feedback, and always has time for her current and former students. She strikes that amazing balance of giving enough structure but also leaving room for her students to figure things out for themselves. Although I know that I will fall short, I can only hope to emulate Paula in my career.

Another large debt of gratitude is owed to the two scholars who most helped me decide to pursue a career in history: Mary O'Neil and Sean Cocco. While I was at the University of Washington, both Mary and Sean were incredibly generous and enthusiastic in encouraging my interest in history. I am grateful that they encouraged me to follow a career that I love.

In a similar vein I must thank my father, my mother, and my sister, without whom I would never have taken the risk to follow my love of history and eventually write a book. Through pursuing a career that he obviously enjoyed, my father inspired me to find similar joy in my own life. My sister was continuously enthusiastic about my choice to follow history even when I was sometimes doubtful about it. To my mother I owe the greatest debt. She has read and edited endless drafts of papers, has provided financial aid at times, and was always unwavering in her support of this project and my career and in her love for me. I would not have accomplished this task without her.

I would like to thank my two small boys, Oliver and Charlie, who were born while I was writing this manuscript. Their love and enthusiasm have helped keep me motivated, made me feel humble, and reminded me to look for the human in historical writing.

Finally, I would like to acknowledge the fundamental role that the support and companionship of my wife, Tarrah, have had in the completion of this book. Tarrah's love and friendship have made my life inestimably better and saved me from becoming a crotchety old academic. To her and to my mother I dedicate this work as a small token of my gratitude and love.